THE YEAR OF THE GHOST: AN OLDUVAI DIARY

The year of the ghost: an Olduvai diary

Derek Roe

A Beagle book, published in Bristol, England 2002

For Biddy and Nick

Published under the Beagle imprint by the
Western Academic & Specialist Press Ltd, Bristol, England

©Derek Roe 2002

The right of Derek Roe to be identified as the author of this work has been asserted

ISBN 0-9535418-5-1

British Library Cataloguing in Publication Data

A catalogue record for this book is available from the British Library

Design and typesetting in Verdana and New Baskerville by Melegari Design

Printed and bound in the UK by Short Run Press Ltd, Bittern Road, Exeter, England

Contents

Publisher's note to readers

The diary which forms the main section of this book (pages 39-145) can be read in isolation, but Derek Roe has also written an introduction to Mary Leakey and to the archaeology of Olduvai Gorge, one of the most famous archaeological sites in the world. These can be read before the diary, afterwards, or even not at all. Derek completes the story in his aftermath and epilogue sections, taking us through to the end of Mary Leakey's long and accomplished life.

The photographs in this book were all taken by Derek on his travels in East Africa. Most are slides which have been used many times to illustrate his various lectures and have therefore become somewhat battered from use, so please take the worn quality of these illustrations as a reflection of the great interest they have evoked over nearly 20 years.

Acknowledgement

We would like to thank Cambridge University Press for giving us permission to use two of Mary Leakey's own drawings of stone tools from Olduvai (see pages 31 and 32). These were originally published in *Olduvai Gorge Volume III: excavations in Beds I & II 1960-1963*, written by Mary Leakey, which was published in 1971.

INTRODUCTION

Mary Leakey with Matthew

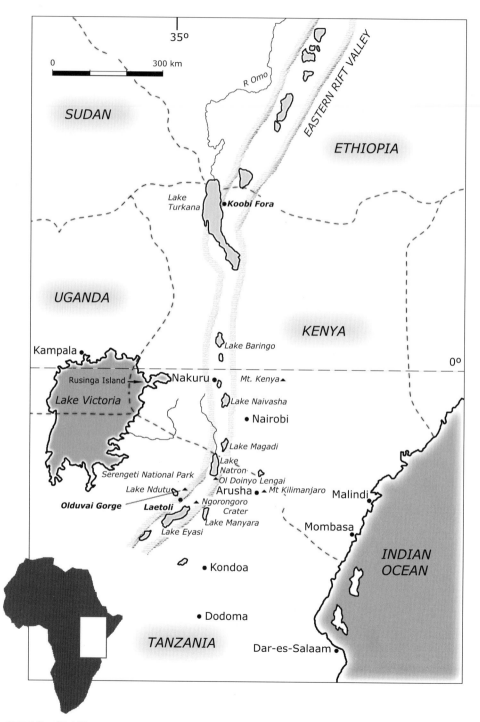

Figure 1 Map of East Africa

I suppose everyone gets to take on something extraordinary at least once in his or her lifetime. In my own case it all happened at quite short notice: I was aged 46, comfortably obscure and modestly successful as a teacher and researcher in Old Stone Age Archaeology at Oxford University, when I suddenly found myself commissioned to create the autobiography, written in the first person singular, of a particularly distinguished colleague who happened to be a woman, aged 70 and, if that was not hard enough, she was the famously formidable and notoriously reticent Mary Leakey.

This book is an account of the time I spent doing that (in 1983), and is built around the diary I kept of three remarkable trips to East Africa, where Mary was. In this introduction, I aim to provide the background information without which much of the diary might be rather hard to understand. I need to give some account of Mary herself, who died in 1996: by any reckoning, she will surely be remembered as one of the great women of the twentieth century, and she packed enough in the way of discoveries and adventures into her 83 years to fill several ordinary lifetimes. Her story is of course told more fully elsewhere - including in the pages of the autobiography – so I need only provide a basic outline here. It is also important that I should set the scene with regard to Olduvai Gorge, in Tanzania, where most of the action in the diary takes place. This is one of the outstanding archaeological sites of the world, vital to our knowledge of the earliest stages of human activity and development; it also happens to be one of the most beautiful wild places I have ever visited. Again, there are many accounts of Olduvai available, ranging from brief summaries in popular books on archaeology to a series of highly technical monographs, but a brief account is certainly required here, if the significance of the diary's physical backdrop is to be appreciated.

Finally, I ought to explain in this Introduction how it was that I myself first met Mary Leakey (which happened in 1969), and how it came about that, 14 years later, I was given the task of acting as her ghost-writer. I can document from our correspondence how she on the one hand, and I on the other, viewed the project at the time when it was set up, and that is of considerable interest to the way things developed and finally turned out. The occasion of our first meeting is not a bad story in itself, never previously told, and may explain some of the attitudes with which I set out on my task.

It is already clear to me that this Introduction will need to be balanced by at least a brief epilogue, though my main purpose is to offer the diary itself simply for enjoyment, which is something the handful of friends who have read it privately over the years have invariably encouraged me to do. The diary text is essentially as I wrote it at the time: just a tidied up version of the hand-written original, which remains in my possession. By 'tidied up', I mean that I have regularised the use of tenses, to remove quite a lot of jumping between present tense and past tense, according to mood at the time of writing: I now find that merely distracting. I have corrected a few spellings of names that I got wrong in early entries and right, after enquiry, in later ones. I have not omitted any of the incidents or thoughts I recorded at the time, and only very rarely indeed have I added a few words or altered a phrase, always for the sake of clarification; twice I have omitted a personal name to avoid causing needless embarrassment, when it simply was not significant to the story. There are, however, absolutely no wise-after-the-event second thoughts inserted into the diary text, and no hindsight editing of fact or opinion as originally recorded: it would not be a true diary if that were the case, and any later reflections of mine about the whole episode will be found in the Introduction and Epilogue.

I will give the brief statement of Mary Leakey's life and career first, and then tell the story of my meeting her and working with her prior to 1983, and the setting up of the autobiography project. The account of Olduvai Gorge can follow. The only other preliminary point that occurs to me is that I have not so far mentioned the details of the finished autobiography: it was published by Weidenfeld & Nicolson in 1984 as *Disclosing the Past*, by Mary Leakey. What, you've never read it? Never seen a copy? Well, I'm not too surprised. Perhaps, if you read this book, you will find out why that might be so, and perhaps you will also want to try and find a copy somewhere. It isn't really the book I wrote for Mary, but it's not at all a bad read.

*

Mary Leakey

Mary was born on 6 February 1913 as Mary Douglas Nicol. Her father, Erskine Nicol, was of Scottish descent, her mother, Cecilia Frere, was English and her maternal grandmother (Cecilia Byrne), Irish. Erskine Nicol was a successful professional painter, like his own father, who bore the same name. Through the Freres, Mary could claim descent from John Frere, who in the late eighteenth century found palaeolithic stone implements in association with the bones of extinct animals at Hoxne in Suffolk, and accurately perceived the true implications of the discovery at a time when the account of the Creation in the Old Testament book of Genesis still ruled, and any denial of it was widely regarded as heresy. Various nineteenth-century Freres held senior positions in colonial administration in Africa, and among them were some outspoken opponents of slavery.

Mary and her father were very close, and he taught her the basic skills of drawing which she afterwards applied particularly to prehistoric stone artefacts: her drawings of palaeolithic tools are amongst the very top flight of all such work, and likely always to remain so, most of all, perhaps, for her ability to convey the textures of the fractured surfaces of many different rock types, not merely flint and chert. Mary's father also transmitted to her in quite early childhood his own strong, if general, interest in antiquities and archaeology, which dated from the time he had spent in Egypt before she was born; he travelled frequently abroad to paint different places, though the First World War halted that for a while. After it ended, he made regular annual extended trips to France, taking his family with him, and thus Mary at an early age encountered, in her father's company, the Upper Palaeolithic painted caves, and palaeolithic stone artefacts, for the first time; she also became fluent in French. From her father she also gained a great love of animals, especially watching them in the wild. It was her mother's sisters who, very early on in her life, introduced her to dogs – creatures which, especially if they were Dalmatians, she later more than once claimed to prefer to people.

Given the somewhat mobile pattern of the Nicol family's life, it is easy to see that there was little opportunity for any ordinary school education for Mary at this time; she was learning much from her parents, especially from her father, which can be seen to have been of great formative importance, but she did not even begin to learn to read until she was seven or eight. Eventually, her parents decided that something more formal was required, and they hired a succession of governesses for her. Mary made it her business to drive each one to distraction and rapid departure. Everything changed, however, with brutal suddenness in 1926, when her father, aged only 58 and apparently in excellent health, suddenly developed the symptoms of some form of cancer, and in a few short weeks was dead, after a painful last illness. Mary was just 13 when this first great tragedy of her life struck the family.

The following years saw Mary and her mother living in straitened circumstances back in England. Mary was made to go to two Catholic convent schools, and quite rapidly contrived (to her great satisfaction) to get herself expelled from both, on the second occasion for deliberately causing an explosion in a chemistry lesson. Private tutors had little more luck, and eventually her mother gave up the idea of formal education for Mary and allowed her to pursue seriously her growing interest in archaeology, by whatever means she could devise, in the absence of any formal educational qualifications whatsoever. She attended lectures at University College and the London Museum, and more importantly she took part as a volunteer in excavations at several British archaeological sites, most significantly for four seasons at the Neolithic site of Hembury in Devon, where she learned to dig to a high standard of precision under Dorothy Liddell and her gifted site foreman, WEV Young. She also drew some of the flints that were discovered during the excavation for Miss Liddell, and thereby came to the notice of Dr Gertrude Caton-Thompson at Cambridge University, who was impressed enough with Mary's work to ask her to draw the stone tools from her own recent excavations at Fayoum in Egypt. Something of even greater significance was to follow in this particular chain of events, for a research fellow then at Cambridge, at St John's College, was one Dr Louis Leakey, and he was quite specifically looking for someone to draw stone artefacts for a book he was writing, *Adam's Ancestors*. Gertrude Caton-Thompson recommended Mary, and so she and Louis met for the first time, in May 1933, Mary being just 20 and Louis some 10 years older. Louis's upbringing had been in East Africa, and he was already well known for his archaeological work there, including a number of important discoveries.

It seems to me that, even in the very brief and selective preceding account of Mary's family background and early years, one can pick out certain factors which were very important, not only in the shaping of her professional career as described in the autobiography but also in determining the personal nature and the attitudes and responses of the Mary with whom I was to work. I only learned the facts I have just summarised as the work proceeded, of course. If the period referred to above seems rather far removed from 1983, when I confronted my task, it is perhaps worth mentioning that, even before she met Louis, Mary had already made certain life-long friends who, by her special request, read the draft text of the autobiography by instalments, as I completed it. One of these was Gertrude Caton-Thompson, who had introduced her to Louis, whom Mary would always visit faithfully every time she passed through England; in 1983, Gertrude was already into her nineties. Another was Professor C Thurstan Shaw, a friend of roughly her own age, whom Mary first met at the Hembury excavations. Both were very helpful to me in my quest for information, and in their comments on the draft text. It was Thurstan who delivered a moving and much admired address on 3 May 1997, at a Memorial Service for Mary held at Cambridge in the Chapel of Jesus College. Other close friends whom she wanted to read the draft text instalments were people she met at later stages, but her inclusion of Gertrude and Thurstan strengthens my belief that in Mary's case the early years really were of great importance.

The meeting with Louis Leakey, or more accurately the attachment that quite rapidly developed, was undoubtedly a major turning-point in Mary's life from every point of view. In the shorter term, it led of course to her marrying Louis (1936), and it certainly turned her from girl to woman; it took her for the first time to Africa and indeed to Olduvai (1935); it began her professional career in archaeology (admittedly as Louis's partner and co-worker rather than as the holder of some formal post); it also brought her into immediate and dire conflict with the overwhelming majority of her friends and relatives, and thereby firmly established in her adult life the capacity she had already revealed to follow her own chosen path with absolute determination, not exactly regardless of the opinions and advice of others, but, after consideration, with deliberate disregard. It is hard, at the start of the twenty-first century, to understand quite what a terrible thing the liaison between Louis and Mary seemed to their friends and to the academic world of Cambridge in the early 1930s, the simple problem being that Louis was already married and was the father of one child, with a second one on the way. Today, rightly or wrongly, relatively few eyebrows would be raised and the two protagonists would simply have to remember to adjust the wording of their *CVs* – well, perhaps that's an exaggeration, but certainly a comparable event would not now lead to widespread social ostracism, or have immediate specific adverse effects such as the loss of Louis's position as a Fellow of St John's College or – horror of horrors – the withdrawal of his membership of a tennis club in Hertfordshire.

Since many accounts exist of this part of the story of Louis and Mary, I shall not dwell on it here. It was to be my role to coax a version of it out of a predictably unwilling Mary for the autobiography, which those who wish can consult; there are also the versions provided by Louis himself in the second volume of his autobiography *By the Evidence*, by his biographer Sonia Cole in *Leakey's Luck*, and by Virginia Morell in her book *Ancestral Passions*, which is about the Leakey family generally. At the risk of stating the obvious, there would not have been a charismatic Leakey family to give rise to so much literature – or there would have been a very different one – had it not been for the events that befell Louis and Mary between 1933 and 1936.

So, Mary married Louis, to the despair of many friends and relatives, and off she went to Africa. In fact, her first visit there was in 1935, before the marriage, and it gave her the chance to learn more about the skills of excavation, this time from AJ Goodwin, by joining his team in South Africa for a few weeks before travelling on to meet Louis in Tanzania (then Tanganyika) and go with him to Olduvai Gorge. Part of their journey together to Olduvai included the Arusha to Ngorongoro stretch which I describe in the diary, but they were faced by a much rougher version of the road than that of 1983 or today, and had appalling difficulties in the rainy conditions. Apart from Olduvai, on her first visit to Africa, Mary went with Louis to several other sites, including brief visits to two that would later prove of great significance in her life: Laetoli, where some of her greatest discoveries would be made over 40 years later, and Kondoa, where some remarkable examples of Tanzanian rock art were located, the later detailed recording of which (in 1951) and their eventual publication (1983) she always regarded as constituting one of the highlights of her career.

Mary and Louis returned to Africa in 1937, and in the event they stayed there, partly because the outbreak of the Second World War in 1939 made a return to England impossible. They had little regular source of income in those early years, and worked on any project they could, using any money that could be raised, or often none at all. From 1941, Louis officially worked as Curator of the Coryndon Museum in Nairobi (later the National Museum of Kenya), but at first in an honorary capacity, with only the use of a poor-quality bungalow as a tangible reward. Initially, Mary was able to apply her excavation skills to a number of important later prehistoric sites (Late Stone Age and Iron Age) in Kenya: Hyrax Hill, Njoro Cave and the Naivasha Railway Rock Shelter. Since she was later to become best known for her discoveries relating to human evolution and human origins, right at the other end of the timescale, the sheer quality and importance of her work at these much younger sites tends to have been forgotten. More life-long friendships of Mary's date from this period, one of them being that with Mary Catherine Davidson (who later married Bernard Fagg), another invited reader of the draft autobiography text in 1983. Mary's first ownership of a Dalmatian in Africa dates from this time too: a security measure, after a burglary at her camp site at Hyrax Hill.

The war years were difficult ones, and financially precarious: Louis was involved in intelligence work for the Kenyan Government, for which at least he was paid, but he and Mary, with others in a similar situation (including Mary Davidson), contrived to continue various archaeological projects or mount short expeditions, especially when a period of leave occurred. For a while things were tense, since there seemed a real threat of invasion of Kenya by Italian forces from Ethiopia, but that later receded. In 1940, the Leakeys' first child (Jonathan) was born: Mary recorded that she quite liked being a mother, but was not going to let it get in the way of her archaeological career, and fortunately Jonathan proved an amenable and cooperative baby. Discoveries dating from this time included the great Lower Palaeolithic site of Olorgesailie, in the Rift Valley not far from Nairobi. There was also the first of many expeditions to Rusinga Island, in Lake Victoria, to search for Miocene (see glossary) fossil apes, some of which, notably *Proconsul*, were important to the ultimate origins of the human line, at a stage prior to its final separation from that of the apes. Louis discovered an important *Proconsul* jaw in 1943, though Mary's own later discovery of the major part of a skull in 1948 far eclipsed that. In 1943, a second child, Deborah, was born but died three months later from dysentery. Richard Leakey was born in 1944, and Philip Leakey, the youngest of the three brothers, in 1949.

Though there were plenty of highlights for the Leakey family in the period between the end of the war in 1945 and 1960, it is not easy to discern a clear pattern. Some of the major events affected Louis rather more directly than Mary, and in a small number of cases the converse would be true. And all the while, the three Leakey boys were growing up and experiencing far from ordinary childhoods, as the prelude to their own remarkable careers. The family's move to Langata, on the outskirts of Nairobi, took place in 1952, making an enormous difference domestically. While we are only indirectly concerned here with Louis Leakey's own career and achievements, it is much in my mind that Mary always referred to her marriage, all phases of it, as 'the partnership with Louis'. In this attempt to write a brief summary of Mary's life, I am also crucially aware of a number of defining moments, or major turning-points, such as the death of her father and the meeting with Louis, and I believe that the next one did not occur until 1959. That is not to say that there were not major highlights meanwhile, but by 'defining moments' I mean events that were to have a profound long-term effect as well as bringing immediate success.

Gradually, in the years following the end of the war, the Leakeys moved to a state of what might loosely be called financial viability, though there was never much money to spare, since Louis and Mary both tended to spend any sudden surpluses on their research of the time. Their reputations in the archaeological world were steadily growing, assisted by such things as the great success of the First Pan African Congress in Nairobi in 1947, which led to the setting up of the British-Kenya Miocene Expedition to continue the work at Rusinga on a properly funded basis. Mary's subsequent discovery of the *Proconsul* skull, which she then took personally to London, created an international stir and very helpful publicity. People like Charles Boise began to give substantial financial support to the Leakeys' work. At the same time, the early and middle 1950s were the time of the Mau-Mau troubles in Kenya, with which Louis was deeply involved, and dangers were never far away from the Leakey family. Archaeological work proceeded on many fronts: 1951 saw Mary back at Kondoa in Tanzania, at last able to give herself and Louis the long-promised treat of studying and recording the rock paintings which he had taken her to see in 1935, and from 1951 to 1959 there were several expeditions to Olduvai, with excavations mainly in the deposits of the second oldest stratigraphic unit (Bed 2). The Leakeys went again to Laetoli from Olduvai in 1959, but finding neither hominid fossils nor stone tools amongst the many early faunal remains there decided not to attempt any formal excavation. Louis himself was never to visit Laetoli again, and it was one of Mary's lasting regrets that he did not live to see or take part in the amazing discoveries that were later made there. But it was in 1959, right at the end of that year's Olduvai field season, that the next turning-point quite suddenly arrived when Mary, out walking the dogs one July morning, while Louis lay in bed at camp with 'flu, noticed with her sharp eyes part of the skull of an archaic-looking fossil hominid protruding from an eroded surface of some of the oldest sediments towards the base of the Gorge, in the area known as FLK. This was the specimen now known as *Australopithecus (Zinjanthropus) boisei*, or just 'Zinj' for short, and also sometimes called 'Nutcracker Man'. Louis had long before named that area of the Gorge Frida Leakey Korongo (FLK) (Korongo meaning gully), in honour of his first wife: what a place for his second wife to choose for a turning-point in her career, especially when one reflects that elsewhere in the Gorge there were already MNK (Mary Nicol Korongo) and MLK (Mary Leakey Korongo). Possibly Fate has a sense of humour.

'Zinj' was an outstanding find by any standards, and by 1959 the international community of palaeoanthropologists was more than ready to receive such a discovery and to take sides on what should be its correct nomenclature and its position on the family tree of human ancestry, so the international interest was enormous, and the effect on the whole field operation at Olduvai was profound. Louis Leakey was exactly the right person to exploit the new discovery, and to perform the task of showing it off around the world, though Mary joined him for the initial presentation. When, in November of the following year, the even more significant remains of *Homo habilis*, with signs of a larger brain, upright walking and considerable manual dexterity, were discovered at another site in the same productive FLK area of the Gorge, the fame of Olduvai and the Leakeys knew no bounds. Further hominid fossil finds soon followed. The understanding of early Pleistocene geology and environments, and the improvement of techniques of chronometric dating, were all at this time at last making much needed progress, and the long and well-preserved sequence of deposits at Olduvai, spanning the better part of two million years of time, offered a wonderful testing ground for them and a training arena for younger scholars in many disciplines.

Mary was more than content to leave the globetrotting and the showmanship to Louis, and to spend all the time she could down at Olduvai, directing excavations of the highest quality at carefully chosen sites, designed to answer particular research questions. She could do this because the immense interest that began with the discovery of Zinj had been accompanied at last by major institutional support for research at Olduvai, most notably from the National Geographic Society of America. There were also substantial contributions of one kind or another from other funding bodies, and also from wealthy individuals; apart from that, many distinguished scholars in various fields of Quaternary Research were delighted to visit Olduvai and to contribute their own expertise to the research there. The geologist Dick Hay, then at Berkeley, California, is a good example: he first visited Olduvai in 1962, and remained a close friend and active research colleague of Mary's for the rest of her field career. Jack Evernden and especially Garniss Curtis, experts in the then still new technique of potassium-argon dating, were others who first established contact with Mary and visited the Gorge in the early 1960s. In short, at this time, she could call for virtually any specialist expertise she needed at Olduvai, and the grant-giving bodies would see to it that before too long the right people arrived. Mary was in her element: every step she had taken to carve out an archaeological career was being justified and was bearing wonderful fruit. Meanwhile, it was Louis's energetic travelling and brilliant lecture-theatre performances that kept public interest high and the money coming in, especially in the USA, where he was a coast-to-coast star, in eager demand.

Luckily, or perhaps, more accurately, unluckily, he thrived on hero-worship.

All of this, because of the effects that followed, explains why I earlier classed the discovery of Zinj as a major turning-point as well as a great highlight in Mary's life. With hindsight, it is all too easy to see how Louis and Mary began to be driven apart by the vast and rapid change that had taken place in their lifestyles, and how Olduvai Gorge, rather than Nairobi, quite rapidly became Mary's real home. She and Louis inevitably spent less and less time together; Louis through his travels and contacts became involved in many other projects in which Mary had (and indeed in most cases wanted) no part. Through his personal charisma, he formed many relationships which in one way or another quite rapidly destroyed the integrity and simplicity of the partnership with Mary, and all the while his health was deteriorating and his restless energy was hastening that process.

All these things are recounted in the published sources which I have already quoted: the actual destructive events were many and various, and were sometimes more subtle in their nature and effect than Louis's numerous harmful but relatively straightforward liaisons with other women at this time. One particularly influential episode that Mary referred to many times while she and I were working on the autobiography, and clearly felt as deeply as anything, was the business of Calico Hills and Louis's determination to provide southern California with its very own Early Human site, to please and satisfy the many kind friends he had met there on his travels, most of them generous supporters of his and indeed Mary's research projects. He convinced himself that he could discover genuine traces of a really early human presence in California, in defiance of the generally prevailing belief that humans had not reached north America until a mere 20,000 years ago at the very earliest, and probably rather later than that. He persisted, embarrassingly, against all the run of the evidence (as Mary's detached mind and clear vision assessed it) and eventually summoned an international congress in California in 1968, expecting it to vindicate his views. I myself was actually there, by invitation, as a young British researcher with an interest in stone artefacts, of whom Louis had vaguely heard: he telephoned, out of the blue, to ask if I would go, if expenses were paid, so of course I did. The conference returned a tactful verdict of 'not proven' on the Calico Hills site, but many of the delegates would have expressed that as 'disproved', if it had been anyone but Louis, already a sick man. He nevertheless contrived to parade the verdict as acceptance in the press next day. Mary, in her own words, simply lost all of her former great respect for Louis's capacity to think and work scientifically, and it was in the aftermath of the Calico Hills affair that she moved permanently to Olduvai. The camp there was soon afterwards transferred to a new site and given a greater degree of permanence: over the next few years, it was further elaborated, as opportunities arose, to become both her home and her research institute. I do not doubt that, for her, loss of scientific respect was every bit as significant as falling out of love.

The 1960s were therefore a period of many triumphs, but so far as the partnership of Louis and Mary was concerned a summit was reached early in the decade, and beyond it, against all expectation, the way led rather rapidly downwards through somewhat rugged country. There were other very important factors at work, which I cannot explore in detail here, notably the passage of the three sons of Louis and Mary from boyhood to manhood, and in particular the emergence of Richard Leakey as a fierce and fast-moving challenger to his parents' dominance of their research field, with a driving need for his own territory and for the fame that went with spectacular success. He was soon in open conflict with Louis, in particular, on a number of issues. Virginia Morell has told Richard's story in *Ancestral Passions*, and there is also his own autobiographical volume *One Life*. Mary too gives her account of many of the relevant events in *Disclosing the Past*.

I will move on to the next great turning-point for Mary, as it seems to me: the death of Louis in 1972. In that it brought to an abrupt end various unhappy situations, and given that they had been living almost entirely apart for at least four years, some might feel that the death of Louis would have been sad but would not have had a profound effect on Mary's life. While sudden, the event was hardly unexpected, since he had nearly died on several previous occasions from heart attacks, and once from an attack by a swarm of bees. But in fact it did affect her greatly both emotionally and in practical ways, because right to the end Louis had kept up his role as the international traveller, publicist and fund-raiser – indeed, he died in London just a few days into yet another such trip. While Richard Leakey was by then fully capable of taking care of the fundraising for his own research operations, with Louis's death that side of things would simply grind to a halt for Mary and Olduvai, unless she was prepared to do something about it herself. But that would mean emerging from the productive seclusion of life down at the Gorge, into the glare of the spotlights which Louis had so loved but which she loathed and dreaded. It would mean much travel every year over Louis's routes, and saying the right thing day after day to great numbers of people whom she would really rather not meet at all. All things considered, therefore, it could only be seen as a disastrous turn of events, quite apart from the sorrow she felt at the final loss of the Louis who once was, rather than the Louis of the final years.

Many people have found to their surprise that disasters are opportunities in disguise. The outcome was that Mary did indeed take on the role that Louis had played, initially with dread, but subsequently with enormous success. Few who knew her during the last few years of Louis's life, and certainly not Mary herself, would have predicted this. Against all expectation, on her own admission, she ultimately found some genuine enjoyment in at least parts of the travel, and quite a few of the people she met along the way became firm friends, to be revisited by choice as often as possible; she even came to find some degree of exhilaration in the public speaking and the performances on radio and television. Her style was very different from that of Louis, but the sheer quality of her work invariably shone through in her presentations, and, throughout the 1970s and early 1980s, she was never short of compelling new information to share with her audiences, as the work at Laetoli followed that at Olduvai. It may be that at first she relied on finding a sympathetic audience as Louis's shy and sorrowing widow, but if that ever really happened, it was a brief phase, and before long Mary was a coast-to-coast star across America in her own right, well able to assess dispassionately the fundraising potential of the many invitations that came her way. By 1981, she was the holder of several honorary degrees from major universities and the discerning refuser of others from what were deemed to be lesser institutions. Apart from her public lectures, she was also a much admired speaker at the major international archaeological congresses she attended. The money for research continued to come in: for Mary, by design, it came for a much narrower range of projects than those with which Louis had latterly concerned himself. As time passed, she became perfectly willing to make academic enemies, and to maintain her side of forceful debates on the interpretation of hominid evolution, sometimes standing shoulder to shoulder with her son Richard, as other workers (not least in Ethiopia) began to excavate sites which in their own particular ways were just as rich and just as important as Olduvai or Laetoli, and in some cases to challenge her views aggressively. During my work with her on the autobiography, as noted in the diary, I was considerably startled by the strength of her antipathy to the views, and even more to the behaviour, of various colleagues, none more so than Tim White and Don Johanson. Both sides gave as good as they got.

During the years that followed the death of Louis, Mary at first continued to work at Olduvai, concentrating on the beds there that come later in the sequence than those which had yielded Zinj and *Homo habilis*. But the crowning glory of her later years of active field work was Laetoli, the site that she and Louis had twice visited without much reward. Now it came into its own, and during five seasons of digging in 1975–1979 yielded important hominid fossils which were substantially earlier than any of those from Olduvai. But the most spectacular discovery at Laetoli (in 1978) was the famous footprint trail of three upright-walking early humans or pre-humans, preserved with startling clarity in a band of volcanic ash, which had been deposited almost 3.7 million years ago. This same ash horizon also produced some tens of thousands of animal footprints. For once, Mary was not personally the initial discoverer of the footprints, as she had been of the *Proconsul* and Zinj fossil skulls, but it was during her Laetoli expedition that the 'Footprint Tuff' was found, and she will be remembered as the excavator of the hominid trails.

Mary continued to live at Olduvai for another four years after the end of the Laetoli dig, also spending some time each year on international travel. During those years she was mainly busy with post-excavation study of finds, and writing, working on the publications of Laetoli, the Tanzanian rock art, the autobiography, and the fifth and final volume of the important *Olduvai Gorge* monograph series. These were all works of book length, and there were of course various shorter academic publications. *Olduvai Gorge, Volume 5* did not finally appear until 1994, and before the end I myself was to become her co-editor and see it through to completion and publication for her, as her last major work.

At the end of 1983, with life becoming ever more difficult in Tanzania, especially for those who were not Tanzanian nationals, Mary finally left her beloved Olduvai and returned to the family home at Langata, where she lived for another 13 years. She continued to travel and visit her friends, to write, and to attend conferences, including one held in her honour at Arusha in 1985. By now there were many grandchildren, from her three sons' various marriages, and she involved herself with the family during her closing years much more than some had expected. Of her sons, all had distinguished careers: Richard, in particular, has never ceased to attract international attention, whether as palaeoanthropologist, politician or saviour of Kenyan elephants from extinction at the hands of poachers. There is little I myself can write from first-hand knowledge of Mary's life in Nairobi after 1983, and for the purposes of this book I do not need to tell the story beyond that date, because my task is simply to introduce the Mary with whom I was to work and to pick out some of the main events of her life that one might expect to dominate the autobiography. After my task was completed, I saw her again only occasionally, during some of her visits to England, though we remained in touch over matters like the completion of the last of the Olduvai monographs. Her health gradually deteriorated, though she was able to remain remarkably active right to the end. Nairobi, however, had become even by 1983 a city with formidable social problems, and, as time continued to pass, things got only worse, and the rate of violent crime soared. The Langata to which Mary returned for her final years was a very different place from the Langata where the Leakeys had built an idyllic home in the early 1950s. Mary died, after a short final illness, on 9 December 1996. In accordance with her wishes, her ashes were scattered at Olduvai. All things considered, no one should find that very surprising.

*

The autobiography

I first met Mary Leakey in 1969, being of course already familiar with her work – as anyone needed to be who was teaching graduate students about early humans in Africa in a course on Palaeolithic archaeology. The background to that first meeting was that Professor J Desmond Clark, already by then one of the most active and important scholars of the African Early Stone Age, had been appointed as external examiner of my Cambridge doctoral thesis, which I had submitted in 1967. My research for the doctorate included the devising of certain new methods of studying the principal stone tool types of the Lower Palaeolithic – handaxes and cleavers – using a system of measurements and simple statistical analyses. It sounds ordinary enough now but, in those pre-computer days of the early 1960s, such an approach was only just beginning to make an impact on prehistoric archaeology and Glynn Isaac and I were among the pioneers of such techniques, in a small way, when we were Cambridge final-year undergraduates, subsequently developing our ideas as graduate students. My own measurements were devised for the stone tools of the British early Palaeolithic, but broadly similar implements were to be found in many other parts of the world, especially in Africa: Desmond Clark was sufficiently impressed to realise that the same kind of approach would be useful for the study of the handaxes and cleavers he had excavated in the 1950s and early 1960s in the Early Stone Age levels of the remarkable site of Kalambo Falls, which is right on the Tanzania–Zambia border, the excavations being on the Zambian side. He therefore invited me to go out to Livingstone in Zambia, where the Kalambo Falls stone tools now were, and use my new methods to study them.

This was a wonderful opportunity for a first piece of post-doctoral research, and I gladly accepted the task. The best way to fly to Zambia from England was via Nairobi and thence across to Lusaka and on down to Livingstone. I'm not sure exactly how Mary Leakey got wind of the plan, but she did, and she instructed Louis to get in touch with me and suggest that I break the journey in Nairobi for a few days: he was to arrange a trip down to Olduvai for me to meet her, since it seemed likely that the Olduvai handaxes and cleavers would also respond to the kind of approach I was using. This was another amazing opportunity, which I was happy to grab with both hands. In due course, I was on an aeroplane for Nairobi for the first time.

I shall tell the story of that first trip to Olduvai at some length a little later in this chapter, so here I can jump a little way ahead. The essential thing was that Mary and I got on very well on our first meeting in 1969, and after this first look at the Olduvai stone implements, and the study of a pilot sample, it was soon agreed that I would take on the task of studying all the Olduvai handaxes and cleavers as soon as funding could be arranged, as a separate project from the Kalambo Falls work. As it turned out, it took three further visits to achieve the collection of all the data, since relevant excavations were still in progress, and there were artefacts needing to be measured and studied, in Nairobi and in Dar es Salaam, as well as those that were actually in the storerooms of Mary's camp at Olduvai. I was therefore back working with Mary in 1970, 1972 and 1974, and we were regularly corresponding about this project right through the 1970s (and indeed later). My long report on the Olduvai stone implements was eventually published in the final volume of the Olduvai monograph series (Vol 5), to which I have already referred above in the brief account of Mary's life, and there are occasional mentions of it in the diary. In fact, because of the exciting but somewhat unexpected way in which the Laetoli project took off for Mary, after its start in 1975, and since she followed it right through to publication, *Olduvai Gorge, Volume 5*, got set aside, and only finally appeared in 1994 – 20 years after I had completed my work on the Olduvai stone tools.

Because of this project and the friendship that had developed, I also saw Mary fairly regularly whenever she came to England during the international travels which, as we have already seen, became a regular part of her life after Louis's death in 1972. Mary soon fell into a regular pattern for what might loosely be called the social side of the English stage of her annual travels, although the working side of each visit would vary according to what she had taken on in the way of lectures, conferences or consultations with various specialist colleagues in London. I thus found myself with a very precise role, which I was happy to perform: I was invariably required to drive the 20 miles or so from where I lived to arrive in mid-morning at Court Farm, in Broadway, Worcestershire, the beautiful Cotswold house where Gertrude Caton-Thompson spent her later years, living with her long-standing friends the de Navarros, Toty (properly, José, though no one ever called him that) and his wife Dorothy. Toty died in 1976, but Mary's visits to Dorothy and Gertrude at Court Farm continued. Mary would have spent one or two nights there, and I would stay to lunch and then drive her to Oxford and deliver her to her next port of call, the home of Bernard and Mary Catherine Fagg – the Mary Catherine Davidson of wartime Nairobi – where she would stay the next night or two before heading back to London. In London, her hosts would be Michael Day (who was working with Mary on the Olduvai fossil hominids) and his wife Mickey, in Hampstead. Occasionally, if Mary was in Oxford long enough, I might also see her for a meal or a talk all to ourselves, but the routine in any case gave us a chance to catch up on news and any archaeological business.

When I first met Mary in 1969, and during my other early visits to Olduvai, I knew little or nothing of her life story, or the stage it had reached, as opposed to her archaeological achievements. It is therefore worth pausing briefly to relate that period, 1969–1974, to the account of her life given above. In 1969, the disastrous Calico Hills episode had only recently taken place, and Louis was already in decline, with failing health. Richard Leakey's career and fame were surging ahead, and he had already begun the important East Rudolf (subsequently known as East Turkana) excavations, with Glynn Isaac as co-director. When Louis sent me down to Olduvai to meet Mary, she had already decided to make the Gorge her permanent home, whether he realised it or not, and in fact she and Louis would never again spend more than brief periods of time together.

The great burst of field activity at Olduvai that had followed the discovery of *Zinjanthropus* in 1959 was over for the moment; huge quantities of excavated finds were being studied, and publications prepared, with Mary herself deeply involved in the production of volume 3 of the Olduvai monograph series (it was published in 1971). There was still enormous international interest in Olduvai and many visitors would arrive there during the course of each year, often bringing special expertise to contribute to the research effort. Funding for such visits was still not difficult to obtain. Indeed, I suppose that my own visits to study the handaxes can be viewed in that light, since junior scholars were involved as well as senior ones, if they had something to offer. Between my second and third visits, however, everything changed for Mary, with the death of Louis, as I have described. The Mary who came to England as an international traveller each year in the middle and later 1970s was accordingly a very different person from the Mary I met in 1969, though in some ways she had not changed at all. But it was only later on, after the autobiography project got going in 1983, that I could understand these things or see them in context.

It was in 1980 or 1981 that I first heard a rumour that Mary was thinking of writing her autobiography with the help of a ghost-writer: a publisher was keen for her to do it, and she had been persuaded that it would make her some money for her retirement, not that she had any immediate plans for that. I thought at once that I would have enjoyed being involved in that project: Mary and I had once idly discussed writing a general book about Palaeolithic archaeology together, but had never followed up the idea. She subsequently made one such attempt by herself, setting out to describe her work at Olduvai for a general rather than an academic audience, and it didn't work out very well, as she was the first to admit: the book was her *Olduvai Gorge: my Search for Early Man*, published by Collins in 1979. It starts off well enough, with lots of anecdotes about life in camp but, in Mary's own words to me, she got bored with it after the first 30 pages, and it accordingly turns into a very technical summary of things such as the Olduvai fossil animal bones, not really detailed enough for the specialist but far too much so for the general reader. Few people now seem even to have heard of it. That experience was the reason why she was now seeking for a ghost-writer for her autobiography, but it sounded as if she had already found one, so I thought no more about it, beyond wishing I had heard about it sooner, as I might have offered to help.

Mary was in Oxford during the summer of 1981, because Oxford University gave her an Honorary Degree at its summer Encaenia, along with various other distinguished people: I went along to the ceremony, and we had a chance to talk the following day. I asked her about the autobiography, and it turned out that she was far from settled with the arrangements. She had not liked any of the professional writers the publishers had so far produced for her – I don't know who they were, or how many she interviewed – and she was rapidly going off the whole idea, though still under pressure to go through with it.

'Why don't you let me do it, Mary?' I said. 'We once talked of writing a book together, if you remember. It might be fun.'

Mary looked completely nonplussed, but only for a moment.

'Oh, would you?' she said. 'That really might solve everything.'

We talked a bit further, and she was clearly warming to the idea as we did so. She said she would tell the publishers, Rainbird, after her next round of travels, and ask them to contact me, which eventually they did.

Desultory correspondence followed, and it was not until early the following year that things began to take a definite shape. Karen Goldie-Morrison, from Rainbird, came to Oxford to inspect me and discuss the idea seriously, and it was agreed that I should submit some appropriate specimen text, so that they could decide whether or not I would be 'too academic'. We agreed that the most relevant thing I could write would be an account of my first meeting with Mary. If they liked that, they would talk to Mary and me together in London, when she was next in England, which would be in September 1982, and a final decision would be reached. So, when Karen had gone, I reached for my trusty blue biro, word-processors not being available in 1982, and got to work. I will reproduce here the text that I sent them, because the story of the first meeting is quite relevant to many things in the diary, and it began the pleasant working relationship with Mary that had encouraged me to think I could take on this project. It also shows broadly the style in which I was proposing to write, if appointed. Written in May 1982, the only title it has on my faded photocopy is 'Derek Roe: sample text'.

> If you are going to visit Mary Leakey at home in East Africa, it's no good making your way to Nairobi and expecting to find her at the attractive low courtyard house at Langata which Louis Leakey built in 1952. The 'White Highlands' on the edge of Nairobi, where the elegant houses have large cool rooms and big gardens bright with carefully tended tropical flowers, might strike many people as one of the most desirable residential areas in all Africa – and very English, too, if you happen to find that an extra advantage.

Cucumber sandwiches and appropriate primary education can be
obtained, but are not compulsory; half an hour will get you comfortably to the airport when the older children fly home from boarding
school. The city of Nairobi too can wear a pleasing face, provided
you don't stray too far from the centre; indeed, even the centre is
not the safe place it used to be, least of all after dark, though by
day the public buildings, the big hotels, the gardens around the
museum, the shops and the main market all give the air of an attractive capital city in which it might be no hardship to live, provided
you could do so on your own terms. It has certainly come far in the
seventy years or so since it was a collection of corrugated iron
huts at the end of a railway line. But to Mary, Nairobi has become
somewhere to avoid as much as possible – even Langata, even the
spectacular view of the Ngong hills with their grassy volcanic
peaks; even the cool courtyard house with the shy but tame hyraxes,
which Louis trained to use the loo for exactly the purpose its makers had in mind.
Mary cannot avoid going to Nairobi several times a year, but she
makes her visits as short as she decently can. So you *might* happen
to find her there, but she will only be passing through, pursued for
every moment of her stay by colleagues, visitors, secretaries and
staff of the Institute where her office is, who have been saving
their messages and enquiries for weeks or months and know that this
may be the only chance of even a one-word answer until a similar
period has passed. Mary will be tense, and you may find her distinctly unhelpful, unless you are one of the few she really wants to
see. Of the rest, she has been dodging half of them for years and
has no intention of seeing them now if it can be avoided or of doing
what they want if it can't. Others who are waiting she has never
met, and doesn't know quite what to expect or whether she is going
to like them, even if she is aware from letters why they have come;
the remnants of her natural shyness will often get such interviews
off to a sticky start. In other cases, it is she who wants or needs
to see the visitor, to hear news, to seek research assistance or
financial backing or to discuss new discoveries and interpretations.
With these people, there is never enough time to get everything
done, and the rest have to be fought off, while she tries: the
office will cope splendidly, as they always do, after she has made
her escape.
Apart from all of that, and the latest family news and crises (the
Leakeys being no ordinary family), Mary is likely to be tense simply
because she is merely in transit, and another journey begins tomorrow or the next day. Perhaps it is an outward journey, to America
via England: business with publishers in London and Cambridge, followed by a long and taxing programme of lecturing and fundraising in
the States, with the occasional television interview and, from time
to time, an honorary degree to be received. There will be non-stop
hospitality, well-meant but inevitably tiring: too many strident
voices asking predictable questions and too many endlessly smiling
faces. Where do they get all these faces from, in American cities,
for goodness' sake? Somebody must be mass-producing them and import-
ing them and making a lot of money out of it – the Japanese, perhaps. Do they actually have bodies and homes, or do they just dema-
terialise and reappear in the next city? But where the delighted
audiences are, there also the research funds may be sought; besides,
amongst it all, there are a few valued friends, whom it really will
be a pleasure to see again.
Mary does her part of these month-long trips superbly well and gives
her hosts excellent value, earning in one way or another every penny
of the research money that comes in, but it is a feat of endurance
rather than an exercise in enjoyment, and a little harder to sustain
each year. Louis began it of course, and was in his element on such
tours. Mary, however unwilling, simply had to continue them after

his death, if the Olduvai project was to survive, let alone other research operations, because that was what the customers had come to expect. These triumphal tours are as much a price that has to be paid for continuing research support as is the continual need to make discoveries that are spectacular as well as merely being of outstanding scientific importance. Richard Leakey is every bit as good as Louis was when it comes to the arts of public communication and fundraising, but he has his own research projects to finance, and Mary is expected, and expects, to make her own way.*

If Mary's presence in Nairobi is the prelude to one of these international trips, is it any wonder if she seems a little tense? Perhaps, however, the trip is behind her and she is homeward bound. If so, be sure that she is counting the moments till she can start the last lap, the drive down to Olduvai itself. Every corner of the car will be crammed with supplies for the camp, with items of archaeological equipment ordered months ago, with mail, with edited typescripts, with books and offprints gathered abroad, and even with one or two people: perhaps a member of her African staff at the Gorge, returning from leave in Nairobi, and some long-term visitor bringing welcome expertise of some specific kind. If you are lucky, perhaps you yourself will be a passenger, and if it is your first visit you can expect one of the most fascinating day's drives that you are ever likely to experience. Mary of course has made the journey far too often to be excited in that kind of way, but it is in her mind that she has done everything that had to be done in Nairobi and left the rest in good hands, and that now she is going home: home to Olduvai. In nine, ten, eleven hours, depending on the chances of the journey, she will be with her four beloved Dalmatians again, home at last, shaking off the dust of Nairobi and the even more clinging dust of the world beyond. Things are beginning to look up by the time the car turns off the main Mombasa road, with Nairobi already twenty miles behind.

It is Olduvai Gorge in Tanzania, then, not Nairobi in Kenya, that has been Mary's real home for more than 20 years, though it is much longer than that, fast approaching fifty years in fact, since she first went there in 1935. Her camp at Olduvai is a remote place. The Gorge lies at the edge of the Serengeti Plains, below the volcanic highlands of Tanzania, and the camp is a fairly rugged twenty-eight miles from the nearest telephone, which is to be found at Ngorongoro, where the mail arrives (on those occasions when it does) and where there are also limited other facilities. It used to be necessary also to go that far for fresh water, and tanks for rainwater storage at the Gorge were only installed in 1975. True, there is now a radio telephone at Olduvai, which offers a slightly hit-or-miss way of making outward calls, but the world cannot ring you up unless you have decided to listen and, predictably, Mary is inclined in normal circumstances to regard the machine with dislike, suspicion and feigned incomprehension. So Olduvai remains wonderfully, blessedly remote and that is why it is reached by no ordinary journey, though today the business of getting there lacks the heroic qualities it certainly possessed when Louis Leakey first visited the Gorge in 1931, or indeed when Mary made her own first trip four years later, the story of which has been told by Louis, by Sonia Cole and, very briefly, by Mary herself in *Olduvai Gorge: my search for Early Man*, which is the nearest she has come to writing a 'popular' book. Now, there are reasonably good earth roads all the way after the tarmac ends and even the precipitous rocky track that takes vehicles across the Gorge itself and up to the camp has had the attention of a heavy grading machine, so that a saloon car loaded with (for example) people, dogs, excavation equipment, rock samples for palaeomagnetic dating and a dead porcupine found by the side of the track, whose bones will be useful in the lab, goes up it as easily as a Land Rover.

*This comment is based on something Mary herself once said to me, when discussing the Leakey family, including herself: 'Each of the Leakeys needs to have his own empire, and Heaven help other members of the family who come into it without being invited. Olduvai is my empire.'

But however good the roads, I doubt whether it is actually possible anywhere in East Africa to drive all day without incident, excitement or adventure of some kind. Around Olduvai itself, far shorter journeys than that usually produce something quite exceptional to see, or exceptional at least as far as the experience of mere visitors goes. I learned the uncertainties of African travel very quickly on my own first visit, in 1969... Louis, with the warm-hearted generosity which he extended to all comers, met me himself at the airport, though I had only been briefly introduced to him once a few years before and was the most junior of colleagues. He made me welcome at Langata for that night and the following morning, after a visit to the Centre for Prehistory, sent me off to Olduvai in his own new car, with a string of instructions, supplies for Mary, a member of the Kenyan staff of the Centre who knew the way, and a specially hired Kenyan driver from Nairobi, said to be very experienced with Mercedes cars and well able to handle Louis's big Volvo. Both of the Kenyans spoke a little English, which was as well, because I knew no Swahili. We had a picnic lunch, and should reach Olduvai by early evening. In 1969, Kenya, Tanzania and Uganda still enjoyed generally harmonious relations and formed an economic federation which made movement from one country to the next easy; so the route from Nairobi to Olduvai went to the Kenya/Tanzania border at Namanga and then on via Arusha and Ngorongoro to Olduvai – usually about nine hours' run, though one of the Leakey boys was said to have done it in just under five ... Even before we reached the border, my faith in the Mercedes expert had become somewhat shaken, starting from the moment when I had to show him how to switch on the ignition, but it was not until we reached an empty stretch of the Arusha road somewhere beyond the slender and beautiful peak of Longido mountain that disaster struck. If you drive a Volvo with the hand brake on for enough miles, you may indeed destroy the clutch, and that is what this particular driver had achieved. One feels entitled to wonder whether the same fate might not have befallen a Mercedes. It was 1.30 on a Sunday afternoon, other road users were few and far between, my first visit to Africa was less than 24 hours old, and those might or might not be vultures, now one came to think of it.

Never yet, after several attempts, have I succeeded in getting through Arusha without some sort of undue delay, and I know that others can say the same. In retrospect, therefore, I can see that it was not particularly unusual to arrive there for the first time in a new but crippled Volvo on the end of a tow-rope attached to the well-worn Land Rover of a night-club proprietor from Dar-es-Salaam who, if looks counted, could have had for the asking a starring role in any film featuring Middle Eastern bandits. But his nature was kind and honest: three times during the thirty-mile tow the rope had broken, and three times he had not availed himself of the opportunity to drive on with the only moderately exorbitant fee, payable in advance, which had secured his services. A telephone call to Louis from Arusha miraculously found him at the only number I knew, and produced instant instructions on what to do next, where to stay, and whom to contact when shops and garages opened on Monday. By dusk, I was installed in a comfortable hotel and had been delighted by the efforts of three African waiters to extract an energetic stray sheep from its gardens, and by the fact that a large hornbill had deliberately thrown a nut at me from the topmost branches of a flame-tree. I had also undergone the shock of discovering that in Africa the moon is quite a different way up from the one I knew in England. It stands to reason that the stars will be different, but I still do not understand the geometry that tilts the moon through nearly ninety degrees. Perhaps it has disguised itself in the hope of getting past Arusha unhindered. The next day, following Louis's instructions, I left his car for repair at Subzali's Garage, and went on to

Olduvai in a hired white Volkswagen Beetle, with a different and excellent driver. The two Kenyans were not to let Louis's car out of their sight till it was mended. We reached Olduvai in the late afternoon after a marvellous run through increasingly dramatic scenery. Mary had ceased to expect me: at Olduvai you expect people only when they reach the last level couple of hundred yards into camp. She at once made me very welcome, and this was our first meeting.

Mary was alone in camp at the time, apart from her usual staff of Kenyans and Tanzanians: some were guides for the tourists (not very frequent at that time), while the rest made up her expert and highly trained excavating team, plus her cook, who was famous for his superb white bread, made in a biscuit-tin oven, and never forgotten by visitors. It transpired that Mary's own car was actually in Arusha collecting equipment, and was expected back sometime in the next week, so the only vehicle in camp was a large Bedford lorry. The Volkswagen was needed back in Arusha, and left at once; one could see that the matter of getting back to Nairobi in time to catch the flight to Zambia might in due course pose interesting problems, especially since at that time the radio telephone had not yet been installed, but there was really no point in worrying about it. My visit had already been shortened, and there was so much to see and only two hours of daylight left. In a matter of moments, Mary had packed me into the Bedford and was driving it herself on a tour of selected sites in the Gorge, handling the heavy vehicle with superbly delicate control in places where at that stage I would have thought twice about even walking. It was an unforgettable afternoon. I knew enough from my studies at Cambridge about Olduvai and the African Early Stone Age to please Mary with the questions I asked. Everything about the Gorge and the landscape and the animals we saw, quite apart from the archaeology, impressed me profoundly. It was perhaps the most beautiful of all times of day for a first visit. Mary's heart always warms to those who are deeply impressed by her beloved Olduvai, and I could not have concealed its effect on me even if I had wanted to do so. She had expected to have to persuade me to undertake the study of her handaxes, but for me the project of course represented a golden opportunity to apply methods of my own devising to material from one of the most important sites in the world – and a chance to return to this beautiful place for a much longer visit. By the end of the afternoon, Mary and I had become firm friends. In the evening, I looked at some of the stone implements in question and became so absorbed in taking measurements from a small pilot sample that, when Mary came in to offer me a drink, I did not even hear her, and she tells me she tiptoed out, deeply impressed. That night, I slept in a tent under the big acacia tree by the camp, warned by Mary to be sure not to go out in the dark without a torch because sometimes there were cobras. I didn't see any cobras, but next morning we found fresh tracks left in the dust by several lions, who had passed soundlessly through the camp in the middle of the night, which they do not often do, without even disturbing the dogs. Undoubtedly, wild Africa was stretching out her hands to me as she has done to so many on their first visit. Those who grasp them in an equal response soon find themselves locked in a warm embrace that engages all the senses and may last for ever, while few can wholly ignore or ever forget the first appealing gesture, even if their paths do not lead them this way again. One can see indeed that Nairobi and Langata are not a part of wild Africa. Next day we were off soon after first light to see more sites in the Gorge. During the morning, Mary suddenly became restless: she could hear the engines of several tourist vehicles somewhere in her Gorge, and she was *not* in the mood to meet tourists. This was 1969: Louis was at the height of his powers and in charge of all the fundraising. Mary, still immensely shy of all publicity, asked only to be left in peace at Olduvai to carry out the scientific excavations that were so badly needed, to her own exacting standards, to interpret her discoveries with the help of scholars of her own choosing - like Dick Hay, the geologist, from Berkeley, California - and to test by selective research the major theories of human evolution and cultural development that she was beginning to formulate. Exciting new techniques in Quaternary Research were beginning to make definite answers a real possibility. Tourists interrupted all that, and wasted precious hours, if not whole days. Tourists penetrated uninvited to the camp, which was private, and expected to shake her hand. They had even been known to take surreptitious pictures of her washing her hair on a Sunday morning... Since 1969, Mary's attitude to tourists has altered radically in a fascinating way which, to me, is completely understandable in terms of the changes in her career since Louis's death. It is not that Louis was holding Mary back, but that after 1972 she had to take on, as she must have known for some years that she would, certain things that she had been able previously to leave alone.

But all that lay some way ahead, and on this particular morning in 1969, we fled from site to site, Mary with an ear cocked for the sound of engines, achieving a more rapid but also more extensive tour than had been planned. Perhaps that was how I came to leave my hat behind somewhere near FLK I, the find-spot of the famous 'Zinjanthropus' skull: what a resting place for a piece of headgear! No doubt a Maasai herdsman eventually found it: on a later visit to Olduvai, I once saw one wearing proudly an American golf hat and a pair of glasses with very thick lenses which cannot have been doing much for his eyesight, though he was otherwise attired just as any good ethnographer would have expected.

Mary's car returned to camp that afternoon, and she generously offered to take me all the way back to Nairobi herself next day, if the Volvo did not turn up repaired, since my flight to Zambia was unalterably booked. In fact, late that evening, the Volvo did reach camp, complete with the supplies and the two Kenyans: Louis had somehow contrived to send down a new clutch assembly from Nairobi to Arusha. The car now, however, had a substantial dent in one side, which the driver swore was someone else's fault. Mary was glad not to have to make the journey to Nairobi. My own feelings were somewhat mixed, but we set off on time next day. The driver was now so nervous that he drove all the way to Ngorongoro in second gear. Arusha, needless to say, was ready for us. There had been some incident in the area of the bazaar, which had attracted a large crowd of excited local people, and two Tanzanian policemen were operating a simple diversion of the traffic. The driver completely ignored their clear signals to turn left, whereupon they blew whistles, stopped the car, demanded his licence, confiscated it and informed him that he should collect it and pay a fine the following morning. They then disappeared into the crowd, which was jeering happily at this downfall of a car with Kenyan number plates.

If one is to be the only white person in such a situation, while still new to Africa (though learning fast), I suspect that one should be armed with H Rider Haggard's *Allan Quartermain* as well as *Teach Yourself Swahili*, or at least with a more assertive temperament than mine. Somehow I caught up the policemen and informed them in the most English kind of English I could contrive that this was the car of the famous Dr Louis Leakey, a personal friend of the President of Tanzania, lent to me as a visitor to their beautiful country - and a visitor, moreover, officer, who has a plane to catch in Nairobi shortly. The fame of Louis stood me in good stead: the policemen had heard of him and were slightly impressed. After a certain amount more talk, they quite suddenly threw the licence back at the driver and strode off. The driver was also slightly impressed. If anything, his performance rather deteriorated after that.

Certainly, I was very glad to see Louis's front gate again at last. The driver may have been less certain of his reception by the *bwana*, but he marked our arrival by overshooting the entrance and then backing firmly into the gatepost. There was only just time for me to get to the airport after giving Louis a rapid account of the main adventures and my thanks for everything; I last saw the driver about to begin his explanation of the car's condition. No doubt all of this is no more than an average example of the hazards of travel in East Africa, and my account is not really a fair one, because I have failed to dwell on the beauties and fascination of the landscape, which were unfailing whenever one dared to look. It transpired later that my own British driving licence would in fact have allowed me to take over the driving of the car at any time – Louis had been under the impression that this was not so.
The next time I made the same journey, Mary and I shared the driving in her car and I enjoyed every moment. But we were still held up in Arusha for a couple of hours. That, however, is another story, and so is the time when we were charged by a rhinoceros while driving along the edge of the Gorge, and the time when we got stuck in the mud at Lake Masek some miles from anywhere and had to be rescued by George Dove, or the night puncture in the middle of Serengeti, or the day we saw the pack of wild dogs on that exhilarating run across country to Laetoli, before the excavations there made the site world famous. There are, you see, really no ordinary journeys in East Africa.

Reading this text through again so many years later, I see nothing that I now know to be inaccurate in it, unless it is my describing Louis as 'still at the height of his powers' in 1969. Certainly, he was still operating at full speed in things like his fundraising efforts, but I have already suggested in the summary of Mary's life that he had begun to decline in other ways by then. Aside from that, I think there is one important omission in my account of the first meeting with Mary: the fact that the 1969 team of Dalmatians greeted me in a friendly manner, and I got on well with them throughout my short stay. If that had not happened, since Mary always respected their judgement, her welcome to me would have been less warm and there would always have been some sort of barrier between us. I really am not exaggerating when I say that I am quite sure I would never have become her ghost-writer, if the dogs had disapproved of me on any of my visits. Inevitably, some of the incidents just described get a mention again in the diary, but only in passing. Some themes that run through the diary are certainly anticipated above, like the ride from Nairobi to Olduvai, the hazards of car journeys in East Africa, including the tendency of Arusha to have a baleful influence on travellers, or my puzzlement over the African moon, but I class that as continuity rather than repetition, and still think it is worth using this 'specimen text' as part of the introduction to the diary itself.

Immediately, back in May 1982, I sent off my finished text to Rainbird as promised, and received a favourable reaction, which was followed by a meeting in London. I reported on this to Mary, and decided that it was only fair to send her a copy of the specimen text, since she was the person who really needed to be happy with my writing style. Peter Jones, who features frequently in the diary, was shortly due to return to East Africa from Oxford, to resume working as Mary's assistant at the Gorge, after a break and some travel, so I entrusted the letter and text to him. Peter is the son of a then Oxford colleague of mine, and I had known him since he was a young schoolboy with a serious interest in the flint implements he picked up in the fields near his home in Oxfordshire. He also spent a year studying at Oxford for our Master's degree in Prehistoric Archaeology, during which time I was his principal teacher. I will quote my letter to Mary and her reply here, partly for the contents and partly to serve as an example of our correspondence. It is entirely predictable that my letters would in any case have tended to be longer and fuller than Mary's, but one practical reason for that is that she always wrote on one of those air-letter forms with a printed stamp, which offer you a maximum of one and a half sides of space. Often, Mary used about a third of that, though this time she used the whole of it. No one could say that over-succinctness is one of my failings as a letter-writer.

```
60, Banbury Road, OXFORD
31 May 1982

Dear Mary,
Jambo, habari? - and all that African talk that reminds me of man-
goes. This is a brief note (by my standards) by hand of Peter to
report on affairs with Rainbird, from whom you should have heard
independently.
When we were last in touch, you were rejecting authors over lunch,
and were going to phone me once more on your last evening, but you
evidently didn't get a chance or couldn't get through, not that it
mattered. Nothing then happened for a couple of weeks, after which
Karen Goldie-Morrison phoned and later visited me here. No, I know
you don't care for her, but I get on quite well with her. We had a
long talk, from which it emerged that I had to prove I wasn't too
academic and that involved writing some specimen text - I also gave
her some odds and ends of a suitable nature I had written. I argued
at great length that the best result would be if I were given a free
hand to write a book about you, full of direct quotations and so
forth, rather than attempt to put words into your mouth. She was
inclined to agree, but doubted if it would suit the publishers. To
amuse you (well, probably) here is a copy of the specimen text I
sent. Since it couldn't really be a sample of what they had in mind,
it was agreed I should write about you and experiences of my own on
my visits to you, so I did. See what you think. Bear in mind that it
is supposed to convince a publisher (a) that I can write in a
saleable non-academic manner (b) that I know you well enough to per-
form the task and (c) that I have appropriate qualities as an
observer of scenery and people. I do not say that it proves any of
these points - see what you think - but I thought it would convince
Rainbird, and it evidently did. So I went and had a very pleasant
lunch with them and we went over all the same ground again, with the
predictable result that they would be very pleased if I did it, but
it must be an autobiography written in the first person ostensibly
by you, even if I write every word. They agree that I could probably
write a splendid biography of you, and that it would be a much bet-
ter book than a ghost-written autobiography, but as saleable com-
modities they say there is simply no comparison. An autobiography
will sell over 100,000 copies and will make you your money: a biog-
raphy, however elegant, might sell 10-15,000 - 'not really worth
doing'. (I should say of course that if I had been allowed to do a
biography, all the proceeds could have gone to you, so it wasn't a
difficulty of that kind.)
So, there you are. We can do it, and I will of course do my best for
you, but we can't do it the way I would wish and the way I know I
could do effectively and successfully. All the things they liked
about the sample text will be hard to achieve (though not necessari-
ly impossible) because it will sound forced and artificial if I put
that sort of stuff into your mouth - or that's the way it seems to
me. Can you hear yourself saying that sort of thing, transposed into
the first person? How far will you go for an estimated $150,000-at-
least? It won't fool anyone who knows you, for a moment. Still, that
will be an infinitesimal proportion of the customers.
We have been in some odd situations in the past, Mary - the mud at
Lake Masek, for example - but I'm not sure this isn't the oddest. No
doubt we can make a go of it, and I will if you will, but you'll
```

have to be fairly forthcoming and be prepared to tell at least some
of it the way I write. Yes? No? Think for an hour or two and then
write me as long a letter as you have time for, assessing the entire
situation. (Perhaps we should do it in verse: Mary, Mary, quite contrary, how does your story go? Oh dull enough, except the stuff made
up by Derek Roe. Mary had a little lamb: its name was Derek Roe; it
had to write what Mary said – or else it had to go. Well, that's
prose, really, isn't it?) Why don't publishers know what's good for
them? Just think of the film rights we shall lose. In my version,
you could have been played by a team of actresses from child stars
upwards, Louis by Lawrence Olivier, Richard by someone from one of
the James Bond films and I could have appeared briefly, played by
Donald Duck. And just think of the other possibilities of who could
play your various colleagues and visitors at Olduvai and American
sponsors ...
This letter is now becoming irrelevant, so I will stop. But do
write, if you're still ready to go ahead and still want me. I can do
no more at this end till you come in the autumn, unless you can send
me anything in the way of diaries, letters, journals that already
exist – you won't have time to write or record anything. I could
perhaps write a bit about the scenery and the Olduvai operation, by
way of a start, to be fitted in somewhere, but there's very little I
can do without yourself.
All more or less well here otherwise. Peter is in good form and has
enjoyed his stay in England. I'm very impressed with all he is
doing. Love from us all, Derek.

Here is Mary's reply.

P.O. Box 30239, Nairobi, Kenya.
June 3rd/82

Dear Derek,
Peter brought me your letter and masterpiece. I feel that it is a
bit degrading for you to be asked to 'ghost' and I think it is very
good of you to agree. If you want to back out, I'll quite understand, but I hope not.
I think I told you that my motive in undertaking this project is
purely mercenary. The $150,000 will see me comfortable for the rest
of my days and save the annual lecture grind. I can only contemplate
doing it with you – for some reason we can get along together. I
know it won't be easy and we may start hurling books at one another.
But I hope not and believe we can avoid actual violence! You can put
such words as you think fit into my mouth, provided they are not too
outrageous. Besides I think you could have me relating impressions
of [the] Gorge etc as passed on by visitors. At any rate Derek, if
you are game to try, I am too.
I tried to phone you before leaving London but got no reply on both
occasions. Peter seems well and happy. He really needed to get out
into the big world. He leaves for Olduvai today, whilst I grapple
with what Rainbirds have done to the rock painting book. Meave [wife
of Richard Leakey] has seen the 'edited' version and prefers to be
out of Nairobi when I set eyes on it!
Please be honest and back out if you feel you would rather not
undertake this job. I would hate to think I had pushed you into it
against your will.
Love, Mary.

In September, Mary and I did go together to a meeting with the publishers, and it
was finally agreed that I should take on the task of ghost-writing her autobiography. I
remember the looks of astonishment on the faces of the Rainbird editorial staff at the easy

way in which Mary and I talked together: they had obviously been treating her with great awe, and seemed to have difficulty in believing that she would ever allow anyone to tease her or make her laugh. It was agreed that I would need at least three visits to her in East Africa to do the work, which would have to be fitted in somehow with my ordinary duties during an Oxford academic year, and we discussed timing and deadlines and the drawing up of a formal contract. The work would have to be completed in the calendar year 1983, and the first visit would take place as early in January as could be arranged between Mary and myself. Over the remaining months of 1982, I did all the background reading I could, and even sent Mary a long list of what seemed to me likely to be major themes, topics or highlights, but she sent only a few words in reply and clearly nothing much would get done before I made the first trip.

The drawing up of the contract seemed to me needlessly complicated and very long drawn out, but that was mainly because I wasn't greatly interested in it, and would have done the whole project on trust, though it was not my first experience of writing a book and I knew perfectly well that publishers don't work in such a way. Academic archaeologists of my kind are very gullible, and for the vast majority of what they write professionally, however excellent, the question of payment simply doesn't arise. The same goes for the giving of opinions and advice, which they tend to do regularly for free to all comers, often good factual information which the enquirer might well not be able to obtain anywhere else in the world. Lawyers, accountants and the like are genuinely horrified when I tell them this, and a large proportion of the world is no doubt quietly laughing itself sick and pocketing the profits. A few archaeologists have gradually learned the lesson, but not many had done so by 1982. So, the contract didn't interest me greatly. Visits had to be made to a solicitor working for the Leakeys in London, who explained that, although Rainbird was the publisher, the contract would be with a Company in Holland called Sherma BV, which was 'simply a medium through which the Leakeys ... are virtually forced to make contracts because of the very complicated tax and exchange control problems which would otherwise surround their earnings'. This Company seemed to have a parent company in Jersey, to complicate things further.

One way or another, the contract was not eventually signed until the middle of May 1983, by which time I had completed one trip and was planning the next. The delay, I gathered, was something to do with 'the recently renegotiated Double Taxation Treaty between the Netherlands and the United Kingdom which has forced Sherma to make a thorough reexamination of its operating terms'. Well, fancy that, I thought: it seemed to have little to do with my writing up Mary's life story for her. The contract, when it finally appeared, specified the completion date as the end of December 1983, as already agreed; I was to submit the final version to the Company two weeks before it went to Rainbird and 'make any reasonable revisions or corrections that the Company deemed necessary'. I was to write captions for the illustrations and to read and correct the proofs within two weeks of receipt; I was to receive 'printed in all copies of all editions of the Work an acknowledgement in a form to be mutually agreed between [myself] and the Company and Mary Leakey' for my contribution to the work. Copyright in the text of the work would vest in the Company, and by signing the Contract I would assign the copyright of my contribution to the work to the Company, in consideration of the following payments: $US3000 on signature of the Agreement, $5000 on delivery of the complete typescript, and $2000 on publication. In the event, none of these payments reached me even remotely on schedule, though they all came in the end, as did the refund of expenses, though only after reminders each time. Just how closely the terms of the contract were adhered to, is perhaps a part of the whole story. In any case, the contract was only in a draft stage when 1983, the Year of the Ghost, dawned, and I began to think about packing for departure, pen in hand. At least I had received an air ticket, even if rather at the last moment and apparently from somewhere in Ireland, as opposed to Holland, the Channel Islands or even London. It looked as if the whole thing really was going to happen. The odd thing is that I can't actually remember when I decided to keep a diary of my trip.

*

Olduvai Gorge and its archaeology

General introduction

The purpose of this final section of the Introduction is to describe the Gorge in its present day form and to mention some of the principal discoveries there which have made it so important to the archaeology of human origins. These things provide the background to the diary, in the sense of describing and explaining the setting in which it was being written, but quite apart from that, anyone who may wish to make an evaluation of Mary Leakey and her achievements certainly needs to understand the significance of Olduvai as one of the world's outstanding archaeological sites. It is true – as we have seen – that Mary had many outstanding successes at other sites, but Olduvai was (to use a favourite word of hers) 'special'. It was, after all, here that she insisted her ashes should be scattered.

The whole of Olduvai Gorge constitutes a very substantial geological feature, some 50 kilometres long, or considerably more than that, if one allows for the combined lengths of both the Main and Side gorges, which form a rough Y-shape (see figure 2). At its deepest points, it approaches 100 metres in depth. It has been created by the combination of earth movements and faulting with erosion by a river: the earth movements altered the area's drainage pattern, and an existing river was given enough new erosive power to create a Gorge. As figure 2 shows, the sides of the Gorge are not straight, but are deeply indented by many erosional features, gullies of different sizes, some of which are steep-sided and some shallow. The local name for one of these gullies is a *Korongo* and many of the individual archaeological sites have Korongo as part of their name. Louis Leakey

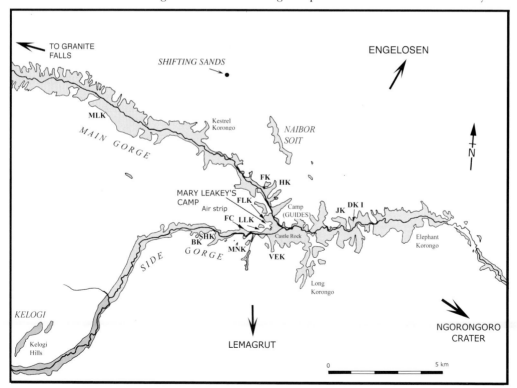

Figure 2 Sketch map of Olduvai Gorge

named most of them after friends and colleagues, often in honour of a particular discovery, and it is the initials that are normally used: thus, the full name of SHK is Sam Howard Korongo, while BK in full is Bell's Korongo.

The actual formation of a Gorge at Olduvai occurred relatively late in the whole chronological sequence that is represented there. The main significance of the Gorge feature is that it is a great natural excavation trench, so to speak, cut through the deep sediments that had already been deposited, with very few breaks, between some 2.0 million and 400,000 years ago. These sediments represent a succession of past landscapes, which were inhabited by early humans and by the animals of the region. Here and there can be found rich concentrations of archaeological material, featuring stone artefacts in association with animal bones, and these are the individual archaeological sites which the formation of the Gorge has made accessible. They still need to be discovered, essentially by careful examination of the sides of the Gorge itself, but that is not nearly such a simple matter as it might sound, since the Gorge's sides are often precipitous or in places covered by thick thorny bushes, or other vegetation which completely masks the sediments themselves and their archaeological contents. Usually, therefore, the sites come to light where there has been modern erosion of the Gorge sides, for example, after the rains of each year. Even after a site has been found, it may be a formidable task to cut back the side of the Gorge, digging down from above, to reach the archaeological horizon and expose a substantial area of it in properly controlled excavation trenches. The *Zinjanthropus* site at FLK, already mentioned earlier in this chapter, is a good example both of the way in which important material may first come to light, and the magnitude of the task of excavating it.

Exactly why there should be a substantial accumulation of archaeological material at some particular place in the landscape is something the archaeologist needs to determine. It is possible for natural agencies to bring the objects together, but it is to be hoped that intentional human action is also involved, and it is by the study of such evidence that light can be cast on the capabilities and behavioural patterns of the early humans. It is also of course the case that there are important changes in the nature of the archaeological material as one passes from the older levels at the base of the Gorge upwards through the younger ones that overlie them. For example, the progress of human evolution will be marked by changes in the hominid types; the animal communities, as represented by the various bones, teeth, horns, tusks and antlers, will also change, partly through evolution but also in response to changes in the local environment and climate. The technology of human artefact manufacture, too, undergoes important developments as time passes. In all these respects, Olduvai Gorge has quite extraordinary evidence to offer: conditions of preservation are generally very good, and the sheer length of time represented there is exceptional. In the creation of the Gorge, nature has opened up a window in sediments representing over one and a half million years of time, and indeed the sedimentation continued after the Gorge itself was formed, so that around two million years of time is represented in all. Even though there are now several sites in Africa which antedate Olduvai, the particular span of time represented here is of crucial importance to our understanding of the whole African Stone Age and indeed of the earlier Palaeolithic of the whole Old World.

So far as the early humans of Olduvai were concerned, they were occupying a landscape lacking the Gorge of today, but richly endowed with natural resources, on the grassy plains below the volcanic highlands. There were lakes; during the earlier part of the sequence, one of them was located close to where the Main and Side gorges now meet, where the main concentration of archaeological sites is. Such lakes might be filled with either saline or fresh water, but even if the former were the case, there were streams and rivers draining to them, whose water was certainly fresh. The vegetation was probably much like that of today, the grassy plains being dotted with acacias and other trees, and game animals were clearly abundant. Plenty of good rock for tool making was obtainable, whether directly from outcrops (like the white quartzite of Naibor Soit or the green phonolite lava of Engelosen), or from the beaches of the streams or rivers.

Some of the local volcanoes were active during the period represented by the Olduvai sediments, and indeed the sediments themselves include a major component of volcanic ash. Sometimes the ash falls hardened out to form rock (known as tuff). If the volcanic activity may perhaps sometimes have inconvenienced the early human population, from the archaeologists' point of view, it is of great importance, because lava and tuffs can usually be directly dated, using such methods as potassium-argon dating. Where the ash fell gently, it often sealed in and preserved archaeological horizons – with a covering that is likely to be precisely datable. The Olduvai region also saw several episodes of tectonic activity (earth movements) during the whole period of sedimentation. One of these, as I have already noted, led to the changes in

Exposed beds of Olduvai Gorge

drainage which caused the Gorge to be cut; an earlier one caused the lake that was present at the beginning of the sequence to shift its position by several kilometres, so that in the main area of archaeological sites a point is reached in the stratigraphic succession where one is no longer looking at evidence for lake-side environments but at sediments which represent grassland with stream channels, and both the faunal evidence and the nature of the human activities alter to reflect this *(see Figure 3)*.

Dry season. The plants are aloes, and the mountain is the Lemagrut volcano

Olduvai Gorge was first discovered in 1911 by a German entomologist, Otto Kattwinkel, who came upon it very suddenly when in pursuit of butterflies on the Serengeti Plains. He noted the presence of fossil animal bones on the surface of the sediments and collected some specimens. What is now Tanzania was then a part of German East Africa, and German scientists, following up his report, carried out a first exploratory expedition to Olduvai in 1913, led by Hans Reck; by coincidence, that was actually the year in which Mary Leakey was born. But before they could return to continue their work, the First World War broke out, and after that the area passed to British control. Louis Leakey, following up the old reports, succeeded in locating the Gorge again in 1931, and it was he who first found stone artefacts there, in that year, establishing that Olduvai was an archaeological site as well as a palaeontological one.

Geological sequence

It was Hans Reck who, during the 1913 German expedition, first divided the Olduvai sedimentary sequence into five Beds, numbered in Roman numerals, Bed I being the lowest and oldest. These divisions are essentially still in use today, though with some refinements and with tighter definition, based on the work of the Leakeys and their teams of colleagues over the years, with the geologist Dick Hay a notable contributor. The Bed IV of current terminology is only the lower part of Reck's original Bed IV, and the upper part now has the name (of local origin) Masek Beds; similarly, Reck's Bed V is no longer referred to, having been replaced by two further locally named units, the Ndutu Beds and the Naisiusiu Beds. In Figure 3, a diagrammatic section of the Gorge is given, to show these major stratigraphic divisions in the simplest possible form. Plenty of technical literature is available to those who wish to study their complexities, a good starting point being Hay's own definitive study *Geology of the Olduvai Gorge*, published by the University of California Press at Berkeley, California in 1976. I will give here a brief summary of the Gorge's stratigraphy, followed by a glance at the archaeological sequence.

At the base of the sequence, as shown in the diagram, in the lower part of Bed I, there is an actual lava flow, of considerable thickness in places, which has been dated by potassium argon to about 1.9 million years ago. One is often walking or driving over exposures of this black basaltic rock, when one takes one of the tracks along the bottom of the Gorge down below the camp, which is situated on the spur of land between the Main and Side Gorges. Elsewhere, the lava may be masked by sediments of relatively recent age deposited by the present Olduvai river, or by material displaced from the Gorge sides by erosion or slope processes of various kinds – this latter may contain archaeological material, but obviously only in a disturbed context, if so. Older sediments do exist beneath the lava flow, but they are rarely exposed and have not yielded any significant finds.

In Bed I, in the main research area, the sediments consist of clays, relating to the Olduvai lake of this time and its surrounding flats, plus much volcanic ash, which in places has hardened out into distinctive tuff horizons. The last are important: not only are they directly datable but also they act as important marker horizons, when separate sites need to be correlated with each other or placed in stratigraphic order. Tuffs IB and IF are good examples, shown on the diagram; the second of these formally marks the top of Bed I. The lower part of Bed II, however, is very similar to Bed I in terms of sediments, representing the same lake-margin environment, with continuing volcanic activity. Middle Bed II contains many important units, varying from wind-blown ash to torrent gravels, which I will not discuss in any detail here: suffice it to say that a major environmental change took place at this point in the sequence, with a shift in the lake's position and the establishment of grassy savannah where it had been. In the upper part of Bed II, the savannah conditions prevail, and the archaeological sites are often associated with stream channels of various sizes.

'Castle Rock' with red sediments of Bed III

In Bed III, the most distinctive sediments have a strong red hue, and form a striking feature in many of the classic views of Olduvai, though in fact Bed III is only exposed in a rather limited area of the Gorge, and some of its other sediments are grey. A large, isolated block of sediment known as Castle Rock, capped with red Bed III

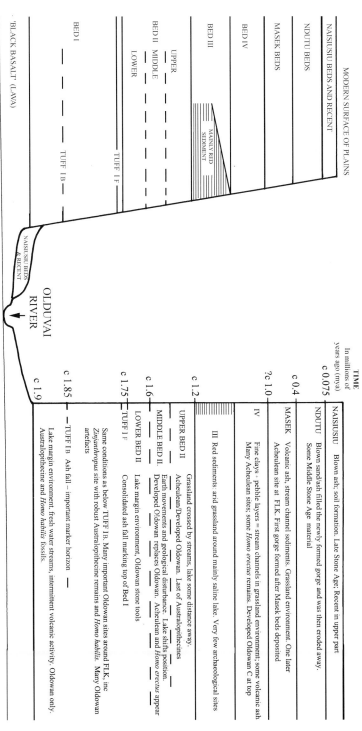

SIMPLIFIED DIAGRAMMATIC SECTION OF OLDUVAI GORGE

Figure 3

sediments, is a particularly prominent Olduvai landmark figure. The red colouring found in Bed III appears to represent conditions that were unpleasantly dry overall, and is believed to have been caused by the alternate wetting and drying, over a long period, of essentially saline alluvial deposits, something that can be seen in the red-coloured flats around the present-day Lake Natron. It is certainly true that the red sediments of Bed III have yielded little evidence of either human or animal occupation of the area, though in the grey sediments at JK an extraordinary complex of apparently artificial pits and runnels was found, tentatively interpreted as a place where the early humans obtained salt, by a process involving the evaporation of water.

Bed IV suggests much more amenable conditions for human occupation of the Olduvai area: stream channels, large and small, are a particularly important feature, the actual sediments of this bed accordingly consisting largely of the fine clays and sandstones, and the conglomerates with heavier stones, which such streams deposited in their beds. There is also a contribution of volcanic ash, including some distinctive tuff horizons, which have helped greatly as markers in correlation between Bed IV sites in different areas of the Gorge. The Bed IV archaeological sites are closely associated with the stream channels, where their occupants doubtless found various amenities ranging from water to shady trees and useful toolmaking rock in the form of cobbles and boulders.

The overlying Masek Beds show a greatly increased proportion of wind-blown ash, with conditions apparently rather drier again, and the stream channels fewer in number. It is at the end of the Masek deposition that renewed tectonic disturbances led to the formation of a Gorge for the first time, when the main drainage way gained enough erosive power to cut down through the underlying deposits. Soon after this first Gorge was cut, it was filled up again by the Ndutu Beds, which consist of relatively soft, wind-blown volcanic ash, whose origin can be traced to the only one of all the local volcanoes that remains occasionally active today, Ol Doinyo Lengai. This blown ash is believed to have reached Olduvai at least partly in the form of migrating dunes: at Shifting Sands (mentioned in the diary), the last active survivor of a more recent dune field of similar origin can be seen, situated not far from the Main Gorge edge on the opposite side of it to the camp. Yet another episode of tectonic activity subsequently led to the Gorge being scoured out again, more deeply this time, with the removal of much of the Ndutu Beds ash that had been blown in. Not all was eroded away, however: while the proper stratigraphic position of the Ndutu Beds is high up the sides of the Gorge, overlying the Masek Beds, in actual fact surviving consolidated remnants of the blown ash may be found at almost any height, unconformably overlying any of the earlier beds. While this can create geological confusion, the compensation is that the shallower slopes provided by these patches of Ndutu Beds may sometimes offer an extra route for vehicle or pedestrian access to the bottom of the Gorge, avoiding a long detour.

The Naisiusiu Beds, which conclude the sequence, were formed much later on by a broadly similar but much less intense episode of deposition of wind-blown ash, again from Ol Doinyo Lengai: this occurred towards the end of the Pleistocene, during the Late Stone Age. In the sides of the Gorge, the Naisiusiu Beds can be found at the very top of the sequence, and they also occur in a few places down on the Gorge floor, as patches which have not been removed by the modern Olduvai river.

Archaeology

Stone artefacts, which are the commonest reliable evidence for early human activity, are present at Olduvai right from the start: that is to say, they first occur at sites in Bed I just above the back lava flow mentioned above, and can be found in all the subsequent major stratigraphic units. When the Bed I sites were first being explored by Louis and Mary Leakey, the artefacts they yielded were the oldest known anywhere in the world, but subsequent work has revealed several earlier occurrences elsewhere: at the time this is written, the oldest stone tools date from a little over 2.5 million years ago at Kada Gona in the Afar region of northern Ethiopia. That date makes them some 700,000 years older than those of Olduvai Bed I, but in no way diminishes the interest or importance of the latter.

The oldest artefacts at Olduvai consist of cobbles, often of lava, from which a number of flakes have been struck, and also quantities of lava and quartzite flakes, either unmodified or roughly shaped by simple trimming of the edges. It is an open question whether some of the flaked cobbles are intended to be tools – for example, simple sharp-edged choppers, with a convenient hand-hold formed by an unflaked smooth area of the cobble's surface – or whether their role was simply to yield the even sharper struck flakes, which were used as tools with or without further trimming. Either way, the stone tool industry is an extremely simple one in technological terms, and seems just what one might expect to find with the contemporary hominid fossil remains, which are those of early humans of small stature and small brains, by comparison with their successors; it has been given the name Oldowan, sometimes spelt Olduvan, since it was first found here at Olduvai. ('Oldoway' is an anglicised spelling of the name of the Gorge, which was in use when Louis and Mary Leakey were first working there; 'Olduvai', which follows the correct local [Maasai] spelling, subsequently replaced it. Given the date when the stone industry was first named, 'Oldowan' is

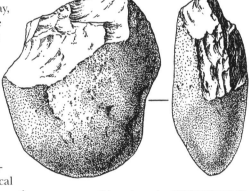

Olduvan chopper from FLK Zinjanthropus site, Bed I, 85mm long, drawn by Mary Leakey

probably technically correct; however, I myself always write 'Olduvan' when I think editors will let me get away with it.) The simple Olduvan industry of Bed I shows little or no advance over the much earlier Kada Gona stone artefacts just mentioned, and indeed the term Olduvan has now been stretched to include them and comparable finds at other early sites in Africa. For all its simplicity, this toolkit evidently provided all the equipment the earliest humans needed to carry out such tasks as cutting meat, scraping hides or working wood and plant materials.

This Olduvan industry is present at all the sites in Bed I where artefacts occur, and continues in the lower division of Bed II. In the Middle and Upper sections of Bed II, however, there are two changes to note. First, the Olduvan becomes 'Developed Olduvan', by virtue of having a wider range of deliberately shaped tools, although there is really no change in its basic technology, the working of cobbles or other pieces of rock directly from the natural units in which they could be picked up, whether to make them into tools or to obtain flakes from them. There are two kinds of Developed Olduvan, designated A and B, on the basis of their respective ranges of tool types. In B, it seems clear that at least a few of the selected pieces of rock were being deliberately shaped as heavy-duty cutting tools, by flaking on both main faces.

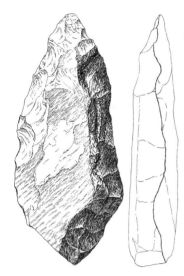

Acheulean handaxe from site TK, Bed II, 250mm long, drawn by Mary Leakey

The most striking innovation in Bed II, however, is the first appearance at Olduvai of true handaxes and cleavers, in the industry known widely over Africa and many other parts of the Old World as 'Acheulean'. The handaxes and cleavers are by no means the only stone artefact types in the Acheulean, but they are certainly the ones that have come to characterise it. They are well-shaped, large cutting tools, often with a high degree of symmetry, and in Africa they are in almost all cases made on large, heavy flakes of rock which had been specially struck as blanks for their manufacture. Classic African Acheulean handaxes tend to be of oval or tear-drop shape, fairly flat, with useful cutting edges extending round much or all of their circumferences. The distinctive feature of cleavers is a transverse or oblique axe-like cutting edge at the top. The way in which these tools are made shows that the Acheulean stoneworkers were employing quite a different kind of technology from that of their Olduvan counterparts, and a higher level of planning and perception.

Although I must resist the temptation to discuss such things in detail here, important questions obviously arise about the significance of the sudden appearance of the Acheulean at Olduvai. Is it a dramatic invention by the local human population, at a time which the geological evidence shows to be one of environmental change? Or does it mark the arrival in the area of new hominids, who were a stage further along the path of human mental and physical development? Whatever the answer, at Olduvai there was no total replacement of the Olduvan by the Acheulean: there are broadly contemporary occurrences of both in Middle and Upper Bed II, and the same could be said of Bed III, in so far as it has any well-stratified traces of contemporary stone tool assemblages at all.

In Bed IV, the Acheulean really comes into its own, with many fine sites, associated with stream channels, yielding distinctive assemblages with fine handaxes and cleavers made from a variety of rock types – indeed, the study of the Bed IV Acheulean lay at the heart of the research project that first took me to Olduvai. Yet, right at the top of Bed IV, Mary Leakey excavated a series of sites whose stone tool industries seemed far more reminiscent of the Developed Olduvan of Bed II: true, they had handaxes, but there was little or no sign of the technique of making them on large, specially struck flake blanks. Instead, they were roughly shaped on cobbles or any other suitable piece of rock that could be found. Mary named these industries Developed Olduvan C, suggesting that, even as late in the sequence as this, the Olduvan tradition had not finally expired.

Only one site has ever been excavated in the Masek Beds, and it yielded a remarkable Acheulean industry of large pointed handaxes, made from the white quartzite which comes from the Pre-Cambrian inselberg of Naibor Soit, two or three kilometres away, and now just across the Gorge from the camp. This is an extremely difficult rock to work, because of its tendency to shatter, but the Acheulean craftsmen of the FLK Masek site controlled it superbly to create precisely the sizes and shapes of handaxes that they wanted. The Ndutu Beds contain a small amount of Middle Stone Age material, in which further advances in stone tool technology make their appearance, and there is at least one worthwhile Late Stone Age site in the Naisiusiu Beds, but the main archaeological significance of Olduvai, and of Mary Leakey's work there, concerns the period represented by Beds I–IV and Masek, the remainder of the sequence being mentioned here only for the sake of completeness.

I said earlier that stone artefacts are the commonest reliable evidence for early human activity, and this is true, largely because they have a greater capacity than the more fragile kinds of evidence to survive not merely the passing of time but also the huge range of potentially destructive processes that are implied by bland phrases like 'geological disturbance'. They are not necessarily the most informative kind of evidence for actual human behaviour, however, and one of the joys of Olduvai is that some of its sites have produced rare and important information of other kinds. This is not the place to discuss them in detail, but here are some examples. All of them were discovered in the course of work which Mary directed, or in which she was deeply involved, and in most cases the evidence is either unique or hard to equal in quality, for sites of the same age, anywhere else in the world.

The oldest site in the Gorge is at DK, just above the black lava in lower Bed I. Here there was not only a virtually undisturbed living-floor with stone artefacts and bones in association but also a ring of roughly piled lava blocks, which it is hard to explain convincingly as the result of natural processes: it is widely regarded as the best surviving evidence for a shelter deliberately constructed by early humans – the circular base of a hut, shelter or windbreak, the upper parts of which were probably formed of leafy branches. What *were* the actual domestic living conditions of the early humans some 1.8–2.0 million years ago? Even a hint of actual evidence is precious. Higher up in Bed I, in the productive FLK area, excavation revealed the major part of an elephant carcass, some of the bones still articulated, with many stone artefacts in direct association, and traces of stone tool cut-marks on the bones. While it is now widely believed that at this stage of the Palaeolithic period the humans were more often scavengers of carnivore kills than hunters of large game animals in their own right, here at FLK North the humans seem at least to have got to a carcass first and to have exploited it for meat, whether they killed the elephant or not. In the overlying Bed II deposits at the very same site, there was a rather similar occurrence, though for once only poorly preserved, featuring a *Deinotherium*, an extinct form of proboscidean which is not a true elephant. Another Olduvai site with important evidence for the question of how the early hominids obtained their meat is BK at the top of Bed II, a Developed Olduvan site. Here, the remains of many large animals were found in the deposits of what had been a marshy, muddy area, including several examples of *Pelorovis*, a giant buffalo (now extinct). It is possible that at least some of the animals had been deliberately driven into this soft ground by humans, so that they became trapped: the most striking find was a largely complete *Pelorovis* skeleton still in an upright position, surrounded by stone tools.

In Bed II, a less spectacular site, but one of great interest, is the 'Chert Factory Site' at MNK. Chert is a highly siliceous fine-grained, sedimentary rock, which flakes very easily and predictably, and is everywhere prized by stone toolmakers. At Olduvai, it is extremely rare, but good nodules of chert had formed in the beds of the lake that was present in the main archaeological area prior to Middle Bed II times. When the lake shifted its position, the chert nodules became accessible, and they were systematically exploited by the human population, who worked them where they were found, taking suitable flakes back to the living sites for use, and leaving behind the unwanted debris: this is one of the oldest clear examples of a quarry or factory site for stone toolmakers, and is surely relevant to any assessment of the extent to which planning ability and social organisation had developed amongst our early ancestors by around 1.6 million years ago. I have already mentioned the extraordinary 'salt extraction pits' (if that is indeed what they are) at JK in Bed III: their possible implications for human mental development are also considerable, and no other comparable site of this age is known anywhere.

These examples will suffice to show the high quality of the archaeological evidence which the Olduvai sediments have yielded over the years. Much could also be said of the importance of the faunal remains for their own sake, quite apart from the associations of some of them with traces of human activity: large and small animals and birds are well represented, and fish remains come from several of the sites. But there is another category of evidence that has completely overshadowed these: the hominid fossil remains.

It is true that there are now several sites in Africa which have produced hominid fossils in greater quantity than Olduvai, and also specimens of far greater age, but many of these discoveries belong to the last two or three decades, and for a long while Olduvai was undoubtedly the leading site in this field. The newer finds have in no way robbed the older ones of their significance, but have simply changed the context in which we view them, and to some extent relaxed the intensity of the original controversies about their interpretation. The Olduvai hominids remain vital to our understanding of early human evolution. Up to the time that Mary left the Gorge, 61 separate hominid fossil finds had been made (catalogued as OH 1–61, OH simply standing for Olduvai Hominid). Plenty of technical literature exists about most of them, and only the briefest summary is required here.

In the most general terms, then, the hominids present in the early levels at Olduvai (Bed I and Lower Bed II) are of three kinds, attributable to two genera, *Australopithecus* and *Homo*. The australopithecines can be divided into gracile forms and robust forms, and at the risk of grave oversimplification, I as a mere archaeologist can say here – if you promise not to tell anyone – that the robust forms look more ape-like and the gracile ones somewhat more human (though the evolutionary lines that lead to the modern great apes on the one hand and to humans on the other had diverged from their common stem somewhat before five million years ago). Physical anthropologists or human palaeontologists are far from agreed on the correct terminology even for the broad hominid types of this period, let alone the precise attributions of individual finds. Many in fact prefer to use the generic name *Paranthropus* for the robust australopithecines. '*Zinjanthropus*' was a name dreamed up by Louis Leakey for the famous find made by Mary in 1959: it is a name at the genus level, which has simply not stood the test of time. Louis rather liked his finds to be new genera, let alone new species, but his colleagues quite rapidly recognised that 'Zinj' was simply one of the more robust of all the australopithecines then known.

The earliest *Homo* represented at Olduvai was discovered first at the site known as FLK NN, which is less than 100 m from the *Zinjanthropus* find-spot, and slightly lower down in Bed I, so actually a little older. It was named *Homo habilis* ('Handy' or 'Skilled' Man) because amongst the remains were hand bones which suggested a surprising degree of manual dexterity. Foot bones were also present, and indicated a fully bipedal gait; these things, along with details of the lower jaw and teeth, the shape of the skull and size of the brain, led to the *Homo* classification. Remains of *Homo habilis* subsequently turned up on the same floor that had produced 'Zinj', as work there proceeded, and most people assumed that *Homo habilis*, rather than an australopithecine, was the maker of the Bed I Olduvan industries, then thought to represent the absolute beginning of stone tool manufacture. In 1959–1960, these finds, together with the new chronometric dates of c 1.7–1.8 million years for the sites that had yielded them, were nothing less than sensational, and their interpretation was accordingly no small matter. Much has happened since then: many more early hominid species are now recognised, and the status of *Homo habilis* is controversial again, if for rather different reasons.

While the archaeological sites of Bed II are not always as well preserved or undisturbed as those of Bed I, the question of the Bed II hominid cast of characters is just as interesting. The types that can be found in Bed I are also present in Bed II: even at the very top of the latter, at BK, robust australopithecine remains have been found. But there is an important addition: the first occurrence of a much larger and more fully developed early hominid, *Homo erectus*, though some would prefer the designation *Homo ergaster*. Louis Leakey personally made the first find (OH 9), the major part of a calvaria (part of a skull), in December 1960, at the site known as LLK. Although it was not directly associated with stone tools, the new find occurred at very much the same level in the Gorge stratigraphy at which the first Acheulean industries are also to be found. *Homo erectus* or *ergaster* is of great importance, being apparently the first of the early humans to leave Africa and thereby initiate the great slow spread of humans that was to populate much of the Old World and eventually, much further ahead, the New. It would, however, be for other hominid types to complete what *erectus/ergaster* began. More than 40 years after its discovery, OH 9 still remains a very important example of this hominid type.

Whether or not *Homo erectus* or *ergaster* was the bringer of the Acheulean to Olduvai is still hotly debated, but there are several examples of fragmentary remains attributed to this species in association with Acheulean sites in Bed IV, Bed III having produced no *in situ* hominid material of significance. It was a rare event for Mary Leakey to leave a specific ambition unfulfilled at Olduvai, but she never realised her hope of finding hominid remains with any of those crudely made handaxe industries from the very top of Bed IV which she called Developed Olduvan C (see above). It was her own belief that they had been made by a hominid of different and presumably more archaic type from the makers of the Bed IV Acheulean, some species which had survived in this part of East Africa alongside *Homo erectus*. Other explanations are certainly possible, but we may simply never know whether Mary was right or wrong about this.

THE DIARY

Beginning of Olduvai Gorge at Granite Falls

Tuesday, 4 January

That ancient Oxford process 'effluxion of time' (certainly one of my favourite items of the University's official language) has finally brought the beginning of this long-talked of trip, in which I am to begin my task of writing Mary Leakey's autobiography for her. How could anyone possibly have predicted that, when I first met her on my way to Zambia in 1969? It is hard to believe that that was thirteen and a half years ago.

The flight to Nairobi was to be an evening one, but first I had visitors to meet in Oxford: Jeffrey May, a colleague from Nottingham University, and his wife Brenda, friends of mine for many years. So, we had lunch at the Lamb and Flag and idly discussed the marvels and improbabilities of modern travel. This time tomorrow, we noted, I *should* be south of the Equator, in Tanzania, and on my way to Olduvai, having flown six or seven thousand miles and passed in and out of Kenya by special permit (since Kenya and Tanzania are not currently speaking to each other). Where would I really be? Would I have even reached Heathrow? The conversation convinced me that I really was about to make a journey, and that this travel stuff has to be taken seriously, so, being me, I decided to have a haircut and buy a battery electric razor and a strap for my suitcase, and actually achieved all three.

Ray Inskeep, friend and immediate colleague, kindly drove me to the bus station. I was due at Heathrow not later than 5.30 pm – I, with my Irish ticket for a Kenyan airline, my suspicious-looking portable tape recorder and no less than 24 cassettes and endless batteries; the set of Scanning Electron Microscope photographs I am to take to Mary's assistant – my former student Peter Jones – which probably look like spy-satellite pictures, and the whisky and a hundred small-size cigars for Mary herself, without which I think we should not get off to a good start when I got to Olduvai. The whole project, when one stopped to think, was clearly ridiculous. So, it was hardly surprising to find that the man on the telephone had been wrong about the bus times: there was no such thing as a 2.50 departure arriving at Heathrow at 4.05, only a 3.15, via Abingdon, Wallingford, Henley and Maidenhead, arriving at 5.04. I joined it. Not content with such a varied route, it also turned out to drop people at South Hinksey and pick up homeward-bound schoolchildren at Culham. Would we ever arrive?

In the end, we did, about 5.15, and there was no great rush and no hanging around, which was good. The plane proved to be a 707 – goodness, I thought they were obsolete, and bits of this one did rather look as if they were stuck on with Sellotape. Unless my ethnographic senses were deceiving me, however, at least half of all these many people would be getting out at Athens. Where on earth could they all have come from, in January? Is the pound low against the drachma? The pilots were clearly Kenyan, and looked cheerful. I found myself hoping that they would fly better than rather a lot of Kenyans seemed to drive, on my previous visits.

By luck, I ended up with a whole row of seats to myself, in a nearly full plane. Then we were off, nearly on time, and soon into wintry cloud, losing any view of the lights of London. A welcome gin-and-tonic materialised over presumable France and dinner over goodness-knows-where, but it's all Europe anyhow, isn't it? We were dead on time to Athens, where security seemed minimal: anyone who wished could easily have made an unofficial entry into Greece, I reckoned. More than half the passengers got off, and less than a dozen got on. I put my watch forward to East African time, and off we went again: there was some very good moonlight-on-the-sea-with-islands stuff, then cloud: but I had noted that the moon is already getting to be what I would regard as the wrong way up by the time one reaches Athens. I associate that with Africa: no one warned me to expect it, on my first visit, and indeed no one else even seemed to have noticed. I still can't quite work out the geometry of it. For the moment, it didn't seem to matter too much: at least on three seats, with three pillows, one could stretch out and even sleep quite well, for a few hours.

Wednesday, 5 January

Dawn began a little before 6.0 am, and it was spectacular. The sun came over the edge of the world as we passed by Lake Turkana. Earlier I had glimpsed some of the oil fires in the southern Sahara, which regular travellers on this route tell me they always see. If you ask me, the sun was in no hurry to arrive this morning, and the colours had begun to fade before it did, but, once up, it gave of its best and turned rapidly from red to silver. We were just too far south to make out the Koobi Fora spit on the east shore of the lake, which would have told me where all the early Palaeolithic sites are about which I lecture, and anyhow we were flying some way west of the lake itself. It looked as if it had been raining down there. The summit of Mount Kenya was firmly in the cloud. We descended to Nairobi through some splendidly beautiful cumulus clouds, with a very low base, landing a mere 49 seconds late: the *cognoscenti* among the passengers were critical of the pilot's angle of approach, though it seemed OK to me. He did it at Athens too, they said knowledgeably. One never escapes completely from *cognoscenti* when travelling.

Security at Nairobi also seemed to be tending towards the minimal. The customs officers were too bored to open my case, so the tape recorder and other dubious looking items entered Kenya unchecked. Would anyone be there to meet me? Mary, who is down at Olduvai, was sending her secretary, whose first name is Hazel, but I had never met her and had no idea what her surname was. But she was there, and picked me out easily: apparently Mary had said I might look a bit academic ...

Hazel, whose surname proved to be Potgieter, said that there were various things to be done in Nairobi before we started the journey to Tanzania. She would be taking me to the border at Namanga, and Peter Jones would meet me from the other side and complete the journey. First, therefore, we went to the National Museum, where I saw Richard Leakey briefly and got some local Olduvai information and gossip. All was believed to be well with Mary, except that when they were last in touch she had thought she might be sickening for a dose of malaria - if so, picked up at Baringo in Kenya during a visit over Christmas, since the Olduvai mosquitoes don't carry it. Coffee in Hazel's office followed, while we waited for a police permit that would allow me to cross the border, and then we went to Mary's Nairobi home out at Langata, which I have visited several times before, to collect distilled water and other supplies. That afforded a welcome chance to change into lighter clothes. Finally, we left in Hazel's car at about a quarter past eleven, taking as passenger a new driver, who is joining Mary's African staff at Olduvai, and a great deal of luggage.

Nairobi seemed much as I recalled, with a few new buildings, though the museum complex was much enlarged and altered. Some of the purple jacaranda trees were flowering – they do it twice a year, I learned. There have been good rains, on time, for the first time for several years, and Kenya was green. There was a decent growth of green grass out on the Athi plains, which I have only previously seen looking dry and rather brown and empty of game. Now there were a few kongoni, several gazelle, a single wildebeest, some marabou storks – they always seem to be there – and four vultures in a tree; also there were swallows and other small birds, and several brightly coloured butterflies. January in England already seemed a remote impossibility. Half way to Namanga, there is an abrupt change of landscape to acacia savannah, which I suppose must coincide with a change of bedrock. Suddenly, the bare plains were gone and there were trees and termite heaps and more hilly relief. Plentiful Maasai were out and about, in their usual bright colours. Soon Longido Mountain, with its dramatic tine-like peak, came into view, and Mount Meru beyond: Kilimanjaro, as usual, was in cloud, except the bottom third. All these are in Tanzania, so we were nearing the border. How well I remembered this landscape. And so to Namanga, in just two hours, a very good run. Traffic was minimal: maybe fifty vehicles in the hundred miles we had covered, once out of Nairobi and off the Mombasa road. The reason for this, of course, was that the border is still closed – hence my special permits, arranged by Mary and Richard Leakey.

The rendezvous with the vehicle from Olduvai was for 1.0 pm, and we were only marginally late. This was too good to be true, and quite unlike the normal course of travel in East Africa, which never goes according to plan. What gremlins were waiting? Arusha still lay ahead on the Tanzanian side, and I had never yet got through Arusha without trouble and delay: quite a lot of people find the same thing, I believe. Something would soon go wrong, I thought to myself – just wait and see. But meanwhile we passed through the Kenyan border post and customs and drove on to the Tanzanian one.

There you are – what did I tell you? We immediately met one of Peter Jones's passengers, who was due to be taken back by Hazel to Nairobi, but he was on foot, and he was bearing the news that Peter was stranded, five miles back in Tanzania: an oil pipe had fractured on his Land Rover and, as the messenger graphically put it, 'all the oil has fallen out on to the ground'. Ah, well. But at least the border could offer Coca Cola and light snacks and a small area of shade (it being hot summer in East Africa), and even a garage which had some oil, if anyone could get it back to Peter. But before we had worked out how to do that, he arrived in person, in his vehicle, on the end of a tow-rope, cheerful. The damage to the oil system was evidently substantial, however, so a committee of mechanical expertise convened, consisting of Peter, the members of the African staff who were with him, the new driver we had brought, and a few interested bystanders – Tanzanian *cognoscenti*, I shouldn't wonder. Those of us who were onward bound took the opportunity to pass through the Tanzanian customs meanwhile: no one wanted to open and check my case, it being a bit hot for that sort of thing. After two and a half hours, a temporary repair to the Land Rover was effected, in which (I am proud to record) my Swiss Army knife played a distinguished role, and Hazel left for her return journey to Nairobi. We attended to final documentation at the border police post, where a Tanzanian policeman respectfully referred to me as 'the *Mzee*': this Swahili word literally means 'old man', but is in fact also a general term of respect, as once applied in Kenya to the late Jomo Kenyatta and now in Tanzania to President Nyerere. Well, fancy that: only a few weeks ago I was impressed at being called 'young man' twice in quick succession by a lady from Yorkshire, who visited my college at Oxford, when I was helping to greet the guests after a funeral. What is one to think?

On we went, in Peter's perhaps not completely repaired Land Rover. Somehow we seemed also to have acquired three Tanzanian policemen who wanted a lift, one of them armed with a sub-machine gun. It appeared that they had some bandits to hunt, further down the road. Fair enough: I count that as local colour. We started well, but the engine got more and more sick, and quite a lot of things started to rattle ominously. When we dropped the policemen off, the engine would not restart at all. Push, everyone – that did the trick. There were thirty miles or more to Arusha, and hardly any traffic about at all to offer assistance, should we break down completely, but one could only press on hopefully, which is how much of life seems to work in East Africa. We crept noisily along. We over-

New Arusha hotel, 1983

heated: push start again. Would we make it? It was by now a beautiful golden evening, and in many ways a pleasure to be going slowly, but this would not really be the best place to spend a night, even if the bandits turned out to be good company ... Eventually, some two and three-quarter hours later, we limped into Arusha, and the garages were of course long closed. So, there I was, staying the night unexpectedly at the New Arusha Hotel, with an ailing vehicle, which is exactly what happened in 1969, on my very first day ever in Africa, a story told in the Introduction. *Plus ça change* ... well, not quite, because the hotel was now, I noted, actually fourteen times as expensive as it had been then. But this time I have an expense account – well, probably. Peter and I had a cheerful dinner together, catching up on news, views and the philosophy of life: tomorrow would be another day, and maybe, one way or another, we should reach Olduvai. And then again, we might not. I recalled the conversation at the Lamb and Flag back in Oxford, some forty-eight hours ago, but a world and an age away. There was really nothing to be gained by worrying, and no way of contacting Mary Leakey. Anyhow, who ever got through Arusha in a single easy shot?

Thursday, 6 January

I awoke to bright sunshine, after a long sleep. Breakfast included pawpaw and some of those tiny bananas that grow in Tanzania and seem to taste so much better than any banana that was ever imported into England. Peter, who had been up earlier than I, arrived at 8.45 with the news that the Land Rover was being worked on at his favourite garage and might or might not be ready today. We agreed to meet again at 11.0, when a fuller report would be available. Peter had various calls to make in Arusha. Meanwhile, I looked around the town and was offered a great number of highly advantageous currency deals for Kenya shillings or English pounds, which it seemed wise to decline. The shops had some quite attractive Makonde ebony carvings.

When I met Peter at 11.0, he was accompanied by two Englishmen, who were also suffering from the local disease of vehicle problems. To my amazement, I actually knew both of them, for different reasons, from a long way back. They turned out to be Graham Dangerfield, the zoologist, whom I had last met when our school careers overlapped in 1955, and a writer, John Goldsmith, whom I had met briefly in London in 1968 when Brian Fagan took me to his club for lunch, and John was about to publish his first novel, *Mrs Mount, Ascendant*, which I subsequently read and enjoyed. They were in Tanzania to consider possible books and films on Serengeti. From a start of mutual unrecognition, we actually managed to piece together our previous encounters. Arusha, and in particular the New Arusha Hotel, is just the sort of place where such unlikely meetings, based on improbable coincidences, take place. John Goldsmith and I provisionally arranged to have lunch again after another fourteen years, if not sooner, perhaps in Tierra del Fuego, as he says he wants to visit there.

Peter reported that the fractured oil pipe and other consequential damage could be mended, at a cost of about 1500 Tanzanian shillings (16 shillings to the English pound is the official rate, though up to 85 shillings to the pound can readily be obtained from unofficial sources, I gather. No wonder everyone in Arusha seemed to want to buy pounds when they found out I was from England). One particular loud clanking noise which had accompanied us into Arusha has now been diagnosed as indicating a fractured main engine bearing, not surprisingly. It could be repaired, if we could find a spare part in Arusha, though it is apparently a major task to get at the thing. Peter and I walked down the town, away from the glossy tourist end, to begin the search, with one of the garage mechanics who, after a hundred yards, observed cheerfully, 'You couldn't have walked this far and survived, if you had been Indian.' Peter explained that the Asians, many of them Indian, are much hated in East Africa at present, though their trading skills are heavily relied upon by everyone. There were some curious items in the shop windows, including a proudly displayed tee shirt marked 'Dallas', with a picture of JR from the *Dallas* soap opera, whose grip on the world's imagination evidently included Arusha. There was also a bookstall selling only copies of a football magazine called *Shoot!* Surprisingly, a spare main engine bearing for the Land Rover was forthcoming almost immediately, though it cost a further 875 shillings.

The garden of the New Arusha Hotel is a nice enough place to wait about, and indeed to start drafting an introductory chapter to the autobiography of someone else, based on guesswork and preliminary reading. My efforts in this direction proved somewhat intermittent, as news of progress at the garage came from either Peter or from Graham Dangerfield and John Goldsmith, whose vehicle is also being worked on. As they are also going on to Serengeti, one possibility was that I should go on with them to Olduvai and let Mary know what was happening, if it turned out that our own repair was going to need another day. There were many bright butterflies in the garden, and several kites soaring and circling overhead, plus the occasional hornbill amongst the branches of a big tree: I remembered a big hornbill throwing a nut at me from that same tree, back in 1969. Eventually, it became clear that our own vehicle would be ready in mid- to late afternoon. The other one was actually ready first, but not by very long. It would not, however, be possible to reach Olduvai until far too late, so Peter arranged that we should all stay the night at a privately owned safari lodge, Gibb's Farm, run by Mary's good friend Margaret Gibb on the slopes of Ngorongoro, where fruit and vegetables for Olduvai are always bought when anyone passes. That was some three to four hours' driving away.

So at last we left, at about 4.30, for the Arusha to Ngorongoro stage of the journey, which I well recalled as a spectacular ride. Late afternoon sun and some violent though brief rain produced a magnificent rainbow, and Mount Meru was crowned with a dramatically shaped, flaring cumulus cloud. It was nice to see baobab trees again in the Rift, and to reach Mto wa Mbu with the last of the sun catching the wings of a dozen or more storks flying together. Mto wa Mbu is one of my favourite place names in all the world because of its exotic sound, even though it only means something like Mosquito Creek. The market was already closed, and traffic was extremely light, the reason being that there is no petrol to be had anywhere – except by the resourceful Peter, through his own contacts in Arusha. Incidentally, the whole cost of labour for the repairs to the Land Rover, many hours' work, was paid for by Peter with one packet of Omo soap flakes and four bars of ordinary soap, which he had obtained back at the border at Namanga at the special urgent request of the Arusha garage mechanics. Such commodities are quite ordinary in Kenya, but completely unobtainable in Tanzania at the moment, and like gold: the garage was extremely satisfied with the deal. Again I reflected that Oxford was already a lifetime away, though, oddly enough, I was about to be reminded of it.

This happened when we stopped next, which was at the edge of the Manyara Game Park, to pick up Patti Moehlman, an American researcher from Yale, who has for some years been studying jackals near Lake Ndutu, out on Serengeti beyond Olduvai, and is not only a good friend of Mary but also in fact her nearest neighbour, a mere hour and a half's drive away across the plains. Peter had brought her to Manyara on his outward journey, and her own Land Rover was at Olduvai. She was far too experienced in things African to have seriously expected him back on time, but was glad to see us safe and sound. I had even met her once, in the somewhat different surroundings of Merton College Garden, in Oxford, at the Encaenia Garden party (an occasion for full academic dress) in 1981, when Oxford gave Mary an Honorary Doctorate, and various friends and supporters gathered. Patti had promised then to show me her jackals if ever I came out to Serengeti while she was there, and now perhaps she will. Peter's wife Annie – they married only quite recently – was somewhere in the Manyara Park, studying the occurrence of tubers and edible roots as part of her doctoral research at Berkeley (University of California), which my old friend and Cambridge undergraduate contemporary, Glynn Isaac, is supervising, but she was not findable or indeed expecting to see Peter: she will come to Olduvai shortly, when her work here is finished.

The Land Rover had run well to Manyara, but now once again the engine would not fire on the self-starter, so we all had to push it almost as far as the area of the park where the elephants are, before it would agree to get going. Off we went up the steep climb that is the Rift escarpment, and soon into darkness, torn by the occasional flash of lightning where there were distant thunderstorms, and so eventually to Gibb's Farm, a delightful place in an area of rich and fertile farmland. Comfortable rooms were ready for us, with running water and showers. There was a beautiful garden and a friendly lounge, with the odd sight of a traditionally decorated Christmas Tree amongst the African wood carvings and the vases of roses and antirrhinums. Everyone here knows Peter. Now we got confirmation of what Richard Leakey had forecast to me in Nairobi: Mary has indeed gone down with malaria. Oh dear. We arrived at Gibb's Farm at almost the same moment as the Dangerfield-Goldsmith vehicle, and others staying at the lodge included some cheerful American tourists and an Australian family now living in Dar-es-Salaam, the husband being in the oil business. There would be little or no more petrol available in January, he said, and he should know: it's lucky that Olduvai has its own store. A very sociable dinner followed, with everyone sharing two large tables: it included a Tanzanian red wine, which could perhaps best be described as interesting.

Friday, 7 January

This morning, after a good night's rest, I could see what a superbly beautiful place Gibb's Farm is, with a long view over coffee plantations and agricultural land to distant mountains, beyond its own garden which was full of shrubs and trees and flowers. Once, of course, it was a very large private estate, owning most of the land it still overlooks, but much of that has been taken over by the Tanzanian Government.

Off we went again, laden with avocados and fresh vegetables, and this time not needing a push start. We stopped in the local village to add pawpaws to the supplies and then pressed on towards Ngorongoro itself. Soon we met a Toyota truck that had broken down, and picked up one of its passengers, who was, of course, known to Peter: he works for the local administration, and needed to get to Ngorongoro village. We stopped for documentation at the boundary of the Ngorongoro Conservation Area, and then began the winding climb through the cloud-and-rain forest to the rim of the crater. Purely because it was high time for something else to go wrong, we had a quick puncture on the way up, just to show willing, but were on our way again after only about ten minutes' delay, and then paused at the top to cool the engine and enjoy the unforgettable and now increasingly famous view over the great caldera 2000 feet below (photograph page 63). Through binoculars, elephant, buffalo and much other game could be seen; with the naked eye, none of them. The next call was in Ngorongoro village, to drop our latest passenger and to collect the mail from the post office, and then we began the long descent towards Serengeti, Olduvai and home. The recent storms had made the road – unmetalled, of course – very difficult in places: there was frequent deep mud, and also great eroded channels in places, two or three feet deep, but it got drier further down. At the top we saw a substantial herd of buffalo, and on the way down stopped twice for me to take pictures of the distant view of the Gorge in its Serengeti setting, though in fact it was a bit hazy. Since I last stood here, I have become the proud owner of a telephoto lens, and there are lecture slides to be thought of, quite apart from possible illustrations for the book. We also passed three groups of giraffe, and plenty of wildebeest, zebra and gazelle. There were many small, brightly coloured birds, whose names I don't know, plus a handsome Egyptian vulture, and one secretary bird – they always strike me as hilarious, on the ground. But it was time to arrive, and find out how Mary was, and we were soon taking the rugged track across the Gorge itself.

Everything seemed much as I remembered it – was it really eight years ago, nearly nine, that I was last here? That didn't seem possible. There were some new buildings, and I saw that the camp now has a thorn fence and a gate, and there were the two electricity-generating windmills, of course, but I had heard from Mary about those, so they were not too great a shock. The big acacia tree in the centre of the camp had got much larger and broader. Mary's four dogs, recognising the Land Rover, came rushing to greet us, as they always do, but of Mary there was no sign. The camp staff told us, with sombre faces, that she was asleep in her hut. Peter went there quickly, and found her looking grey in the face, and obviously very sick indeed. The flying doctor would not be passing this way for another week, and Peter decided at once that he must go for medical advice (an hour and a half's drive away) just as soon as he could leave this afternoon, and if necessary he would radio this evening for Jonathan Leakey to fly down and take Mary to Nairobi. Things were certainly looking far from cheerful: Mary, who is about to be seventy, had had a high temperature for several days, back-aches, internal pains and a rash. It actually crossed my mind at that point that maybe I had come all this way only to write an obituary, and I think a similar thought occurred to the others too, though no one put it into words: malaria need not be a serious thing at all, but it can certainly prove fatal if it leads to complications that are ignored.

As it transpired, this was actually the low point, and it did not last long. By lunch time, Mary was already on the mend, and even felt able to eat a chicken leg and some salad: she was improving visibly by the minute, and her temperature fell rapidly. Maybe our arrival had something to do with it. Peter still went for the doctor's advice, with a list of symptoms, because it was not clear that ordinary malaria was all this was, and there were several other possibilities amongst the list of tropical illnesses. He left at 1.30, expecting to be back around half past five, and took one member of the camp staff with him in case of breakdown en-route – after all, the Land Rover was far from well itself. Patti and I stayed to look after Mary, who, by mid-afternoon, was cheerful and talkative, and ready for news, conversation and plans. She was also well enough to say that she hoped to goodness Peter wouldn't bring the doctor back with him. We even talked about the autobiography, and she directed me to the hand-written notes she had made since we last met. I already knew from correspondence that she had recently had trouble with one eye, and had lost vision in it, temporarily, it was hoped, and she now told me more about this. She said she was becoming accustomed to the loss of vision, and it was certainly going to be permanent: the 'trouble' was an actual thrombosis, which occurred unspectacularly and without warning one day, while she was having her usual afternoon rest. The blood clot settled on her eye

– it might have gone to the heart, or anywhere, but it ended up on the eye, and nothing can be done about restoring the loss of vision, so in her usual way she is simply managing without, and can already drive her car again, having at first thought it would be impossible ever to do so.

Patti and I took tea through to Mary, and sat at her bedside. Not many visitors get even as far as the door of her personal sanctum, let alone beyond it, so that was an unlikely casual benefit for the aspiring author. Six o'clock came, and no Peter, so Patti and I drove out a few miles in Patti's Land Rover, to see whether he could be seen in the distance, or needed rescuing from anywhere within reach. It was mainly a good excuse to do some game-watching, anyhow, on a beautiful evening. Thundery rain came near during the afternoon, and the wet earth could be smelt on the breeze, but the rain itself, as so often, never reached Olduvai. We saw plentiful wildebeest, zebra and gazelle out beyond the airstrip, but the best sight was a group of vultures and tawny eagles, feeding off a small gazelle carcass: the eagles were superb, and were busy enough with their meal to allow the Land Rover to within a few yards of them. Eventually, I spotted Peter's vehicle in the far distance, and we returned home. He arrived with good medical advice, and was very pleased to find Mary so much improved.

The usual Olduvai tame ravens were busy around the camp during the afternoon, and after dark a pair of genets came for their evening feed of milk and bananas. I had not seen genets before. It was now far too late for Patti to go on to her own camp at Ndutu, out on Serengeti, so she decided to stay the night and go on at dawn. We are all invited to go over and see the jackals and their puppies early next week, if Mary is fully recovered, before Patti returns to the States. A cheerful dinner for everyone took place at Mary's bedside: the dogs approved thoroughly of this, and it was thought to be an unprecedented event in the entire history of the Olduvai camp. There are currently four dogs: three Dalmatians, Matthew, Janet and Sophie, the latest in Mary's long line of Dalmatian teams, plus a sleek light-brown dog of uncertain breed, a stray who had been abandoned by one of the local Maasai groups when they moved on,. He arrived at the camp some months ago and soon signed on. He is a characterful soul, simply known as Brown Dog, which is much in the tradition of Mary's rather factual naming of unexpected additions to her animal community. The Dalmatians make sure in subtle and sometimes less subtle ways that he knows his status to be below theirs: during the day, all four are together, but at night the Dalmatians get to sleep in Mary's hut, while Brown Dog sleeps somewhere in the camp's staff quarters. Brown Dog looks to me like a sharp observer, who might well be quietly writing a thesis in his spare time.

Brown dog at Shifting Sands (see page 96)

A concentrated attack by mosquitoes, hawk moths and other supporting aircraft brought the eventful day to a slightly early close. At this time of year at Olduvai, it is necessary to sleep under a mosquito net, and one has been provided for me (though I noted it has several large unofficial holes) in the small timber-framed, corrugated-iron-walled hut, with a shady thatched roof, which is to be my home and writing room. It was pitch dark, as I made my way there, with no moon, and the stars Africa-bright. It was odd to see Orion almost vertically above, and lying on his side. In Israel, which I visited a year ago, one could see the Great Bear very low on the northern horizon, but here it will remain firmly out of sight, I imagine, or anyhow it is not to be seen at this time of year. These were mostly other peoples' stars, a Southern Hemisphere night sky. Such details, and the various sounds of the night, convinced me, if I needed convincing, that England was indeed several thousand miles away, which is fine, for the time being. There were no lions to be heard, however.

Saturday, 8 January

Patti got safely away about 7.0 am. Breakfast for the rest of us was at about 7.30, Peter having overslept, not surprisingly. Mary seemed cheerful and further improved, and insisted on getting up after breakfast for about an hour, after which she retired to rest in bed, feeling well but weak. I spent my time looking at her notes, most of which proved to be no more than subject headings to guide our work together, and continued various writing, including some draft text for a simple Olduvai guidebook, which is a possible additional project for this trip, depending on how things go, (and for which Mary seems genuinely enthusiastic). Half way through the morning, the doctor whom Peter visited yesterday suddenly arrived, unexpectedly. He said he had been wondering overnight about the possibility of colonic cystitis instead of malaria, and had decided to come and see for himself. Fortunately, he was able to decide that all was well, and that it was indeed nothing worse than malaria. He is a new neighbour for Mary, though she had actually met him before he moved to the hospital where he is now based. He is charming, and clearly a great asset: Swiss by nationality, speaking excellent English and Swahili, as well as German and doubtless French too. He is very interested in archaeology, and had taken the trouble to read up all he could about Olduvai and Laetoli, before moving to the area. At his hospital, he told us the nursing sisters are Mbulu, while many of the patients are, or should be, Maasai: the Mbulu and Maasai are traditional enemies, so that the Maasai assume the sisters will simply cut their throats if they visit the hospital, and accordingly refuse if possible to go there. The doctor, whose name is Philip, stayed to lunch, and invited us all to call on him one day next week if we make a visit to Laetoli, where Peter has promised to take me if time permits, the hospital being at Endulen, only two or three miles from the Laetoli site. Mary enjoyed the doctor's visit so much that she actually gave him some mangoes *and* one of her precious packets of cigars – what more need be said? She felt better all the afternoon, but still tired.

It remained clear and bright all day, with little cloud and no hint of thunder or rain. During the afternoon, I read and wrote some more, and then walked in the Gorge for about an hour, refreshing my memory of the parts of it that are near the camp. There were very numerous bones and stone artefacts in the erosion channels caused by the recent rains in the FLK area, most of the material doubtless washed out of the Bed I sediments. It was not my fate to find any hominid fossils – I didn't expect it would be. I noted a small spheroid of the Naibor Soit quartzite, naturally cemented to a bovid tooth, which was rather nice, though archaeologically worthless, having only the status of a derived surface find. On my way back to camp I passed two very pleasing giraffe, peacefully feeding off acacia shoots.

Today, no less than six ravens flew into camp instead of the usual four: I was the first to notice this, and it caused great excitement, as it means that four young have hatched safely this year, instead of the customary two. A tiny sunbird spent almost the whole day attacking its own image in the wing mirror of Mary's Peugeot car – defending its territory against a supposed intruder. A very tame scrub robin came to be fed at the window ledge of the main camp building, bobbing up and down much like an English robin. In the evening, I had a much clearer view of the genets: their long slim bodies are spotted brown, and they look rather cat-like (often being referred to as genet-cats), till one sees the pointed faces. In fact, they are of the same family as mongoose, weasel and stoat: pretty and attractive creatures, ready to accept the food put out for them, but gone in a flash if there is any sudden noise or rapid movement while they are eating.

The doctor told us a lot about malaria during his visit. It is greatly on the increase, and in many areas resistance has been developed to almost all known protections or cures. He confirmed that the Olduvai mosquitoes, luckily, do not carry it, and that Mary will indeed have picked hers up at Baringo over Christmas. I'm rather glad about that, given the state of the mosquito net.

Sunday, 9 January

There is no real way at Olduvai of telling when it is Sunday, as opposed to any other day: I can well imagine how people lose all count of time, in the world's remoter places The early morning call with tea is just slightly later, and the only major difference is that we get our own lunch and evening meal, the staff being off duty. As for preparing lunch, you still have to remember that it is Sunday early enough to put the traditional baked potatoes on to cook, which Peter efficiently did, to Mary's amazement. Today she got up for breakfast, almost normal except for a painful and bright red rash around one ankle, which looked to be turning septic, and she was wondering whether it might be a spider bite. Anyhow, she was fully ready to make a start, cautiously, on the autobiography, but we got on so well that we ended up having two long sessions, and covered the early years, up to her father's death at Cabrerets in 1926, more or less completely. We took the cards she had made out with headings as a basis, and expanded via questions of mine and the filling in of obvious chronological gaps. The latter is in some ways the hard part, because her memories of that far back are naturally unclear, and there are few other sources from which to recover any missing information; in other ways, it is relatively easy, because the resulting text for this early period does not need to be long, and many of the small details are unimportant. Soon I had better write my notes up into draft text, and see how it turns out. Mary is confident she will approve; time will tell.

Also in the morning I put together a page or two of possible guidebook text, introducing Olduvai. In the heat of the afternoon I read a paperback for a while, as a concession to Sunday: the camp has a large library of these, donated by visitors over the years. Mary is a keen reader of crime fiction, with predictably strong views on the relative merits of the authors. PD James is best, and Agatha Christie so low in her estimation as not even to be mentioned. All six ravens came into camp again to be fed. The scrub robin will almost take crumbs of cheese from my hand: it may take a day or two more to achieve this, and Mary doesn't think I shall succeed. I do.

In the late afternoon, Brown Dog ended one of the autobiography sessions somewhat abruptly by being dramatically sick on the floor. Sploosh, sploosh – and a third one. Exit Brown Dog, in considerable embarrassment. In the aftermath, I was mildly amused to note that the camp staff are only partly off duty on Sundays ...

I walked in the Side Gorge for the last hour of daylight – the camp, not by coincidence, stands on a spur of land at the junction between the Main and Side Gorges, a magnificent situation, looking

Mary outside main work/dining room, author's hut in foreground

out towards the great mass of the Volcanic Highlands, with the big extinct volcano Lemagrut dominating the scene. The Side Gorge is remarkably green, after the recent rains. I saw a dik-dik (the smallest of all the antelopes) running a little way off, and then noted that another was watching me calmly and unconcerned from only about 30 yards away. It's often hard to get a good look at dik-dik. Turning my head, I found that other calm eyes were also surveying my progress: a particularly handsome giraffe. He or she turned out to be one of a group of six, including two young ones, all quite unconcerned by my presence.

A wire screen has now been fixed over the window in Mary's study in the main building, so that I can work on if I wish in the evenings, after the others have retired, with light and without insects (which are far more active than I remember from my previous visits, but then I have never before been to Olduvai at this time of the year). Nine pm is certainly far too early to sleep so far as I am concerned, even when one is going to get up at 6.30 am. So, I availed myself of this for a while, armed with mosquito spray, and the arrangement worked well. Earlier, Peter and I had a long talk about his work and forthcoming publications, and he showed me some flaked lava pieces, some of them closely resembling artefacts, found by himself and Dick Hay (Mary's chief geological colleague over the years at Olduvai) on Lengai, the only one of all these great volcanoes that remains occasionally active today. These objects are thought to have resulted from the mid-air collision of lava blocks, hurled up in an eruption of Lengai, perhaps about 600 years ago. That's remarkable, and quite a new idea to me. It would be rather hard to prove, as Peter said.

Monday, 10 January

Last night there was a stampede of wildebeest past the camp, and another at about first light. I heard the second one, and so did the dogs. The general opinion is that the wildebeest were being chased by lion, of which there are usually plenty around, though I haven't heard them so far. After breakfast, huge flocks of sand grouse passed by, migrating out on to the plains. During the day I succeeded in getting the scrub robin to take cheese from my hand, surprise, surprise. I suspect robins are the same the world over: one day, evolution will replace their two wings with a knife and fork, I shouldn't wonder.

I photographed the sun coming up over the horizon, over Ngorongoro, which it did at exactly 6.45 am, though it gets light a long while before then. At the other end of the day, sunset is close to 7 pm, though today there was dramatic cloud. I photographed that too, though about ten minutes too late, I suspect: the sun sets close to the Kelogi inselberg, down the Side Gorge, so it usually looks good. Between these two events, I spent all the working day writing up the notes I made during yesterday's sessions into draft text, and got perhaps half way. I read some of it aloud to Mary, who seemed to approve quite genuinely, and of course the actual reading out of the story reminded her of extra facts, or showed that we had got events in the wrong order, so it proved a very useful exercise. Mary and Peter were otherwise very busy collating and sorting large plans and drawings from the Laetoli excavation, in connection with the publication of the report, which is now in preparation: they were packing them all into a roll for Patti to take to the States when she goes at the end of this week, calling here on her way to leave her own vehicle and collect luggage.

Mary's ankle and foot were very swollen and brightly coloured, but she was fine otherwise. I noted the afternoon temperatures today: it got up to about 88 degrees in the indoor shade of the large and airy main building, so I don't know what it would have been in the full sun outside. Then cloud built up, and it fell very quickly to just over 80. Heavy rainstorms could be seen in several directions, including thundery ones, with lightning, out on the plains towards Ndutu, but as usual Olduvai remained dry. I photographed a distant dust-devil near the base of Lemagrut, with sunlight catching it and purple shadow all around.

Peter tried unsuccessfully to radio Nairobi in the morning and again in the evening, with messages asking for things to be sent with the next flying doctor aeroplane or the next visitor, but Nairobi Control seems to be off the air. Peter got through very clearly last Saturday. The radio is an essential device, which Mary detests, while accepting its usefulness. She keeps it firmly switched off, so that no one can call her, and simply from time to time calls up Control to ask if there are any messages, and to make any calls she wishes.

I went for an evening walk again, and met up with Andrea, who is the new African driver we brought down with us from Nairobi. He was moving slowly and cautiously, carrying a large metal spike, because of last night's probable lions. He speaks a certain amount of reasonable English, and told me a long and rather complicated story about his friend George, who once won a scholarship, but I couldn't quite follow the details. Andrea has been to Rwanda, Zambia and India, and wishes to visit all the countries of the world, 'but passports are difficult'. There was also something about a grandmother and a daughter in Canada. He was also clearly deeply impressed by the rough state of the road down to Serengeti from Ngorongoro, which he will shortly be trying for himself, on a trip up to get supplies.

In the evening, lions could be heard roaring, a long way off down the Side Gorge. I worked on the writing till about 10.45, and for the last half-hour or so could hear the sound of a heavy vehicle. Mary heard it too, but there were no lights to be seen. Peter says it is a trick of sound here, when there are patches of moist air around, and that it would really have been many miles away on the main road, in quite a different direction, but even Mary feared it was imminent uninvited visitors, something she hates. On my way to bed, I met one of the genets: very bright little eyes in the beam of the torch.

Tuesday, 11 January

No luck again with the radio, which Peter tried valiantly, this morning and again in the evening. '3681, 3681 to Nairobi Control. Do you read? Over.' And again, and again, for ages. The radio crackled with miscellaneous voices, African, Asian and European, all on a similar quest, and no one seemed to be having any luck – the bloke in Nairobi didn't 'read', or even 'copy', which is the other thing they do, and a particularly stupid piece of jargon, in my view: one wants constructive action, not mimicry. Perhaps he really was reading, still in bed with a cup of tea.

I was ready to start work at about 8.0 am, as usual, after the leisurely breakfast, but was not destined to make immediate progress. First there was a tiny red bird which I had not seen before to look at, and that turned out to be a fire-finch. Mary takes the greatest interest in birds, and knows a lot about them, so we always stop for anything different, even it's only me for whom it is new. Then I suddenly saw seven of what I took to be ravens, flying straight and purposefully across the camp, followed by five more and then a few others. But we only have six ravens. Mary was on her feet at once, because now and again, not every year, there is a great and extraordinary raven convocation somewhere nearby, for which they arrive in dozens, and sometimes sixty or seventy can be seen at once – not usually in January, however. I'd like to see that. Little is known about such events, but they are evidently something to do with mating: ravens are monogamous, but widows and widowers get new mates on these occasions.

Anyhow, further research from a clearer viewpoint, beyond the big acacia tree, soon showed that the air over the Gorge was alive with birds of prey: at least a hundred vultures and eagles, soaring and circling, some low, some very high, and more arriving. Our ravens were clearly in on it, and it could only mean one thing: a lion kill, down in the Gorge, or perhaps on the cliff edge, just two or three hundred yards from camp, one of their favourite killing spots. Since the birds were circling and not landing, the lions were presumably still on the kill. Mary knows I want to see lions at work, being just a tourist from England at heart, so off we went at once, she and I in her Peugeot with the box-shaped body, armed with my camera, and with me driving because of her sore leg. Sadly, we never found the kill, though not for want of trying, edging the vehicle to the very brink of the cliff between bushes, and then driving down into the Gorge and looking back up. It must just have been masked by the bushes, which are thick and green after the rains. We must have been very close – so close, indeed, that even Mary deemed it not to be safe to get out of the car and peer round the last bushes. There were marvellous views of circling birds of prey, of course – telephoto lens on, click, click – but no lions. We drove back, eventually, disappointed. Then, suddenly, the sky was empty and all the birds were down: the lions had evidently eaten their fill and staggered into the shade nearby to sleep it off for the rest of the day. Now it was the birds' turn. It would not be a good idea to take my evening walk in that direction, Mary warned me – well, she wants the autobiography written, after all. So far as we would-be spectators were concerned, the whole episode was over, with no sign that anything had ever happened. I never saw either the lions or the birds leave. The whole thing was just a routine event in this part of the world, and many hungry mouths will have been fed. Not surprisingly, the six ravens never once came for food at camp during the rest of the day. As a consolation prize, Mary and I did later see the four young ones give a brief display of the famous raven aerobatic flying along the Gorge edge, rolling and touching each other in flight. Sometimes, though not today, they will throw and catch tufts of grass in mid-air. One of the watching adults rapidly drove off a kite that came too near.

After all this excitement, I worked at writing up the draft text for the opening section of autobiography quite productively, and read Mary the results, which quite plainly delighted her. I just hope things continue to go as well as they are at this stage. Afterwards, I walked in what were reckoned to be safe areas not far beyond the camp perimeter, and watched the sun set in an even bigger rain-cloud than yesterday's. It has not been quite so hot today. During the afternoon, thinking that the thermometer was having too easy a time of it indoors, I carried it out into the mid-afternoon sun, and it shot up to 97: I expect it was well over 100 yesterday, therefore. In the later evening, I succeeded (I hope) in photographing the genets, using a flash, which they didn't seem to mind. There was almost a plague of hawk moths at the time, dozens of them: they congregate around the genets' banana dish, amongst other places, and their eyes are bright red by torch-light when the other lights are out. Mary and Peter were enjoying some hilarious reminiscences of what might loosely be called personality problems and shifting personal liaisons amongst the members of the Laetoli excavation team in 1976 and 1977 – we may well have some fun with that stage of the story, when we eventually reach it. Even Mary stayed up till 9.15, talking. Afterwards, I got back to writing and completed the requested character-assassination of the governess who looked after her, or attempted to do so, in 1924–5. I worked on till 10.45 to complete that chapter with the tragic and sudden death from cancer of her much-loved father, when she was just 13, and retired to bed with a genuine lump in my throat after reading through my own description. Why do certain people say I have no imagination? I hope the women's magazines won't want to serialise this book ...

Wednesday, 12 January

The camp staff always bring a cup of early morning tea at about 6.25 am, and today there was a wonderful yellow-green pre-dawn light when it arrived. This is the date when we said we would try and go over to see Patti Moehlman and the jackals at Ndutu, which is about an hour and a half's drive away across the plains. Mary's leg was better, but not really up to such a bumpy ride, and in any case she and Peter were still deeply involved with the Laetoli drawings, plans and photographs that Patti is to take to America. But they didn't want me to miss the trip, so Lucas, one of the Kamba camp staff who has been here since 1966 and speaks excellent English, was assigned to me as guide, the Peugeot was filled with petrol, and off we went, with clear directions at least to the 30 square miles stretch of Serengeti where Patti should be. And then? 'Just look for a Land Rover, and that will be her ...'

It is the height of the game migration season now, something I have always wanted to see, and I knew the plains would be full of animals. In some years it happens earlier than this, and in others later, and one cannot tell in advance. The main herds passed through Olduvai itself a week or two before I came, but they will not have dispersed, and there should be much to see. The Peugeot proved a good cross-country vehicle, almost as tough as a Land Rover, lacking only four-wheel drive. In due course I succeeded in rediscovering its reverse gear on the steering column gear change – I knew where it was when I drove yesterday – and the rest was simple. The roads were sound and dry, though very rough in places: we started out past the air strip, and joined the main road in about five miles, turning adventurously right, instead of the more familiar left for Ngorongoro. This is actually the main arterial road of northern Tanzania – no tarmac, of course – but we did not see another vehicle or person for the next couple of hours.

We saw much else, however. The first main excitement was a female cheetah, which Lucas spotted lying in the grass away to the right, eyeing several dozen grazing gazelle thoughtfully from a tactical down-wind position: too far to photograph, but clear through binoculars. And all the while, her two young cubs were watching us, unnoticed, from only a dozen yards away: we only saw them when I restarted the engine, and they rose from the grass and trotted into the bushes, also unphotographably. The plains beyond were certainly full of game, mainly gazelle and zebra on this stretch. At Granite Falls, which I remember from a previous visit, the road crosses a continuation of the Main Gorge, here very shallow, but rocky: there is a ford, which has water in it at this time of year, and there are trees and bushes. Here there were impala, a richer brown colour after the paler gazelle of the plains. Out again on to the grasslands, and soon we saw the first of several hyaena, and the first of many Kori bustards, which always look so large on the ground. In the distance could be seen an enormous congregation of wildebeest, certainly two or three thousand. As one's eye traversed the landscape, here and there were small spirals of circling vultures and eagles, doubtless marking the locations of recent kills.

The instructions were to turn left at the signboard towards the lakes of Masek and Ndutu, so we did, moving on to good firm grass tracks which in fact made for much smoother going than the main road. I recognised that junction. 'Look for a long low ridge and at the top, turn right and drive on to the plain itself, leaving the track altogether: Patti should be along there somewhere.' Surprisingly, these optimistic instructions proved as easy to follow as they sounded, and soon we were amongst the growing new grass and the zebra. With so vast a horizon, mainly flat, there were few landmarks to aim at: it was like being on a ship out of sight of land. Naabi Hill was one prominent feature in approximately the right direction, so I steered a little to the left of that. It was easy enough going, but one had to watch carefully for sudden concealed burrows, the diggings of jackals and hyaenas, which are at least axle-deep, and can be invisible in the grass until one is almost on top of them. I just saw a white-coloured tortoise in time to stop, reverse and drive round him (or her – I don't know how you tell, with tortoises, from this sort of distance). Once a hyaena sprang from the ground almost under our front wheels, quite invisible until then, and watched us balefully from 20 yards away. I photographed it, and a nearby bustard.

After a few miles, we stopped to scan the horizon for Patti. Never did I see a landscape containing fewer Land Rovers, let alone golden-haired American jackal experts from Yale: just us and the game, in a vast expanse. Oh well, press on: the reserve instructions were to continue in the same direction until we struck a road, in a few miles, and there to turn left for Ndutu itself. No doubt we would reach the road in due course, but first there was a long black line, perhaps a mile of it, passing across our front some way ahead. As we approached, it resolved itself into the only thing it could be: a string of migrating wildebeest, perhaps a couple of thousand, following their leader in single file towards Ndutu. The chaps up front in the line saw our vehicle while we were still far off, and decided to break into a run. Wildebeest copy their leaders faithfully, and the result was like watching an immense freight train start moving: the engine is well on its way before the forward motion has reached the trucks at the back. So, I should now have lots of pictures of a wildebeest migration – or I hope so. We couldn't wait for them all to pass, so edged forward, and in due course they divided and the second half passed behind us. In their abundance, they made a very impressive sight, and in fact this proved to be only one, and not the largest, of the many such herds we saw during the day. Only a vastness like that of Serengeti could absorb so many animals, such congregations of wildebeest, gazelle and zebra in particular, and leave no impression whatsoever of overcrowding. There was plenty of room, and plenty of grazing, for everyone. It was a situation of plenty for the predators, too, of course, and therefore for the scavengers. It will all be very different when I come next, in a few months' time, in the dry season.

Another surprise to me was the storks: many great flocks of them, on the ground, containing hundreds, and sometimes probably thousands. They were mostly migrant European storks: I know that some that were ringed in Germany have turned up on Serengeti. But I had no idea they came in such numbers: whole areas of grassland were white with them and, as we approached, the hundred or so nearest to us would rise gently, not very seriously concerned, and flop down again a few yards further away. But there was still no sign of Patti.

Then, suddenly, there was the road: it was only a grass track, and quite invisible until we got there, because of the seasonal thickness of growth of the plains grass. Turn left, they said. And there *was* a vehicle in the distance, the first of the day – but it turned out to be a dormobile from the Ndutu Safari Lodge, not a Land Rover. But then, almost at the same moment, there she was, suddenly emerging from behind the wildebeest herd, back on the grassland, not very far away. So, the whole unlikely tentative arrangement had worked out, and we did indeed meet up. Patti had in fact seen us while some distance behind, and was making for the road to meet us. Mary's vehicle is quite distinctive, and Patti reckoned anyhow that it couldn't really have been anyone but us out on the plains.

News of the jackals was bad. Not all the expected pups had yet been born, some animals had died, and this morning all of the six or seven pairs or families Patti was studying were firmly below ground so, after all that, there was nothing to go and see. Indeed, the only jackal we got to see all day was one I had caught sight of some way off before Lucas and I drove onto the grassland. Never mind, perhaps there will be another chance when

I come out again later: the golden and silver jackals have their litters at different times of the year. Besides, there was much else to see, as we followed Patti in convoy to Ndutu, stopping to look at such things as a new-born Grant's gazelle, and a fine view of the shore of Lake Masek. Well, now, that place was the scene of a memorable adventure in 1972, when Mary's Land Rover sank axle-deep into sticky blue mud at no notice at all, leading to my heroically uneventful 50-minute walk across lion-infested country and the subsequent rescue of Mary by George Dove, the then owner of the Ndutu Safari Lodge, accompanied by a senior Swedish diplomat, but that's quite another story. Since then, things have changed quite a lot, because in one recent wet year Lake Ndutu overflowed into Lake Masek, and the old road and causeway got swept away in the process.

There were giraffe and impala amongst the trees, as we followed Patti to the Safari Lodge for a cool drink. It seemed almost empty, and is now Asian owned, but it did not seem to have become in any way spoilt over the years since George Dove left. It looked much as it did when I spent a night there with Mary and others in 1974, en route to Laetoli, because in those days there was no direct road there from Olduvai: that was made a year or two later, when the Laetoli excavations began. Patti also took us to see her own camp, a tent under the trees about a mile away, on a spur of land with a marvellous wild view over much of Lake Ndutu. The lake shore below was black with wildebeest, and more were moving to join them. Then it was time to start for home: we had done and seen all these things, and it was still only just after noon.

Lucas and I drove back by a slightly more direct route, and again saw much more of the Serengeti game. Things that were different from the outward run included a single wart hog, some very large vultures on the ground near the road, several giraffe and the occasional ostrich. In one place three hyaenas were together, looking as if they were thinking of ganging up on a herd of zebra, who were edging cautiously away. I didn't think hyaenas usually hunted like that in the middle of the day, but there was no time to stop and watch the unfolding drama. We met as many as six vehicles in all, so no doubt it was rush hour. At one point, what I took, in the shimmering heat, to be a distant glimpse of the tops of the Olduvai electricity-generating windmills turned out, when we got nearer, to be a pair of giraffe in the middle of an empty stretch of plain. We were home by about 1.45, in time for a late lunch. It had been an uneventful morning at Olduvai, though Andrea, the new driver, had taken a Land Rover up to Ngorongoro to get meat and supplies for the camp, and there was some slight concern because he was not yet back.

In the remainder of the afternoon, I worked on the text and read the results to Mary after tea, before making a start on breaking new ground with her, using the next set of cards. She claimed to be getting really interested in the whole project, which she admitted she had previously been rather dreading, and she is clearly enjoying the reconstruction of her childhood that is gradually emerging as a continuous story, held together by several distinct threads. I must say, I'm enjoying it too, whatever difficulties may lie ahead.

Just before dinner time, there occurred one of those sights that Mary dreads most: the headlights of an unexpected vehicle, which was already rounding the corner and heading straight for the camp, only 200 yards away – no time for her even to hide. Uninvited guests are always viewed with deep suspicion, and most of them rapidly enter Mary's general category of 'stinkers', which otherwise includes most publishers, a number of senior French archaeologists, several members of the local Maasai community who conduct forbidden trade with the camp kitchen staff, all people who don't like dogs and, generally speaking, anyone who doesn't behave exactly as she wants them to. No, it could not be Andrea and the missing Land Rover. That had turned up about 6.30, with a cast-iron alibi: the delay had been caused by the discovery that it was a public holiday in Tanzania, and the butcher's shop was closed. The shopping expedition's members had resourcefully found out where the butcher lived and explained that Mama Leakey (as Mary is respectfully known locally) urgently needed meat, whereupon he had fetched a cow, killed it and cut the carcass into joints for them there and then. Even Mary was prepared to concede that these things take time.

The arriving vehicle turned out to contain two Italians, one called Anna-Maria, who is an old friend of Mary's and has worked at Olduvai as a welcome visitor previously, plus a man by the name of Paolo, who appears to be attached to her. Mary was polite to Paolo, but one could tell that she had reservations. It was remembered that Anna-Maria had been tentatively expected to camp at the Gorge for a night on 14 January; today, however, was undeniably only 12 January, and no Paolos had been mentioned as part of the deal. They could speak fluent French, but little English or Swahili, and it appeared they had been having various difficulties, not least with the *essence* (petrol). I must say, I found I could understand almost every word of their French, no doubt precisely because they are not actually French themselves, something I've often noticed before in my linguistic endeavours. They gladly accepted the use of a hut for the night, plus dinner, and were clearly as *bien fatigués* as they claimed. Mary aired her own excellent French – curiously, we had just been writing up the time when she became fluent in French as a child, during her visits to France in 1922–6. The unexpected visitors posed certain problems in the camp kitchen, as one might expect, but these were efficiently coped with, after a pause. Mary gave the visitors some of her less good whisky, and concealed the mangoes, but they seemed nice people and she has always liked Anna-Maria. They retired to bed as soon as they decently could, to Mary's scarcely concealed delight, but the general disturbance and the effort of switching to French had left her wide awake, long after her own usual bedtime. More whisky out of the better bottle seemed the obvious remedy. She long ago gave up trying to persuade me to drink whisky, which somehow I have never got to like as a drink: she regards it as a basic flaw in my character, I expect, but not to the level of making me a stinker, since there is the obvious advantage that I don't consume any of the precious supplies. At least I drink wine and gin-and-tonic when offered, so I am not beyond all hope.

We sat and talked for quite a while, mainly about current events in the Leakey family. Suddenly Brown Dog wandered soulfully in – what on earth could he be doing out at this time of night? Perhaps some problem with his thesis had left him restless, or maybe the unexpected change of routine had also been having repercussions in the staff quarters where he sleeps: we took him back, anyhow, and there was no sign of anything amiss. Mary retired to bed about 10 pm – very late for her – hoping she would sleep. It was a bit late to start writing again, so I picked up one of the camp's numerous paperbacks to read for a while, which happened to be by Nancy Mitford. That made me wonder how things might be going at present back in Swinbrook, where she lived as a child, not two miles down the road from my cottage. Will they have snow there by now? Mid-January is just the time it comes, in many years.

Here at Olduvai, it had been a very windy day, and for once the wind did not drop at sunset. The windmills were still whirring round at a great pace, as I eventually went to bed. They are switched on only at dusk, one or both, according to conditions, when there is enough wind to work them: for a little while, when they were new, they were run during the daytime, but a raven flew into one and was killed, so Mary immediately decreed that in future they should only be switched on after the ravens and other birds had gone to roost. It seemed strange that on this Tanzanian tropical January evening, with the indoor temperature at 70, one should actually need to wear a thick sweater, but everyone did. Perhaps it's the wind.

Thursday, 13 January

This was a more routine kind of day, after all the events of yesterday. There was an entertaining start, however, involving the radio: Peter actually got through easily this time to Nairobi Control, who was in fine reading form, and via him to Hazel Potgieter. Atmospheric conditions (or whatever) then became such that we could hear her very clearly, but she couldn't make out a word Peter said. We learned that Mike Norton-Griffiths is certainly flying down to Olduvai at the weekend to make a long-talked of visit, on his way to count wildebeest on Serengeti (Heaven help him). It is deemed vital that he should bring us dog biscuits, gearbox oil for the Land Rover and mosquito spray – yes, and that's exactly the order in which I would have expected them to be requested. Hazel, however, could not make out even one of the items from this curious list, however slowly and clearly Peter spoke, and nor could Control, who was in on it all, trying to help. Since everyone who is tuned in can listen to every radio conversation, the efforts to convey the information must have been much enjoyed over a wide area of East Africa. Finally, a helpful Asian voice, somewhere in Tanzania, whose owner could hear both sides, joined in as a link, and the vital details safely reached Hazel. I wondered whether the Asian gentleman would add that his brother's wife's cousin in Nairobi would be honoured to supply such worthy and desirable commodities to such a distinguished customer at a specially favourable rate, but he didn't – a lost opportunity there, I should have thought. All this took place before breakfast and, while it was going on, the two Italians surfaced and listened in amazement. Perhaps that was what influenced them to speak quite good English throughout breakfast: Mary concluded afterwards that all that French stuff last night had been needless effort. After breakfast, they left to camp elsewhere in the Gorge area, claiming to be well supplied with food and necessaries. There was a general air of relief, because there is so much work in hand, and the making of polite conversation, in whatever language, would have been an unwelcome hindrance.

We all worked on our various projects throughout the day, with few interruptions, but Mary and Peter kept finding serious inconsistencies amongst the Laetoli plans, diagrams and tables which had been produced by different contributors: this resulted in frantic unpacking of the rolls of drawings so carefully sealed up for Patti to collect when she passes through, and desperate composition and recomposition of lists of errors, messages to editors, notes for publishers and letters to contributors, as each new problem emerged.

The six ravens were frequently in camp, so evidently there were no kills nearby today. Halfway through the morning, the father of the family left the group and marched pointedly towards the steps of the main building, croaking urgently and almost indignantly for the usual but, in his view, distinctly overdue hand-out of meat, which was quickly forthcoming. A big brown kite, which is often to be seen hanging around the edges of the camp, tried to join in, but the adult ravens drove it off. I suspect it feels itself the victim of racist persecution, and if so one can see why.

Notwithstanding the continuing crisis over the documents for the Laetoli volume, Mary needed to rest her eye, so we had a substantial session together in the afternoon, though I felt her thoughts were largely elsewhere. Still, I got plenty of new data to work on. Once the Laetoli documents have left with Patti, there will be nothing more she can do about them for the time being, and we may get on even quicker, though in fact things are going fast enough at present.

After tea, I wrote up text from some of the notes and simply couldn't stop till about 6.30, because the hilarious details of Mary's precipitate exits from two Catholic convent schools carried me on. I fear the Vatican may wish to ban this book, but perhaps that will simply boost sales elsewhere. In the remaining time, I walked along the Side Gorge, either side of sunset, feeling extremely cheerful: the different sections of the story certainly bring me changes of mood, and maybe that is a good sign, reflecting full involvement. Will the readers be similarly affected? Who can tell? A great, refreshing wind came rushing towards the setting sun from the general direction of Lengai, not cold like an English northeast wind. But a change of colour and loss of clarity in the far distance, which was not just the gathering darkness, suggested that it may later bring dust. For once, there were no animals to be seen.

Instead of the usual comprehensive wash from a plastic bowl, I tried out the camp shower. Hot water, or cold if preferred, is poured into a canvas bucket, which can be hoisted up on a rope and has a proper shower attachment below, turnable on and off. Very civilised, and a great success. Grass screen panels shield the rest of the world from the shock of perceiving my lack of sunburn, even after a week. Work, after all, is under a roof, although the building is entirely open at the front, and the sun has lost its fierceness when I walk in the evenings. Peter is almost mahogany brown in colour, but then he has been here, on and off, for six or seven years, often digging in the heat of the day.

It was a peaceful evening, with no unexpected headlights. Incidentally, when the Land Rover came back yesterday from Ngorongoro, it arrived with quite a nasty dent, which the occupants didn't report to Mary, but she has now discovered it, so they are in great trouble. It appears that Andrea's first attempts at the local roads were conducted at a dangerous speed, in spite of warnings from the others: that surprises me, since he seems such a calm and slow-moving man. Anyhow, I gather he has been given clearly to understand that he will be on his way back to Nairobi if there is so much as another scratch.

I wrote until almost 11.0 pm before retiring, and that counts as distinctly the small hours, here. As was the case yesterday, the wind took the mosquitoes away – not the hawk moths, however, which seem to have quite powerful engines. Japanese, I expect.

Friday, 14 January

This was rather a cloudy day, by Olduvai standards. Two wildebeest were prancing around outside the camp gate, when the dogs came back from their morning walk, but that soon sent them off. Some Maasai were grazing their herds near the camp later: this always causes an increase in the number of flies.

Mary and Peter completed their collation of the Laetoli maps and plans, and Mary wrote yet more messages to go with them. Patti arrived about 2.30, with a great deal of luggage to be sorted out, most of it to be stored at Olduvai till she returns in May. Her vehicle was also stowed safely away.

I got on with the writing, and had another large chunk to read to Mary when we got a chance, in the late afternoon. The session almost ground to a halt when we got to her escapades at the convent schools, because for a while I simply couldn't read for laughing. I suppose it is the stronger visions brought on by reading aloud, which has to be done with a certain amount of expression, and is very different from the silent task of running one's eye over the text to look for errors or for better ways of phrasing something. Anyhow, the main thing was that Mary liked that part too, and accordingly it really may survive more or less as I have written it: an impressionist account, maybe, but in no sense untrue. In fact she makes very few changes to my text anywhere, at this stage: most are additions, plus the occasional change of wording to make sure some person gets either a fairer deal, or, in the case of those she regards as stinkers, a less fair one.

I wrote on for an hour or so afterwards, and reached her first experience of excavation, which was at Hembury in 1930. From this stage on, there will be other sources of information – written accounts, other people's memories, etc. Louis Leakey is about to enter the story, and there is a great deal written by and about him, of course. Today we administered a sharp jolt to the popular hero-worship view of Sir Mortimer Wheeler.

I walked, as has become my usual habit, from about 6.0 pm, taking my camera, to photograph the evening light on the Olduvai plants (wild sisal), which give the Gorge its name, which is in the Maasai language, *Ol duvai*, place of the sisal, and are such a feature of almost every view. Patti joined me for a while. I also looked for suitable places from which to photograph the camp, and speculated on when the light would be best in each case during the daytime. There were no animals about, though some flights of birds went over, very high up.

The evening meal was a very sociable occasion, with all Patti's stories of current life at Ndutu, and news of the various little Serengeti communities, and much gossip about individuals and stories of their predecessors. This is how the extraordinary local 'bush tele-graph' actually works, I suppose: certainly, everyone on Serengeti always seems to know about every event affecting anyone for miles around, almost as soon as it has happened, sometimes sooner, though there are no telephones and meetings between neighbours happen only rarely. Some of the people talked about tonight will doubtless be relevant to my later chapters. The others insisted that I should read out some of the passages I had already completed which Mary and I like best: Peter and Patti had not heard any of it, and were naturally curious. I just hope the ordinary readers will approve as warmly as they did, when the time comes.

As Patti's journey to the States would take her through London, I ended the day by writing some postcards and a letter home for her to post when she gets there, and I also packed my first completed film to go for processing by the Kodak laboratory, so that it will be there waiting when I get back: a few of the slides may be relevant for my own lectures next term to the geographer undergraduates at Oxford who take the Pleistocene option in their Finals. All that took until about 11.15 pm. It had become a very still night, with more mosquitoes accordingly. There was quite a variety of distant animal noises to be heard, ranging from lion and wildebeest to a Maasai donkey, which had doubtless been disturbed by one or the other. At least I could say truthfully on the postcards that I could hear lions roaring as I wrote. That should be the only outbreak of postcard-sending, and in any case, half of this first trip is now over. Quite a productive first half, I think, after the unavoidably slow start.

Saturday 15 January

Peter was to drive Patti to the Kenyan Border: they left more or less on schedule, soon after breakfast, in a well-laden Land Rover, which at least now seemed to be starting first time on the self-starter – just as well. Within minutes of their leaving, we found that Peter had left behind a vital shopping list.

'He always does,' said Mary resignedly.

The camp seemed distinctly empty after their departure, but there was much to be done. Patti had left Mary a beautiful framed colour photograph, which she took herself, as a birthday present for 6 February, when Mary will be 70: it is large enough to hang on the wall, and shows wildebeest and giraffe at either sunset or dawn, somewhere out on Serengeti. A search in the tool store yielded a hand-drill and a screw, and I was able to use some little strips of old bamboo to improvise a rawlplug, to hang it for her. Success.

I wrote, and Mary wrote letters, but after a while she decided on a spell of rest with a book, being tired after all the extra effort of getting the Laetoli papers ready to go, which came a day or two too soon after the malaria, I suspect. After a while, two things happened almost simultaneously: a light but perceptible shower of rain – yes, actual rain – and the arrival of a light aeroplane, flying low over the camp and revving its engine as a sign of greeting and intention to land. It was the promised visit by Mike Norton-Griffiths, and soon he was safely down and taxiing bumpily through a herd of Maasai cattle, which just happened to be all round the airstrip. The Maasai particularly like watching aeroplanes coming and going, and are now quite used to them, even in as remote areas as this. Mary reappeared at once, and we drove out in the Peugeot, since much luggage was expected – and indeed there was a great deal of it: parcels, packages, boxes, some for Mary and some to be delivered in due course to Margaret Gibb. There was also mail, and even a spare part for one of the windmills; there was a badly needed battery for the other Land Rover; there was the requested mosquito spray, cans and cans of it; the gearbox oil that had also been asked for; and certainly enough dog biscuits to open a pet shop. Mary was delighted.

Mike, whom I had met two or three times before, had brought his sister Anne for the ride: she had reached Nairobi yesterday, having driven all the way from Paris, arriving only two minutes late, he said proudly. It turned out that this was an unofficial flight, just for us: you'd never get that lot through the customs anyhow, it was agreed. They were to return to Nairobi later today, in time for a dinner invitation and to take Mike's children to the cinema to see *The Empire Strikes Back*. Mary and I listened respectfully, because Olduvai doesn't have too many cinemas. Mary then revealed that she couldn't stand *Star Wars*, which someone took her to see in Los Angeles, and had left before the end. Mike and I exchanged a look of silent sympathy.

Much unloading of the Peugeot followed, back at the camp, before a drink of freshly made lemonade before lunch. There were exchanges of news, but I didn't know many of the people mentioned. Lack of total commitment to the conversation accordingly enabled me to spot a small light-brown animal walking along the near edge of the Side Gorge about 200 yards away and, when it sat down, tentatively to identify it as a cheetah, which it indeed proved to be, when binoculars were fetched. It looked either very well fed or else pregnant, and remained for quite a while, sunning itself, before suddenly disappearing. It was much too far away to photograph, even with a telephoto lens.

The visitors left in mid-afternoon, scattering the Maasai cattle somewhat as they took off: they had decided to take a route over Serengeti to see the migrating herds of wildebeest, but I don't think Mike was really going to try counting them. Mary decided that Anne looked years younger than when she last saw her, and announced that this would be because almost at one stroke she had recently disposed of three daughters to husbands, and her own husband to a blonde.

'It has done her all the good in the world,' said Mary, wisely.

It was now hot and sunny, but particularly clear after the recent rain shower, so I went with my camera to take some of my previously planned shots of the camp from points along the edge of the Gorge, and a few other pictures. Afterwards, I got back to the writing, and actually brought the opening section to its end, which comes where Mary meets Louis. That makes at least 15,000 words, probably more, written and generally agreed, without difficulty, but the two remaining major sections of the book will be much longer and, at various predictable points, much harder going. The target length is supposed to be around 120,000 words, so there's a long way to go, but it's a small landmark. I read the new pages to Mary, and made a few changes accordingly, mainly deletions this time.

After all that, the evening meal was a bit late, and afterwards we sat and talked over a wide range of subjects, past, present and future, much of what was said providing me with considerable insights for the sections to come. Then we suddenly noticed it was already 10.35 pm, and long past Mary's bedtime. There was the sound of distant lions again, and cloud was obscuring the stars for the first time.

Sunday, 16 January

I was woken by the sound of violent rain during the night, and was surprised to find, on consulting my watch, that it was only 12.42 am. I doubt that I would even have gone to bed by that hour, back in England, but there I was, waking up and supposing that it must be nearly dawn. Next time I woke up, it was. For once, it was not possible to see the sun come up, as there was a bank of mist and steam after last night's rain, which the rain gauge showed to have been over half an inch.

After breakfast, I began work with Mary on the difficult section which concerns her meeting Louis and subsequently marrying him, notwithstanding the fact that he happened to be married already when they first met – a very different matter in the 1930s from what it would have been if it were happening today. She would really prefer to omit the whole episode from the book, but even she knows she can't get away with that.

'My mind is a complete blank,' she announced firmly, as we sat down.

By the end of the morning, however, we had managed to reconstruct the whole sequence of events, and I had got down notes that should enable me to write an account that passes Mary's censorship. We had also established that there are a number of factual errors and some important omissions in the accounts that occur both in Sonia Cole's biography of Louis and in Louis's own autobiography – the latter written, certainly, when his memory was failing. If I never achieve anything else during my career as a writer (if that's what this is), then the patient coaxing of the story this morning from Mary, who is notoriously difficult and reticent about divulging even ordinary personal information, may well count as my highest achievement.

There was more rain, on and off, during the day. I noted that the six ravens were absent, so there must have been a kill not far away, but there were no circling vultures to be seen. Not one raven came to camp, all day, anyhow. I did see a wiretail, a bird rather like a swallow, but much more brightly coloured.

I read for a while after lunch, while Mary was having her usual afternoon rest, and then began writing up the morning's notes into draft text. I walked down into the Gorge again in the evening, when the weather had cleared up, and in the course of my wanderings saw the new moon. They're at it again: the thin crescent is absolutely on its side, like the grin of the Cheshire Cat in *Alice in Wonderland*.

We get our own evening meal on Sundays, and traditionally Mary cooks something simple for it, but she is well aware that I can cook, so somehow it turned into her putting the things out and me doing the actual cooking: fried liver, bacon and tomatoes were decreed. It worked out pretty well, for a first culinary attempt at Olduvai with a potentially critical audience waiting, and also considering the number of hawk moths in the tiny kitchen, apparently attracted by fermenting bananas amongst the stored fruit. I counted 36 hawk moths, and there were large numbers of other insects: I kept them all out of the frying pan, I think, but if that was not actually the case it's all good protein, isn't it?

I thought it was time I went to bed a bit earlier than recently, to catch up on sleep, and was moving in that general direction, when there was an interesting scuffle-crash-tinkle noise. I confirmed by torch light my diagnosis that one of the genets had knocked over and broken an empty glass. No genet to be seen, of course. We shouldn't have left those mango skins out for them.

Monday, 17 January

I was woken again in the night by heavy rain on the hut roof. This time it was only 11.59 pm – just still yesterday, so to speak. This is ridiculous – fancy my having scored two hours of sleep before midnight! The rest of the night passed without further disturbance, so far as I was concerned, though it subsequently turned out that there had been some action round the back of the camp. During breakfast, I noticed several vultures flying purposefully across the Gorge in the direction of the airstrip, so Mary and I thought a brief trip in the Peugeot would be in order. The camp's staff then reported that there had

Rain over Kelogi (see page 63)

been lions and hyaenas in the night on their side, and not far off. Quick, grab camera, and off, Mary driving so that I could take photographs.

Immediately, we saw a very large congregation of vultures, Marabou storks and eagles, on the ground: the lions were already gone. There turned out to be two carcasses, one a Maasai cow which had got lost the previous day – so we later heard, when a Maasai turned up to ask for malaria pills for a sick child – and the other a wildebeest. So, we scoured the surrounding area, looking for fat sleepy lions in the shade: not a sign, though there were lots of vultures and eagles in trees, all bulging profusely.

'Let's try the other side of the Gorge,' said Mary, and in the end we did a large circle of about 15 miles, seeing a great deal of interest, but not a sign of a lion. There were lots of wildebeest out towards the main road, on the far side of the Gorge, so they clearly aren't all out on the plains yet. There were also plenty of gazelle of both kinds (Thompson's and Grant's); also one golden jackal and, everywhere, vultures and eagles in the branches of the trees, and then another even bigger group of them on the ground at yet another kill, the lions again already gone. Evidently, more than one pride is about. 'Do you want a picture of vultures flying?' asked Mary hopefully, revving the engine of the Peugeot. So we charged through the middle of them, but most were too full of food to do more than stagger aside.

Minor sights during the course of this unexpected trip included a pretty partridge-like bird called a yellow-neck, and another bird called a roller, and a lovely wild flower called an ipomoea, like a mallow or convolvulus, pink, which flowers during the rain and always turns its back to the wind. We got back eventually after about an hour, and it was still only 9.0 am. Mary was very apologetic about the lions, and is now absolutely determined to find some for me, but it seemed to me that there is nowhere in the northern hemisphere where one could go out and see all the things we had just seen – ever, let alone in an hour's unplanned drive after breakfast.

I returned to the writing. Peter arrived after lunch, having been performing various errands in Arusha after taking Patti to the border. He brought with him a mechanic to join the staff, Omari, the expert who had fixed up our vehicle in Arusha on the way down. Peter had apparently heard then that Omari was looking for a new job, and had persuaded Mary to take him on, on trial, if he was still free. He was soon at work, since all the vehicles except the Peugeot need some sort of attention. Peter was also carrying fresh vegetables and fruit, including over a hundred mangoes, most of them destined to be made into chutney (an annual Olduvai event), when they ripen later in the week.

Peter's arrival was followed by that of two heavy, thundery rainstorms, which came up from different directions: they seemed to encircle us in a crescent shape, and then broke.

Evening walk: acacia tree, a distant giraffe

One had an extraordinary sheer edge of falling water to it, beyond the Gorge, which I photographed. It rained hard enough for us to have to roll down the canvas storm screen across the open front of the main building. The temperature fell 10 degrees when the rain came up. Then it all cleared away, to leave a fine evening, which ended in the best sunset yet. When I went out to walk, I found that there is now already quite a lot of water in the small seasonal river at the bottom of the Gorge, and everything was very fresh-looking. The big acacia tree in front of the camp has responded to the different weather conditions by coming into bloom.

The working part of the day, amongst all these excitements, went very well, as I composed more of the difficult section and read it out to Mary. Only one – no, two – of what she is beginning to call my 'purple passages' got toned down a bit. I have the feeling that a purple passage is any piece of descriptive text containing more than one adjective, but I know what she means. I shall keep trying to get away with them, however, or the text will become very flat and dull, and not at all what I was asked to produce.

An arrangement has been made with the camp's staff that, next time they hear lions nearby, they are to wake me early, even if it is still dark, to go out by myself in the Peugeot before the lions have left the kill. That sounds a good scheme to me, and I await the cry of '*Simba, simba*' in the early hours tomorrow, or one day soon. Mary clearly regards the failure of the lions to appear as a personal affront to her as my hostess:

'Everyone else sees them, except you,' she said, fiercely. If I were a local lion, I'd take the hint.

Not surprisingly, the ravens were absent all day.

Tuesday, 18 January

There were very odd noises last night around my hut, of a vaguely animal nature, on and off between 2.0 and 5.0 am. I concluded in the end that it must be a porcupine moving around: a rather shy one is known to live nearby. I couldn't see anything out of the window, and was too sleepy to explore further, and I suppose it might have been something a bit more bitish than a porcupine. No one else seems to have heard it. I'll go out with a torch, if it comes again.

Morning tea arrived at 6.25 as usual, and we were only half-way through the '*Jambo – asante sana – OK'* ritual, which never varies, when distant lion were heard. '*Simba, simba,*' said Kabebo. They sounded rather a long way off, but I was dressed and ready in a few moments, only for it to be decided '*Simba* very far'. So I had a second cup of tea and read Nancy Mitford instead, which was not at all the same thing, but it's a very funny book: I must find some more of hers to read, when I get home.

Only scattered vultures were to be seen, soaring and circling, evidently searching, so there were certainly no kills nearby. The ravens returned in the afternoon. It was a busy working day, of the usual pattern, and we got quite a lot done. Not much of note occurred, I suppose, but there's always something, at Olduvai: more flights of sand grouse went over, chattering to each other, and in the afternoon a swarm of bees passed, moving very fast. In the evening, I walked out on the plain, away from camp and out past the airstrip. I saw at once what I thought might be a cheetah, sitting bolt upright in the distance, but somehow it looked more dog-like, though its ears were rounded. When I got just a little closer, though I was still having to look at it through my telephoto lens at full power, it made off, and then sat again. It now looked like nothing so much as an English collie dog, with brown body and white shoulders, but the oddly shaped ears. It wouldn't let me nearer than about 150 yards, and eventually vanished into some bushes. I decided it must be a stray Maasai dog, but when I described it later in camp, Mary and Peter at once identified it as a single wild dog, rather rare. The rounded ears are evidently a particularly characteristic feature. It's a pity I never got near enough to photograph it, and I doubt that I shall see it again, as they travel for long distances when on their own, apparently.

There were far more wildebeest out beyond the airstrip than there were yesterday: thousands, certainly. Rather nearer at hand was a single zebra, which was inclined to gallop about in a generally satisfying manner, with a nice sound of hooves. There was a pleasing sunset, and a dramatic rain shower over the Kelogi inselberg. We had heard thunder during the afternoon, though only a little rain fell at Olduvai. There is said to be plenty of water in the Gorge river, however, and the dogs apparently swam in it during their walk this morning. In the early darkness, there was the sound of frogs, which I don't remember hearing previously. Tomorrow, all being well, Peter and I are to go over to Laetoli to see what can be seen of the site, on a run which is also to include collecting meat at Ngorongoro (which seems to me to be in precisely the opposite direction). Ah, but will there be an outbreak of *simba* first?

Wednesday, 19 January

No, there were no lions this morning, and in fact there were no disturbances of any kind during the night. We were to start as early as possible for Laetoli, since the round trip via Ngorongoro is a long one. Smothered in anti-sun cream, I was soon ready, and we were away by 7.40 am in the early morning light. If a vehicle is known to be going up to Ngorongoro, there is always no shortage of people wanting lifts. Accordingly, at the bottom of the Gorge, in a place which (whether by coincidence or otherwise) was safely out of sight of the feared Mama Leakey, we collected not only two men from the guides' camp who were to do the shopping at Ngorongoro, but also two young Maasai girls, one of them known to Peter, resplendent in beads, and, one would have to say, morphologically quite resplendent, too: they want to go to visit their mothers or sisters, or whatever, for the day. When I say 'resplendent in beads', I don't mean that they didn't wear other things too, beside the beads, but not a lot, not a lot. Mary would certainly not have allowed them to

hitchhike in any vehicle of hers, on the grounds that if you do the Maasai a favour, they come to expect the same service in future as an absolute right, but Peter has made many Maasai friends. Two dik-dik scampered away as we left the Gorge, and the plains beyond were full of game. I suppose, if one could have counted, we had seen four or five thousand animals before we even reached the main road. It was then necessary to slow down for a very large giraffe – one of many, but this particular one was drinking from a puddle in the very middle of the road, and did not wish to move.

Ngorongoro crater, looking down from the rim

It was an excellent run up to Ngorongoro, past the extinct volcanoes Lemagrut and Sadiman, and we saw many more giraffe. We met few vehicles until we were almost at the Ngorongoro crater itself. Here there was one dead zebra, surrounded by busily photographing tourists – that seemed odd, somehow, when there were several live ones within easy telephoto range. We dropped one of the Maasai girls first and then the other passengers, except the second girl, who had decided she needed to go further and thought she would probably know where to get off. After Ngorongoro, we turned on to a road that was new to me, heading for Ndulen, where the doctor and his hospital are: we were bearing mangoes, petrol and greetings for him from Mary, and if he were free we would take him to the site with us, as promised during his visit on 8 January. The road from Ngorongoro to Ndulen was an earth one, with patches of rock now and again, and seemed

easy going, being reasonably dry except for the occasional deep puddle: the trouble with the puddles was that one couldn't tell whether they were two inches deep or two feet, and there seemed to be both kinds. The Maasai girl didn't say 'stop here', or anything helpful, but eventually we met a group of Maasai who appeared to know her, and she talked to them at great length: it emerged eventually that we had just passed the place she was going to, so out she got, requesting that we pick her up again on our way home.

Peter and I travelled on through beautiful wooded country: this road is on the opposite side of Lemagrut to Olduvai, and the landscape is quite different from Serengeti. On the left, through the haze, could just be made out the edge of the Rift and Lake Eyasi. Peter stopped to show me a Maasai holy tree, dim and shrine-like beyond a protecting curtain of creepers, with many grass-offerings left by passers-by. A local witch doctor who lives near here is widely regarded as very powerful, so much so that he was sent with one or two others to be with the Tanzanian army, when it was fighting in Uganda, to maintain the troops' morale. Peter knows him quite well, from the days of the Laetoli dig. The Olduvai camp staff have absolutely no doubts concerning his power. He has worn his army boots proudly ever since his return from the Ugandan campaign: there can't be too many witch doctors with army boots, I dare say.

Lemagrut volcano, a view across the Gorge

Soon we reached Ndulen, where the hospital was bright with bougainvillaea. Peter knew everyone, of course, and introduced me to several of the nursing sisters. There seemed to be numerous Maasai patients in the waiting room, so perhaps they have got over their objection to the Mbulu nurses; and there too were Philip, the doctor, and his wife and small son. Tomorrow, the new house that is being built for them *might* be ready to move into, so we were shown round it proudly, and it will certainly be lovely, when finished. The specially made kitchen shelves and cupboards were a much admired feature. The men building the house had unfortunately dropped the bathroom mirror, but the best half of it had been put up in the intended place, on the rather splendid grounds that the jagged top roughly resembles the silhouette of Lemagrut. A hole in the centre had been neatly filled by knocking in a nail. The house has a splendid view to the lake, and it might have a beautiful garden, too, if elephant and buffalo did not come right up to the windows and eat everything that is planted. This is evidently a local hazard. We were told: 'One of the sisters is having a beautiful garden, but the elephant is coming in the middle of the night, so the sister is chasing the elephant in her nightgown and the elephant is running away, but the garden is all destroyed and the sister is very cross with the elephant.'

We had coffee (with milk from a Maasai cow), and then headed off for the Laetoli site, with the doctor and his family, who all wanted to come. The route was across grass country, on a good firm very green track; there were three minor streams to cross, but they were shallow and presented no problem. There were many zebra about. The only previous time I visited Laetoli (in 1974, before the excavations took place), I came from the other side, travelling in exactly the opposite direction, so today we had nearly arrived before we emerged on to high ground overlooking the site and at last I could see where we were. The previous time, everything was dry and brown, so today it all looked very different. There were many wildebeest and zebra wandering over the first exposures of the very important Laetoli Pliocene sediments that we came to, and vultures on a kill beyond – no lions, of course, though Laetoli has many. We drove first to Locality 18, where many fossil bones were lying scattered around, greatly impressing Philip, and then on to a general view point, partly for Peter to explain the essential features and partly to look cautiously for elephant and buffalo, since these are not too good to meet on foot. There were none: only one giraffe, later joined by three kongoni. So we drove on to visit the main area of the site, the exposures of the famous 'footprint tuff'. The hominid footprint trails, unfortunately, as I already knew, had been covered over for their own safety, when the dig ended. The areas of the tuff that remain exposed had suffered somewhat from rain and weather since the dig, but were still very impressive and, with Peter's guidance, the geology seemed very clear. There was plenty to photograph: I took slides, so that I can use them in lecturing. We walked a little further, and then turned back to a shady place where the diggers had always set up their camp, to have a picnic lunch. It got quite hot, and the flies became numerous. We could also see that there was rain back in the direction of Ndulen, with thunder, though it didn't reach where we were. I photographed a scarlet bird, a bishop of some kind. Soon it was time to start back: after all, it was nearly three o'clock already, and Peter and I had a long road home to travel, with our various passengers of the day waiting to be picked up. We paused at one point to observe a large whitish bird of prey, which no one could identify, sitting in a tree. I managed to photograph it after three shots, having inadvertently set the camera to time exposure: it was a patient bird, or stupid, as it simply waited in its tree. It looked more like an osprey than anything else, but this is hardly the right environment. Are there ospreys in Africa? I must look that up.

Land Rover stuck in mud, Peter Jones on right

On we went – and then, suddenly, we came to where the rainstorm we had seen in the distance had struck. It must have been violent, for our firm green track had now become very slippery mud and the grass was saturated: it was very difficult to make any headway at all, especially when the four-wheel drive lever suddenly decided not to work. When we got to the first of the little streams, it was now quite deep and full of fast-flowing new water, and one simply could not see where it was safe to drive across. We guessed wrong, and in no time were firmly stuck, the back wheels in almost up to the axle. Push, everybody – no good at all. One couldn't get a grip with one's feet, for one thing.

These are the kind of occasions that remind one of the differences between wild East Africa and not-so-wild rural West Oxfordshire. There was nothing to be done but for Philip to walk on to Endulen, about an hour away on foot, to return with his own four-wheel drive Toyota and tow us out. There was no particular reason why any other vehicle should pass this way within a week, when one thought about it. At least there was no more rain on the way immediately, and also there was a plentiful supply of lovely black mud left, even allowing for what was by then all over us, so that we could fashion mud people to keep Philip's small son amused, he being about three or four, I suppose. Some Maasai herds moved nearby, and there were zebra and lots of the brightly coloured superb starlings to be seen, but not much else. We waited.

Philip was back in only one and a quarter hours, and he did indeed succeed eventually in towing us out, though for some while it seemed more likely that he would slide backwards in to join us. We then made our way slowly on, both vehicles slipping and sliding like ducks on ice. We duly subsided into one of the other streams, but got out of that one by everyone pushing. Eventually, we slid our way past the little Ndulen airstrip, which I noted is built across a hill and has such a rise in the middle of it that you can't see one end of the strip from the other, not even nearly. (I do hope planes don't try to land there after a heavy rainstorm.) And so at last to Ndulen itself.

We enjoyed a cool drink with the doctor's family before it was time for Peter and me to press on: we were now running very late indeed. The earth road between Ndulen and Ngorongoro had been fine in the dry conditions this morning, but what would it be like now?

What, indeed? Peter handled the vehicle quite brilliantly in the now very muddy and slippery conditions, but there was just too much uphill track to be negotiated, and eventually there came a deeply rutted steeply rising stretch where we simply slid sideways and lodged against the bank. No amount of pushing by me would prevent the wheels from spinning, and after half an hour's effort we were wondering what on earth to try next, and watching one of the ruts suddenly fill with a great stream of running water from some rain-shower ahead, when three Maasai men suddenly appeared, two warriors and an elder, complete with spears and so forth. Male Maasai are not normally noted for helping anyone, under any circumstances, though they will always stand and watch eagerly. As they came level with us, however, one of them suddenly and unexpectedly said to me, in excellent English, 'Good day, where are you from? Ah, you are from England. And where are you going?'

He also read out the word Olduvai, written on the side of the vehicle. Peter joined the conversation in his fluent Swahili, and, amazingly, in no time at all, the two younger Maasai were helping to push and to cut branches to put under the wheels to stop them spinning. The elder felt it more dignified to hold the spears. The vehicle, however, remained firmly stuck. At this point I remembered an incident from my 1972 Olduvai visit when I had also suddenly met an English-speaking Maasai in the middle of nowhere. I thought I would try my luck, so during the next pause in the pushing, I asked him where he had learned his excellent English.

'We learn it in my school.'

So I asked, remembering what had happened on the previous occasion, did they by any chance in his school use a book called *Oxford English Dictionary*?

'Yes, we read it.'

'Well, I come from Oxford in England, and from the University where the book was made.'

'You are a teacher from the University of Oxford, where the dictionary in my school comes from?'

'I am.'

Broad grin. We shook hands warmly, and he rushed to tell the others all about it in rapid Maasai. More handshakes, and we all became firm friends at once: Oxford University Press would surely be delighted. At just about this moment, the four-wheel drive on the Land Rover elected to come back into operation, and with the aid of a huge combined Anglo-Maasai shove, we got the Land Rover back on its way. Peter drove it cautiously to the top of the hill, and the rest of us squelched wearily after him. Spears in the back, Maasai elder and warriors on the back seat, Peter and myself in front – off we went.

From this point, the whole journey began to take on a mysterious, shifting, dream-like quality, though I was not at any time asleep. From time to time, we seemed to stop and pick up more Maasai, or drop some of our passengers off, and in due course we collected the girl we had brought from Olduvai for her day trip – and she had decided, of course, to bring her little sister, aged only about five but no less profusely decked in beadwork. This small person chattered excitedly and very charmingly, but literally non-stop, for the next several hours: I don't think she had ever ridden in any form of car before, because she was somehow never quite ready when we started off again after one of the numerous stops. The English-speaking Maasai pointed out his village, in the failing light, and his cattle. I remembered to congratulate him on their number, which is the correct thing to do, and this pleased him greatly. Most of the Maasai got off there, and we had politely to decline an invitation to stop at the village and meet everyone. We managed to pick up several other hitch-hiking passengers between there and Ngorongoro, as we rattled and slid along, most of them apparently known to Peter, who has ranged widely over this area during his time in Tanzania. I have no idea how many different local ethnic groups were represented by the time we reached Ngorongoro. We were something like 3 hours late, by now, but the two men from the guides' camp, who had had all the day to buy the meat and collect the mail, seemed to be hardly ready. It was very late evening when we began the final stage of the journey, the little Maasai girl still chattering cheerfully, neither expecting nor receiving answers to her remarks. We were supposed to collect at Ngorongoro the other of the two Maasai girls who had set out with us in the morning, but there was no sign of her. Her colleague went to look for her, and returned with no news of her but with a length of cloth she had taken the opportunity to purchase. Remarkable people, the Maasai. We waited no longer.

So we clattered our way slowly down the winding road towards the plains, into the very last of the sunset and eventually into the warm darkness. We caught glimpses of giraffe and gazelle, and also saw a flock of Abdim storks, which had been resting in two trees beside the road until our noisy approach. Spectacular distant lightning flickered from four separate storms, fortunately all on the horizon. Zebra loomed up from time to time in the headlight beams, and once there was a bright pair of eyes which eventually proved to belong to a hyaena, who turned and ran for some way in front of us before suddenly plunging off to the left and vanishing into the night. Oh, and earlier, near Ngorongoro, before it got completely dark, we saw a jackal with a white-tipped tail, the rather rare 'side-stripe' jackal, which I had not encountered before. Thus eventually we reached Olduvai, and dropped the two guides close to their camp rather than leaving them to walk across the Gorge, because of the darkness and the lions. It was too dark, also, for the Maasai girl and her loquacious small sister to find their way home to their own *manyatta* (settlement), so they vanished towards the camp's staff quarters to look for somewhere to spend the night, fortunately before Mary saw them. I suppose it was already well past 8.0 pm when we reached home, but our lights had been seen many miles away as we made our descent to Serengeti, and Mary had ceased planning the search party at first light, which she had been contemplating. Drink, hot shower, dinner – in that order, which was undoubtedly the correct one. Recounting of adventures. Bed time. Peter, not surprisingly, was exhausted.

Meanwhile, at Olduvai, the day had not been without incident. Vast numbers of gazelle had crossed the Gorge and gone past the camp, and two snakes had been killed. The birds, led by the scrub robin, had given warning of their presence: a baby puff-adder first, and then a boomslang – both quite nasty. But nothing like the 11 foot (actually measured) mamba that we got a couple of months ago, Mary assured me airily. I'm sorry to have missed the gazelle and the snakes, but can hardly grumble about my own day's quota of adventures. And no writing done, either. Well, we scribes need the occasional gentle, relaxing day off.

Thursday, 20 January

I was inclined to feel, when called in the morning, that a little more sleep would have been acceptable, but I forgot about that a few moments later, when there was a noise of many animals. A very large herd of wildebeest was crossing the Gorge, with a few zebra amongst them. That was something I have long heard about, and always wanted to see, so I was soon dressed and down by the camp gate, watching. For about an hour, they came and went, apparently unable to make up their minds, queuing up, getting in each other's way, suddenly all starting to run and then, no sooner had a group disappeared, than they all came rushing back again, as if there was something down there they didn't like. There was much noise, and loud calling by the leaders. We wondered whether two separate herds had arrived at the same time, and got mixed up, or something like that. In the end, a thousand or two did go on across, while several hundred more, at least, with most of the zebra, stayed on our side, close to the camp, between it and the airstrip, where they remained all day. When the sun rose clear of the mists on the horizon, it picked out the silver white of the zebra amongst the dark wildebeest quite beautifully. And all this happened before breakfast, too.

Peter was feeling not merely tired out after yesterday, but also distinctly unwell, and he suspects that it is the first signs of an attack of malaria. As we had earlier had confirmed, the mosquitoes at Olduvai are not normally infected (just as well, when I consider the number of bites I have acquired, particularly around the ankles). The interesting theory now emerged that some of them could perhaps have got themselves infected by biting Mary once she already had malaria, and might now be busily spreading locally the Lake Baringo variety of the disease. Goodness, I'd never have thought of that. One hopes it is not true. Some pills are to guard against malaria, and others to kill it off when you've already got it, so Peter took some of the latter, which are of course in short supply, and had a quiet day.

I did some writing, and read some of the source material, all day. Up to about 9.15 am, one can sit outside in the sun to work, but then it suddenly gets too hot, and it is time to move back into the big main room, which by then has been swept and tidied by the camp staff. As usual, it got cloudier from about 1.0 pm, but no rain came near, so it stayed warm. Mary spent most of the time working on her proofs for the Laetoli publication: in the early evening, she found an error in one of the tables, which discouraged her enough to decide that the only thing to do was to read a novel instead. I went out to walk for an hour or so as usual, first watching the wildebeest, who didn't seem to notice me, as the wind was blowing from them to me. I then went right down into the Side Gorge, where the vegetation is now so thick and green that one can only get through along the animal tracks, but I eventually reached the stream at the bottom, which at that point was over towards the far side: it had muddy pools, but no flowing water. I returned via the site LLK (Louis Leakey Korongo), the find-spot of Olduvai Hominid 9. A deep recent gully has been cut through the site by the run-off of rainwater, since I was last there some years ago, but the marker for the hominid find-spot is still in position, and looks safe enough. The sun set while I was there, and I noticed what must have been a bat-eared fox watching me with no great concern, only a dozen yards away. I saw two dik-dik shortly afterwards.

At bedtime, I listened for a while to the sounds of the wildebeest nearby, grunting and chattering away to each other, the noise sometimes rising to a brief crescendo, perhaps when one of them said something rude, or maybe when there was a rumour of danger. One could also hear the usual insects in the grass and the trees, and the occasional call of a night bird. There were great flashes of lightning from time to time over Ngorongoro, and a bright young wrong-way-up moon presiding over it all. Definitely an African night – am I really due back in the English winter in five days' time, just when my forearms are slowly acquiring a pale parchment colour that doesn't wash off, which might loosely be described as sunburn?

I almost forgot to mention a minor example of cause and effect this morning – the way in which rather unlikely causes have quite significant effects has been intriguing me in my chronicling of Mary's career and in various details of Leakey family history which I have been reading. Anyhow, the four dogs – the three Dalmatians and Brown Dog – always go for their morning walk while Mary, Peter and I are having breakfast: the camp staff take them. Their return normally ends in a dramatic 'toast race' between Matthew and Brown Dog, to be first for scraps of breakfast toast but, if there happen to be lots of animals near the camp gate, all four are really far more interested in escaping to chase them, which is strictly not allowed, because of the danger to them from cheetah and other animals that would attack them, if they got separated and lost. Today there were plenty of inviting-looking wildebeest to be had and, although I was carefully holding the gate open exactly as instructed, the dogs neatly and quite deliberately eluded everyone and shot cheerfully off. However, as they rounded the corner of the camp fence en route for the limitless forbidden hunting grounds of Serengeti, whom should they meet head on but the two Maasai girls of yesterday, beads and all, off home after their night in camp. The little one, not having seen anything like a Dalmatian before, sprang into the air with a loud Maasai yip, and this was just enough to stop the dogs and divert them back through the gate. Mary looked suspiciously at the Maasai girls – she would have done that anyhow – but said nothing. I merely looked appropriately bemused, which is a very commonplace Oxford skill and as easy to deploy in the open air on Serengeti as in a Faculty Board meeting back at home.

Later in the day, some more Maasai came to the camp, asking for malaria pills, which Mary allows them to do, Louis and she having always run an informal local surgery in earlier days at Olduvai. Well, if they've really got malaria, I reckon the local mosquitoes must be infected.

Friday, 21 January

Something stampeded the remaining wildebeest across the Gorge in the early hours, probably lions. In fact, I heard none of this, though Mary did. The camp staff reported later that chaos had ensued in one of the local Maasai encampments. After breakfast, 20 or so vultures could be seen circling in the general direction of the night noises, so we went out to prospect, but there was no kill to be seen, and the vultures eventually drifted away.

Next, we discovered that the genets had broken into the mango store, where there are numerous mangoes awaiting chutnification, if that's the word I want. Fortunately, on this occasion, the genets seem only to have selected one mango each, instead of taking single bites out of many, as they might have done. We moved the mangoes to a safer place:

Making mango chutney

what a magnificent sight they are.

Peter had recovered from his sickness: if it *was* malaria, he evidently dealt with it appropriately and in time. In the afternoon, Annie, his wife, arrived from the Manyara National Park, where she has finished her work for the moment. The chutney-making has been fixed for tomorrow, as it was thought Annie would wish to be in on it. It was hotter than of late today, with no breeze, the indoor temperature getting up to 87 degrees in mid-afternoon.

Consideration of the arrangements for my return journey revealed an unexpected clash between the time we had forecast to Hazel for my arrival at the Tanzania/Kenya border at Namanga and a talk Peter has been booked to give to visitors back at Olduvai, so I shall have to leave on Sunday rather than Monday. Spurred on by this unexpected reduction in our time, Mary and I resorted to using the tape recorder I had brought, for the first time, so that I will have plenty of notes to take back with me for writing up into text, back in England. We actually made better progress than I had feared, and we shall clearly have to do the same again tomorrow. I'd expected Mary to be put off by the idea of talking into a machine that wasn't going to forget anything she said, but she proved very good with it, and insisted on taking the microphone and talking about anything she considered relevant, rather than waiting to be asked questions.

I walked as usual in the evening, having first taken a photograph of some Olduvai handaxes to replace an unsuccessful lecture slide taken in 1974, and also having photographed Mary and the dogs, which the publishers asked me to do, much as she dislikes being photographed. She was surprisingly cooperative, but I suspect that the light was rather too contrasty. I also got done various other minor tasks that I hadn't yet achieved. It was cloudy for my walk, and during it a lovely soft shower fell, producing a wonderful smell of wet earth. There were numerous gazelle and a small herd of wildebeest near the airstrip: I tried hard not to disturb their evening grazing, but a few edged nervously away. I was back in camp by sunset and we tried unsuccessfully to get through on the radio to Hazel in Nairobi, to tell her of the changed timing for my journey: we got through easily enough to Nairobi Control, but Hazel was not at home.

At Mary's request, I read aloud some excerpts of the draft text after supper to entertain Peter and Annie, and everyone seemed to enjoy them, which is at least a hopeful sign at this stage. The evening was quite warm and humid, with no breeze to turn the windmills that generate the camp's electricity. I heard some flamingo fly over in the dark, sounding like wild geese.

Saturday, 22 January

Last night was rather a disturbed one. First it was very hot, then very windy, and then there was an outbreak of That Animal around the hut again (see 18 January). Mary now diagnoses it as a white-tailed mongoose, rather than a shy porcupine, on the basis of typical droppings found nearby. I'm prepared to believe that, as last night it sounded to be all over the roof of the hut as well as everywhere else, barring inside, and you wouldn't really expect a shy porcupine to be on your roof, even here. I was just too sleepy to go out and look, so I banged vigorously on the wall and whatever it was scarpered somewhat, with a grunt, but soon came back.

At the end of breakfast, only two out of the four dogs appeared back from their walk, so Mary mounted an immediate rescue expedition by car, but they turned up before we had gone more than 50 yards: one of our shorter trips.

The morning was divided between working with the tape recorder and the making of the mango chutney, For the latter, it is necessary to peel and cut up mangoes, garlic and chilli peppers, and these are then cooked in a cauldron with vinegar, sugar, ginger, etc. The whole thing was a splendid ceremony, very sticky-making, but one can of course always lick the fingers. The chutney was all finished and in jars by mid-afternoon, about 20 pounds of it, I think, and there were lots of mangoes over, which is good news. The chilli peppers turned out to be extra strong, leading to grave doubts as to whether the finished product would turn out to be a bit fierce, even though only about half the usual quantity of peppers was used.

The morning also produced a successful radio call to Hazel in Nairobi, with the result that I am due at the border at Namanga at 1.0 pm on Monday. Mary was also highly delighted by the news from Hazel that a visit to Olduvai by King Leopold of Belgium, who had been expected for the nights of 6 and 7 February, had been cancelled. 'Such a nuisance, these kings,' she said, quite seriously.

And just when new mosquito nets had been specially ordered, too. There was some discussion later as to whether she should send him the bill, but it was agreed that the item 'mosquito nets for king' had looked quite good on the shopping list.

Also in the morning, I walked down to the Main Gorge to take some long-planned photographs, before 8.0 am, while the light was right for the shots I wanted, and before it got too hot. In the afternoon, we did some more tape-recording, and I talked with Peter and Annie about their own future plans for archaeological work. I also visited Peter's stone-knapping floor, close by the camp, for a close look at some of the Olduvai rock types and their fracture patterns. There was a sudden hatch of small hornets, one of which actually dared to sting Mary, though fortunately not badly: we sprayed them, and they went away.

After tea, we had our final recording session of this trip, taking the story well into the 1950s, though my writing up of the resulting material into draft text has not got beyond 1935. After that, Mary and I, having admired the enormous numbers of grazing animals out beyond the air strip, decided that we simply must have a last short trip to see them: it was actually her idea, too, though I needed no persuading. We shared the driving. There were thousands upon thousands of animals, well spread out, grazing peacefully for as far as the eye could see, in the evening light, with one or two spectacular rainstorms in the distance. Wildebeest were the majority, of course, but there were also numerous zebra and many Thompson's gazelle (always known simply as 'Tommies'). Amongst them all was a single very large eland bull, the only eland I have seen on this visit. Just for a moment, in the distance, we both thought it was a rhinoceros – wishful thinking, because in this area, where they were once commonplace, the poachers have slaughtered them out of existence for their horns. There were also many storks on the ground amongst the animals, both the white European ones and the smaller kind, the Abdim storks, though not in the huge flocks that had so impressed me out on Serengeti during the trip to Ndutu, 10 days ago. The whole sight, and the sounds of the animals and birds, was unforgettable. Mary said that the game herds have stayed nearby for longer this year than she can ever remember, so my visit could not have been better timed: I have certainly been very lucky, because in another year the timing of the rains might have been quite different and I might have missed everything. Suddenly seeing 20 or so vultures perched in a tree, we made a final detour in search of lions, but there were none, and we drove slowly home across the Gorge.

It was time to start packing, and to do some preliminary loading of the Land Rover for an early start tomorrow. Annie also has to go to Arusha, and the new mechanic, Omari, who has proved a great success, is coming with us to collect some vehicle spare parts there. Dinner had almost an end-of-term atmosphere. Mary and I agreed on the considerable success of the project thus far, and we both felt that we had got a satisfactory amount done, all things considered. It was hot again, today, and once more no rain fell at Olduvai itself. The indoor temperature reached 86 degrees in the afternoon, and was still 75 at 9.30 pm. After the others had gone to bed, I sat for a while enjoying the sounds of the African night: the calls of nightjars and of other night birds that I can't identify, the noise of crickets and of cicadas in the big camp acacia tree, a gentle continuous murmur from the distant wildebeest herd, and the occasional droning flight of a beetle nearer at hand. In the bright moonlight, the familiar shapes of the volcanoes could be made out, up to 20 miles away, while frequent flashes of lightning came from a gathering of storm-clouds over Kelogi. Time to complete my packing, I suppose: it's sad to be leaving.

Sunday, 23 January

Olduvai would not let me go without one last flurry of excitement. As I mentioned earlier, Sundays, by camp tradition, start 15 minutes later than other days, and I still had shaving soap on my face when the return of the dogs from their walk was accompanied by news of another kill out by the airstrip. This time, the vultures were only just arriving, flying low, and hyaenas were said to be driving them off. Possibly, if lions made the kill, they might still be there, or, if not, might only just have left. Mary and I were on our way in a few moments. Too late, again ... When we arrived, there was indeed one hyaena and numerous vultures and eagles disputing the remains of a late wildebeest, but where were the lions? Sundays are clearly too indulgent: if only it had been a weekday, we should have been 15 minutes earlier. We drove slowly along, exploring the bushes in all directions in the customary search for replete lions, but as usual with no result. The low early sun did not help the search, but I don't think we missed anything. Then we saw some of the vultures moving off purposefully and, following them, came across a second kill. This one had evidently taken place earlier, because the carcass was already picked almost clean. No lions there either, so we returned to camp defeated, Mary very disenchanted with her local lion population:

'The place is full of them when you don't want to see them. I shan't ever try to show you one again. It's ridiculous: everyone else sees them. Blasted animals!'

Breakfast was next, followed by the final assembly of luggage, and then we were off at about 8.15, for Arusha, on a bright, clear morning with obviously a hot day to follow: Peter, Annie and I shared the front seat of the Land Rover, with Omari perched in the back amongst luggage of all kinds, for numerous different destinations. The thousands of animals Mary and I had visited yesterday evening were still there and still peacefully grazing, no one apparently having selected them to eat during the night. It's clearly quite a hit-or-miss career, being a Serengeti wildebeest. I wonder how it compares with being a ghost-writer? Doubtless I shall find out, as the year passes. Meanwhile, we turned left at the main road, for Ngorongoro, Karatu and Arusha, the latter some five hours' driving time away. We paused after a few miles, when Peter saw fresh lion paw marks in the dust of the road, but as usual the lions themselves were not to be seen. Having a couple of photographs left to finish on my film, I took one of giraffe and one of buffalo.

It was a glorious ride, and, for once, free from trouble. The first stop was at Gibb's Farm, at Karatu, to deliver some of the items brought to Olduvai by the aeroplane a week ago, this being the first time a vehicle has been passing. We were offered coffee, but declined, as it would have meant too long a stop. There were baboons by the road at one point on the long descent through the forested country the far side of Ngorongoro. It's hard to imagine the young Louis and Mary Leakey virtually carrying their vehicle and luggage up this hill in the opposite direction, through deep mud on a far worse version of the road, back in 1935, two years before I was born. They covered 16 miles in two and a half days. On we went, to the Rift edge above Manyara, and down the precipitous hill to Mto wa Mbu, where the market is. Amazingly, there was petrol at the garage, so Peter joined the queue, and we briefly met a visiting American professor, en route for Serengeti.

The Mto wa Mbu market is full of very attractive objects, including real Maasai beadwork, as opposed to the kind made for the tourists: I suppose the Maasai trade it to the stallholders in return for supplies of various kinds. The stallholders have rather inflated ideas in their asking-prices, but are instantly amenable to requests for 60 per cent reductions. In fact, the local currency, Tanzanian shillings, is held in such low esteem that they much prefer to trade for other goods. I was immediately offered a wide choice of quite nice carved animals in exchange for my hat, but decided regretfully that it would be far too hot across the Rift to part with the hat. I remembered, however, that I had a few surplus tee shirts in my luggage, and consulted my colleagues: it appeared that tee shirts have a high trade value. Omari accompanied me to see fair play. I disposed of two tee shirts and became the owner of a very attractive small turned wooden bowl, a Maasai bead watch and a beaded ear pendant. Wow! I like this trading game. Just wait till my next visit, when I will come properly supplied with trade goods, now that I know what's what. Peter and Annie, of course, are experienced experts. I even wondered if I should also trade a spare pair of Messrs Marks & Spencer's underpants from my suitcase, and reluctantly decided against it, though they would probably have been gladly accepted. My suitcase was for once quite light, since I had decided to leave all the recording equipment at Olduvai for next time, and take just the finished tapes, which I can play back on another machine. It was time to go on: but I gathered there is another market at Arusha, and there might be some time to kill tomorrow morning ...

On we went, crossing now mainly agricultural land. A few ostrich were to be seen, but the wild section of the journey was over. There is some very fine volcanic scenery, however, between Mto wa Mbu and Arusha. We reached the latter around 2.0 pm, with absolutely no trouble at all – an unprecedented event, so far as I am concerned. Perhaps the place is saving up its usual tricks for tomorrow. Peter and Annie know the Arusha that lies off the main streets, so we had a late lunch of chicken cooked in coconut milk and served with japatis, in a very cheerful wholly African eating place. The clientele was inclined to cast what I trust were admiring glances at my not-very-empire-building khaki shorts, which count as rather brief, by local standards. Then we made our way to the town centre. The usual New Arusha Hotel was for once fully booked (another unprecedented event), so I got a room instead at the New Safari, cheaper and noisier, but very adequate. We went anyhow to sit in the beautiful garden of the New Arusha, for coffee and cool drinks. There were dozens of kites circling above – there always seem to be kites here – and the garden had beautiful frangipani and bougainvillaea in full bloom. We arranged a time to meet for supper, and Peter and Annie went off with a long list of calls to pay. I had some written work of Peter's I had promised to read, and could also have a real bath and a rather overdue hair wash.

Supper was a cheerful occasion, with much to discuss and notes to compare on all that had happened over the past three weeks, plus future plans for my next visit, and the gathering of many messages for me to deliver back in England. Afterwards, I finished the reading of Peter's text, disturbed from time to time by loud noises from the street, where bars were open – not at all like an Olduvai night. Ah well.

Peter and Annie heard during their afternoon visits to friends that there had been an attempted coup about ten days ago in the Tanzanian capital, Dar-es-Salaam. It sounds as if it was unsuccessful and has been kept quiet. Certainly there is no sign of trouble or concern here in Arusha, nor was there on our journey today. Perhaps it is only a rumour. It occurred to me that I had heard no international news of any kind since I left England, and it also occurred to me that I had not missed it.

Monday, 24 January

I slept quite well after the noisy bars had shut, which was a little before midnight. After breakfast, I used up my Tanzanian currency on the hotel bill and in the market, which is extremely colourful: a real working market, this one, with fruit, vegetables, dried fish, pots, baskets and supplies of all kinds. It was curious to see stalls selling chips, but made from cassava, not potatoes. I bought – very cheaply – a basket of a widely used local type which I had often seen and admired when previously passing through Arusha. That should shake them up at the supermarket in Witney, Oxon. I also bought four mangoes, unripe enough to travel safely home. I joined Peter and Annie for some of their Arusha errands, followed by an early lunch of samosas and lemon juice, before it was time for Peter to take me to the border at Namanga. Again, remarkably, it was a trouble-free run. Some stretches of the savannah and bush country looked parched, while others were still green. There were hundreds of white butterflies, in one stretch of a few miles. We caught a glimpse of a gerenuk amongst the trees: they are one of the much less common antelopes in East Africa, downright rare in some parts, and I have never seen one before. Many of the acacias were in flower.

Earlier, we saw newspapers saying that 1600 people have been arrested in Dar, following the attempted coup, but this part of Tanzania seems entirely unconcerned about the trouble, whatever it may have been.

We got to Namanga about 1.30 pm, after an excellent run – half an hour late for the agreed meeting time, but only because we had started out later than Peter had originally planned. Hazel, knowing my reputation for adventurous car journeys in Africa, had just been beginning to wonder what had happened this time. She had brought with her a young Spanish archaeologist, who is to accompany Peter and Annie back to Olduvai as Mary's next visitor, Mary having taken pity on him at a conference, apparently after Richard Leakey had told him that his subject of study was too boring to be worth a permit. I think she was now wishing she hadn't invited him, but he seemed very nice. The 'boring' subject was of course the morphology and technology of handaxes, which has occupied so much of my own research efforts ... Well, Mary minds that less than Richard; at least she has met him previously, so he stands a sporting chance of being a success at Olduvai, but I do hope he likes Dalmatians, or he hasn't a hope, and will instantly be classified as a Stinker. On his journey out to Kenya, he had lost all his luggage at Madrid, but fortunately it caught up with him eventually. He told me that he has visited Oxford, and actually came to our research centre at 60 Banbury Road, while I was away, and he knows quite well two of my present research students, Nick Barton and Simon Collcutt, from the time they had all spent studying together at Bordeaux.

Half of the Tanzanian customs seemed to be having lunch, so there was quite a long wait before eventually all my luggage was transferred, or so I hoped, from the Land Rover to Hazel's car, and it was time to say goodbye to Peter, who drove off with his new passenger. Hazel and I made our way to the Kenyan side for more documentation: for once, the customs actually got round to opening my suitcase, but as I had left the tape recorder at Olduvai, I had nothing even remotely unusual to explain. After a cool drink, we started our journey to Nairobi, the ride in Hazel's car on a tarmac road seeming extremely smooth after all the days of Land Rover travel on rough roads or no roads at all.

The country looked still quite green, and we came after a while to damp roads, where it had recently been raining. Here there were large numbers of butterflies again, yellow this time, enjoying all the damp patches they could find, but most especially those which happened to be cowpats. We stopped to examine a large dead bird, presumably hit by a vehicle, but it turned out to be a marabou stork and therefore devoid of pretty feathers to collect. The road became dry for a while, and then wet again, the wet section ending with a sharp line between it and the next dry one, something one often expects to find when travelling through showery conditions in England, but somehow never does: perhaps English rainstorms don't have such sharply defined edges as East African ones. Eventually the familiar outline of the Ngong Hills could be seen in the distance, and then the beginnings of Nairobi itself. We arrived in rush hour and, as we did so, Hazel's car began to make some very odd noises – first a lot of backfiring, and then alarming scraping noises from the clutch. That was much more like what I have come to expect of African car travel, of course, but she contrived to keep going, just about, as we looked for a hotel where I could spend the night, blessed as I am with my author's expense account. We eventually found space at the New Stanley, which looked a bit large and grand, but in fact turned out to be very friendly and not unreasonably expensive: it is high tourist season, and everywhere else that was at all conveniently located seemed to be completely full. Hazel and I arranged to meet at her office tomorrow morning, where, among other things, I am to have a first look at the prolific Leakey archive of photographs, some of which should certainly be useful for the autobiography. Hazel then coaxed her car somewhat gingerly into the traffic queue, the clutch still making alarming metallic noises – I could only hope she would actually make it home.

I had a general sort out and repacking of my luggage, followed by a brief wander round to try and get my bearings before dark. I really didn't remember the centre of Nairobi at all well, having previously usually been driven direct from the Leakeys' home out at Langata to the National Museum. Which way, for example, was the market, which I recalled as being a fairly central landmark?

Finding myself in Nairobi with an unexpected day to spare, I decided to telephone my good friend Robert Soper, a contemporary from Cambridge undergraduate days, now teaching at Nairobi University, and I looked up his home number in the local directory. How remarkable to find a hotel where local telephone calls are free! Eventually I got through, and spoke to his wife, Jane: Robert was out singing with a local choral society. I arranged to meet him at his office tomorrow: it turned out to be very close to where Hazel works, so that would be easy. Another very good feature of the New Stanley Hotel was that its baths are full length ones, and I emerged much refreshed from mine. It also had a nice cafe´ extending to the pavement, built around a very large tree, and called The Thorn Tree. It features a message board, claimed to be famous (and for all I know, it may be), which anyone can use. This looked a better bet that the rather smooth dining room, so I settled for Indian Ocean Fish and Chips, suddenly realising that this was the first meal I had had by myself since the flight out. Afterwards, I brought this diary up to date and sorted out my accumulation of papers from the whole trip, until tiredness quite suddenly caught up with me. Although this was the centre of Nairobi, my room was much quieter than the one in Arusha, as the window faced into the hotel rather than being on the street side. I went out like a light.

Tuesday, 25 January

Though perfectly well aware, when I woke up, that this was my last day in Africa for this time, I seemed to have no sense of an impending journey at all. I had breakfast under the possibly famous thorn tree – it's a yellow-barked fever-tree, if you ask me, but what would I know? – paid the hotel bill and arranged to leave my luggage there to pick up *en route* to the airport in the evening. This really has proved to be a very friendly and helpful hotel, the staff all smiling and nothing too much trouble: maybe I shall get a chance to stay there again.

I walked up the hill to the museum: it was already quite hot, and it seemed to be a drier kind of heat than that of Olduvai. My usually reliable sense of direction misled me slightly, for once – something to do with the sun not being in the south, I suppose – but I was not too far astray, and soon came to a bit I recognised. I noticed there were still soldiers guarding the radio station, after the attempted coup of a few months ago. Apparently, the resulting treason trials are only just beginning, and the university is still officially closed, as quite a lot of its students got involved. Hazel was late arriving, but I didn't have long to wait. Her car had stopped making odd noises soon after I got out, she reported, but this morning it wouldn't start at all. Perhaps my frequent troubles travelling by car in Africa are really something to do with me: maybe I have the same sort of effect on cars in this continent as the late prophet Jonah had on the ship, when he tried his luck at marine travel with such unfortunate results. I must say, that thought simply hadn't occurred to me before. It would explain a lot. In Hazel's office, I handed over all the messages and the letters for mailing that Mary had sent with me from Olduvai. Richard Leakey was away on a short trip to Brussels, it turned out, but his wife Meave looked in and I was able to report on Mary's health and on the progress we had made with the autobiography.

Hazel and I then walked round to Robert Soper's office: he and Hazel turned out to be acquainted by sight but not by name, so I was able to introduce them. We talked for a while, and Robert and I arranged to have lunch together; he also very kindly offered me a lift to the airport this evening, which solved a possible problem. I then returned to spend a fascinating hour or so with Leakey photographs of the period 1935–45, which were in process of being sorted as Leakey Archive material by Joan Merrick, the wife of Harry Merrick. I was introduced to both of them. Harry used to teach my American research student John Dumont, so I was able to give them news of John and promise to convey their greetings to him. Joan Merrick was very helpful, and there were certainly some very usable black-and-white photographs of Olduvai and Ngorongoro in 1935, and of Mary's important Kenyan archaeological sites of Naivasha, Njoro and Hyrax Hill, and of Olorgesailie, which comes a bit later in the story; also, not unexpectedly, several of Dalmatians in 1938. The purely family photographs are at Mary's house at Langata, and she and I must go through those together next time, if we get a chance.

I had lunch with Robert at the Boulevard Hotel under a grass umbrella. The service lacked the quality of the New Stanley's, the meal taking 40 minutes to arrive, but that gave us plenty of time to catch up on each other's news, it being two or three years since he last came to England. Afterwards, I returned to the photographs for another half hour, and then walked back to the town centre for a look at the shops and the market. The quality of the souvenirs in Nairobi has improved dramatically, since my last visit: there were lots of really nice things, particularly at a shop called African Heritage, which everyone seemed to recommend. There were some African objects there of almost museum quality, I thought, though the prices were naturally expensive. In the market, I noted some charming chess sets, carved from soapstone, which seemed very cheap.

Robert was committed to a game of tennis at 4.30, but would collect me from the hotel afterwards, about 6.30, on his motorbike, which would be a new mode of travel during this trip. I had a cold drink while I waited, sitting not far from a group of members of the Nairobi Asian community, who were discussing costs, profits, how to dodge building regulations, and other such matters that I suppose Asian traders like to discuss over an evening drink. The group clearly had its own social structure. 'I never give my opinion free to anyone', said the senior member pointedly, to a young colleague who had evidently asked his advice. I didn't doubt it, but reflected that he wouldn't get very far with that policy if he were an academic archaeologist.

Robert arrived, and off we went in the warm evening breeze. I forget when I last travelled on the passenger seat of a motorbike. Robert said he couldn't think of anyone else who would agree to do so in Nairobi with such equanimity – why didn't he say that a bit earlier? Fortunately, the evening rush hour was almost over. The Sopers lived in a nice house, actually owned by the university, and their four children were variously busy with either homework or animals: there seemed to be two dogs, one cat and one kitten, two mice and one gecko, at least: perhaps there were others that didn't appear. I enjoyed the nice domestic evening, until it was time to go to the airport; seeming almost outlandish after Olduvai, there was even a black-and-white television, showing a football match between the two leading Kenyan teams, one of the boys being football-mad. My own son Nicholas would have approved thoroughly.

The journey to the airport was by car, of course, and Robert drove me first to the hotel to collect my luggage, which is beginning to bulge a bit again after the afternoon's shopping, in spite of the absence of the tape recorder. Could I fit in a couple of Kenyan avocados, I wondered? Yes. Robert's car did not do anything to support my new theory of the Jonah effect, fortunately, and we reached the airport in good time. Documentation for departure was very simple and relaxed. The customs officers were far more interested in whether I could tell them the value of an American quarter-dollar someone had just given one of them. I broke it as gently as I could to them that it was only worth about two Kenya shillings, which caused much amusement and huge beams all round.

About an hour before departure time there was an ominous complete absence of activity in the area of the Departures gate, so it was no great surprise to hear the announcement soon after of a one-hour delay. A subsequent message attributed this to 'operating reasons because the plane had been on another flight'. An alternative explanation that occurred to me, since I had looked out of the window once or twice, was that the plane had been there all the time but the rather nonplussed-looking committee of experts examining one of the starboard engines had not yet finished its deliberations. Perhaps they meant that its last flight had proved a bit too much for it, or maybe it was just a matter of translation from Swahili into English. We eventually took off about 00.40 am, which poses an interesting problem for a diarist: does that count as today or tomorrow, because I had already put my watch back three hours when I boarded the plane, to allow for the time-change. These details matter, if you come from Oxford and are on your way back there.

Wednesday, 26 January

Dinner was served pretty rapidly after take-off, in view of the lateness. The plane was less than half full, but might fill up a bit at Athens, I supposed. Once again, I had a whole row of seats to myself, so could sleep quite well. There was prolonged turbulence over Sudan and the southern Sahara, but, when one is lying full length, it just tends to rock one to sleep. A glass of very refreshing fruit juice was served to coax everyone into a vertical position before we landed at Athens, where we were on the ground for only about 45 minutes. Lots of Greek persons got on, but there was still plenty of room. Why, I wondered sleepily, were they all so noisy at this time of night? Surely they had nothing to add to the works of all the classical Greek authors that wouldn't wait until the morning? In fact, it took the serving of breakfast to shut them up, and that happened somewhere over the top end of the Adriatic, at about 5.30 am. Kenya Airways achieved the remarkable feat of producing individual hot omelettes for everyone, which were really very nice. They never did that on the way out. Perhaps it's an effect of flying to London, intended to prepare visitors for the great British breakfast.

It was only just light enough, being late January, for the coast of Italy to be discernible. A red dawn was behind us, and it looked as if the customers down there might be going to wake up to a nice morning. I wondered whether Anna-Maria, and Paolo, the two who turned up rather unexpectedly at Olduvai a fortnight ago (see 12–13 January), were yet back in Italy, somewhere down there, and whether she had mended her torn jeans, if so – oh, I forgot to mention that, I think. They had appeared suddenly again, on their last day, heading for the camp to say goodbye.

'Quick – hide the coffee cups! And the mangoes!' shouted Mary, rather inhospitably, some might think, when their vehicle came into sight. As for the torn jeans, I suppose Anna-Maria had sat on a thorn or backed into a bush: not too painful, I hope, but the resulting back view was very enticing. Perhaps personable young ladies should be encouraged to come into gentle contact with thorns more often, possibly even with some of those bigger ones with which the semi-arid landscape of Olduvai is so richly endowed, since the tears would be larger. The poet Herrick, who remarked on 'a sweet disorder in the dress', would probably agree with me, but you, Gentle Reader, are entitled to be properly disdainful of such a notion. Oh dear – this literary stuff is clearly going to my head. Returning home will soon sort that out.

The winter dawn struggled to keep pace with us, and seemed to be fighting a losing battle, once we turned in a more westerly direction. In any case, there was cloud over the Alps, which I once saw in clear conditions from a plane window at first light, and they were spectacular. Twice only, on this occasion, I thought I caught a glimpse of snowy peaks through the cloud, but it was hard to be sure. A sudden turning pink of an edge of cloud was about the best that there was to be seen, and after that the light got dimmer rather than brighter. Indeed, there was heavy cloud all the rest of the way, and we descended to Heathrow to find it virtually in darkness, with all the street lights still on, landing at about quarter to eight: that was 45 minutes late, so we had made up some of the lost time. England was damp and rather foggy, but at least not as cold as one would expect at this time of year: 9 degrees Centigrade. Back at Olduvai, it would be 10.45 am, and Mary's indoor thermometer would be climbing towards 80. But that's another world.

Heathrow was extraordinarily efficient: I found myself emerging from customs into the Arrivals lounge, with all my luggage complete and undamaged, just 17 minutes after the aeroplane had come to a stop. There was no direct coach to Oxford to be had at that hour, so I chose the coach and rail link via Reading. The coach left precisely on time, and I was actually a few minutes early on arrival at Oxford Station. A taxi took me to 60 Banbury Road, its radio proclaiming the result of a one-day Test Match in Australia, which convinced me that I really was back home after all. To my delight, I arrived just in time for coffee break.

Monday, 20 June

On waking, I did not feel in the slightest bit ready to start this second visit to Olduvai, and was far from convinced that I was actually about to do so. Perhaps it wouldn't happen, after all? I rapidly decided that I had better assume it would. Last night I had packed, tidied and organised until around 2.0 am, which seems to have become my regular bed-time at the moment, but was still up before 8.0 am, ready to move my car in case the builders, a local firm, who are now working at my cottage, decided to arrive early with their dumper truck, as has been known to happen. They didn't, of course, but the fore-man, Brian, known to the world as Bunny, came at 8.40, and we discussed what parts of the work might or might not be completed during my absence. 'As such' is one of his favourite phrases. Would the kitchen be finished before I got back? Well, not as such. However, I felt happy leaving it all in his hands, because he is a good craftsman and a good organiser, and there should certainly be some progress to see when I return.

The cuckoo, which I had not heard for the last few weeks, was back in Fordwells this morning, but did not seem to have changed its call, which cuckoos should do in mid-June. What a lot of barley there seems to be in the local fields this year, just starting to change from green to yellow, as I leave. Aren't we all, come to think of it? I also noticed that the grass-cutters were out along the roadsides, so the cow parsley season must officially be deemed to be over: it's good that they let it flower completely before they start cutting the verges, and it has been a fine display this year. Things will look quite different when I get back.

I made various final arrangements before departure in Oxford during the morning and early afternoon, posting numerous letters and receiving much kind help with the photocopying that had to be done, from my daughter Biddy, who was out of school early today. There was time for a quick lunch in college, just as if it was any perfectly ordinary day. Jack Hewlett, our caretaker at the research centre and indeed my sole member of staff there in these impoverished times, kindly offered me a lift in his car, to save calling a taxi, down to Gloucester Green, where I could catch a bus direct to Heathrow. In the fine tradition established on the first trip, I found I had got the departure time wrong again, just missing one bus and having to wait quite a long time for the next. This did not matter in the least, as I had allowed abundant time, and one might as well spend some of it at Gloucester Green, even if the waiting room did smell mildly of disinfectant, rather than in the bustle of Heathrow. The bus turned out to be going via Wheatley, High Wycombe and Uxbridge, plus various villages. As well as taking me all the way to the airport, it seemed ready and willing to deliver home New College School boys and Headington School girls, as well as transporting sundry burghers and yeomen of Oxfordshire, and a few visitors from foreign lands, to their various destinations. A cheerful West Indian was presiding over its departure from Oxford, and one could only admire his factual approach to answering questions, something one does not always find amongst one's colleagues. Someone asked him:

'When do you leave?'

'As soon as we start to move,' he replied, only adding as an afterthought: '4.05'.

It was a hot journey, and rather a slow one, because the bus entered into the spirit of various local rush hours along the way, but it was a nice ride, and I admired young foals in fields full of buttercups, thinking darkly that the hyaenas would get them, if this were Serengeti. Who would really want to go to Africa, anyhow, when it's buttercup time in Oxfordshire?

Heathrow was not too busy, and everything worked efficiently. I acquired a box of the right cigars for Mary, which is effectively my entry permit to Olduvai. Departure was not even slightly delayed: this time, the plane was a Boeing 747. I had forgotten how huge they are, as it is some time since I last flew in one, and I felt a little sorry not to be going in the sleek and very small-looking Concorde that was parked not too far away. The passengers included a large tour group of mildly intellectual Americans, going on to Kenya after a stay in England. They were discussing the novels of James Joyce. One of them offered the tentative opinion that James Joyce was quite a ... and another immediately agreed that yes, he really was quite a ... but neither ever finished the sentence, so I was left in the dark as to what they thought he was. At least it reminded me I was now back in the literary mode. I rather fear no one will ever say that sort of thing at an airport about me as the ghost-writer of Mary's autobiography. You never know, though, do you?

Take-off occurred as nearly on time as it ever does, the plane being fairly full, but with only two of us in my row of three seats. The take-off run seemed endless, the plane almost flapping its wings before it lumbered into the air to become immediately graceful. The remains of the day's heat haze cast a thin veil over southern England – I dimly made out Selsey Bill – and then there was cloud, and quite soon darkness, as we headed south-east. There was quite a bright moon, but no sign of Alpine peaks, so doubtless it remained cloudy below. This month's special offer by British Airways was the provision of free wine with dinner to those travelling tourist class. I put my watch forward a couple of hours (not three, this time, it being British Summer Time), which didn't seem to leave much sleeping time, but the flight, which was non-stop, was in fact scheduled to take 8 hours. They showed a film but, looking round, I couldn't see a single person watching it. Only at that stage did I at last suddenly get some sense of being on a journey. It's odd, that: I suppose I had simply had too much to do in the preceding busy weeks of term to think about it.

Tuesday, 21 June

I dozed for an hour or two, on and off, never quite finding a comfortable sleeping position. The captain woke us at 5.08 am, and orange juice and coffee had a semi-reviving effect. We landed at 6.02, with Nairobi still in complete darkness. Eighty people were getting off here, and the rest would be flying on to Johannesburg. The Kenyan Immigration Control didn't look at all ready for the day, but came slowly to life. When I reached the front of the queue, an unexpected problem arose: the officer surveyed with deep disesteem some South African entry and exit stamps in my passport, which related to a visit I made there back in 1977, and directed me unsmilingly to wait until the end of the queue, along with one other man who was suffering from the same problem. Vaguely I recalled reading something a week or two back about Kenya turning away visitors arriving from South Africa, though there certainly wasn't anything said about people who had briefly visited South Africa at some time in the past. It occurred to me this could be awkward. But in 1977 there had been no such restrictions, and besides, I had already been in and out of Kenya unchallenged this very year, so I decided I would smile politely and argue only if necessary. Off we went, when everyone else had passed through, to see some altogether more senior *bwana* just round the corner. Fortunately, he proved very easily persuadable that I was not a threat to national security. The other man had made a transit stop in South Africa only a week or so ago, on his way to Swaziland, and I left him arguing: I don't know whether or not he won.

I reclaimed my baggage, glad to find it still there after the delay, and made my way to Customs, where today the officers were in a mood to open everything and ask questions. I thought it had perhaps been a good move to put the huge jar of Marmite, which

I have brought for Peter and Annie Jones at their special request, into the duty free bag with Mary's cigars, because they never seem to look at duty free goods. For Peter, there was also a sealed pack of spares and accessories for his vehicle, which his father had collected up and sent: it subsequently turned out to include a car cassette player, an ignition system, an oil filter and a few odds and ends.

'I think it's a distributor cap, or something, for a Land Rover,' I said cautiously, holding out the box to the customs officer, having genuinely forgotten what the items were, if indeed I ever knew. 'No, I'm afraid I've absolutely no idea what it cost.'

'That's all right', he said cheerfully, not bothering to open it. Feeling slightly relieved, I emerged from the airport building into grey overcast light and slight drizzle, looking for Hazel, Mary's Secretary, who was to meet me. She was only just arriving, and I had to fend off no less than ten highly competitive offers, some very pressing, of taxi rides to the city centre. Hazel drove me through the drizzle to Langata, where Mary is making one of her infrequent and brief visits to her own house. We passed one marvellously colonial-looking vintage car. It seems to me that at whatever time of year one arrives in Nairobi, there are always masses of bougainvillaea in full bloom, and other bright flowers, and so it was again today. I also noted that they have still not repaired a spectacularly bent bus shelter, which I happened to notice last time, even though it had been erected on the personal instructions of Mary's MP son, Philip Leakey, for the benefit of his constituents.

Mary looked in good health, and was predictably pleased with her cigars. I had a bath and a shave, followed by breakfast, to which Hazel stayed. The Langata house was, as ever, full of animals: there were nine cats at least, though the total was said to rise to about 20, on occasion, at meal times. There were three hyraxes, one of them a baby. Oh, and there was one more cat, on the roof, where it lives, simply named, in Mary's no-nonsense fashion, Roof Cat (cf Brown Dog, at Olduvai). It could be heard stampeding noisily about from time to time, which is no doubt what roof-dwelling cats do.

We spent the morning going through large numbers of Leakey family photographs, to see what might be suitable for the book; indeed, Mary had timed her visit to meet me here particularly for that purpose. I also showed her my own coloured slides, taken on the first trip, some of which we thought might do, while the family albums produced some splendid finds, relevant to parts of the text already written. We are to set off for Olduvai very early tomorrow, and there is a long list of things to do in Arusha en route.

I rested and actually caught up a little on sleep during the afternoon, at the end of which Hazel reappeared with shopping, and we set ourselves to load the vehicle (Mary's Peugeot car) in the very particular manner that I gather experience has shown to be most helpful from the point of view of the checks when one crosses the Kenya-Tanzania border at Namanga. I can't recall ever before tipping 12 bottles of good whisky into an opaque plastic container, marked 'drinking water', but concluded that it must be a local East African tradition. I also helped with the peeling, slicing, cooking and packing of many pounds of mushrooms, which were also to come with us, destined for the freezer at Olduvai, one of the appliances for which the windmills provide electricity. We also made a general plan of campaign for my stay on this trip, quite apart from more immediate planning and writing of lists for tomorrow's journey. The aim is to get at least as far as Margaret Gibb's Farm at Karatu (unless Arusha really does its worst), and just possibly all the way to Olduvai.

There were gleams of sun through the grey clouds during the afternoon, but it was cool enough for a sweater all day and for a big log fire in the evening. There were roses out in the garden, however. One of the numerous cats was found to have a wire noose from a trap round its neck, with a trailing broken end of wire. It was not apparently in any discomfort, but Mary was determined to release it before we left. She eventually achieved this, at the cost of a badly scratched hand, which bled on and off for the rest of the day. I suppose it's lucky it wasn't a cheetah, for which she would doubtless have done the same. One of the Langata cats, incidentally, clearly has one wild-cat parent, as it has spotted flanks and a striped tail. It looks somewhat like a genet.

I set my alarm for 6.0 am, and breakfast time was fixed as 6.15. I was not too tired to write this diary until 11.30 pm. There is a slight water shortage at Langata at the moment, and I was delighted to find, when I turned on the hot tap on the wash basin in the bathroom, that it actually ran *ants*. No, really it did: dozens of them, in a trickle of water, and comprehensively dead. Very curious. Mary is going to have a new pump installed. She told me this evening, without elaborating, that things are getting so difficult at Olduvai that she is now planning to move permanently back to Langata, probably within a year. That was a surprise: when we talked about the future during my previous visit, she had been completely determined to stick it out down at Olduvai to the end of her days, so things must really have deteriorated. No doubt I shall see before long what it is all about.

Wednesday, 22 June

I was deeply asleep when called just after 6.0 am, so must have slept through the alarm. Fortunately, Mary also wasn't up quite as early as planned, and we didn't get away till 6.46. (I wonder why I always note times so precisely on these trips? That could perfectly well have been written as 'quarter to seven'.) Yoka, a driver-mechanic on the Olduvai staff, drove: he is returning to Olduvai with us, after a leave visit to Kenya. It was grey and overcast, but gleams of sunshine broke through as we reached the flat plains beyond the Athi River, turning the grass golden-green against dark rain-clouds. It has rained quite a lot in the past few days, I gather. That stretch is usually empty of game, but today there were frequent gazelle (both Thompson's and Grant's), a scatter of wildebeest and even four giraffe and a few zebra, not to mention two pairs of crested cranes in flight. There was very little traffic indeed on the road, and there did not seem to be any customers for the rather incongruous small shop of concrete-block construction that was proudly offering acupuncture, in one small, nameless village.

We reached the border at Namanga, with no stops, in exactly two hours. The Kenya side was very quick: they all know Mary well, and on this occasion she had brought a signed copy of her small Olduvai book for one of the men, which he received with great delight. Another one informed me, aside, that she was 'a very respectful lady'. That's not quite how I would have expressed it, but I knew exactly what he meant, and it occurred to me that the remark might almost make a title for the autobiography. On the Tanzanian side, much more documentation was necessary, and things were much slower: a new vehicle permit had to be purchased, and so forth. There was no inspection of the carefully packed luggage. Off we set again, an hour and a quarter later. Two off-duty policemen at the border post hitched a lift, and I wondered idly whether they would drink some of the whisky in the water container, but this did not seem to happen, perhaps fortunately, and we dropped them off at Longido.

Once a couple of baboons crossed the road, and once there was a fine circling eagle to admire, but not much else. The weather deteriorated into steady light rain falling from low clouds. At another checkpoint in the road, two more policemen asked for a lift, this time wanting to go as far as Arusha, and space was found for them. For some reason the engine was completely dead on restart, but luckily a quick fiddle under the bonnet by Yoka cured the trouble. No doubt it was just the gremlins flexing their muscles at the sound of the dreaded name 'Arusha'.

The flame trees that line the road on the approach to Arusha were out, looking very good. Well, people call them flame trees, but I believe the real flame tree is an *Erythrina*, and I don't know what genus or species these are. They are about as big as English chestnut trees, with bright splashes of scarlet amongst their green foliage. Also out in Arusha was a large number of vehicles, forming a comprehensive traffic jam, for no obvious reason. We turned round and made a detour to the centre of town, finding it more or less empty and wet. Mary had a long list of administrative calls to make, with which I couldn't really help, so we arranged a rendezvous at the inevitable New Arusha Hotel, and I made my way straight there, aiming to purchase one of the rather nice ebony paper knives with a carved handle, which I know the gift shop there has, for Biddy. I also wanted to send 'arrived safely' postcards to both my children, since sending mail from Olduvai is very difficult, and to catch up on writing this diary, and so forth. First, I went to the bank to cash some travellers' cheques, predictably a slow process, but I completed it successfully eventually. The exchange rate, at 18.6 Tanzanian shillings to the pound, was slightly better than on my last visit, but not much. I was rather surprised not to be offered this time any private enterprise Advantageous Currency Deals in the street – not that I would have accepted them. Has the government's clamp-down on the unofficial currency dealers actually worked, or is it just that no one has any Tanzanian shillings to offer? It might be either, I concluded.

There was no sign of Mary at the hotel, so I wandered around a little more, and the rain gave way to somewhat brighter conditions. It was about 2.15 when Mary finally arrived at the hotel, having had a thoroughly frustrating morning, with nothing achieved: nor would she make any further progress, because the government offices, which open at 7.0 am, close at 2.0 pm each day. There are certain things which she simply *must* get sorted out, so already it is clear that we shall have to stay the night in Arusha. There was a kind of inevitability about that: I'd almost have felt cheated, if we had got straight through, I think. So we had a late lunch and booked into the hotel. At least some of the other Arusha things could be done during the afternoon – a visit to the market, for example, to get some Olduvai supplies. Mary, tired out after her morning, decided to leave Yoka and me to 'do' the market. We acquired two 'debes' of potatoes: a debe is a large all-purposes metal container can, which has become a standard unit of quantity locally for all sorts of things, and it holds several pounds of potatoes, but they were expensive, as each debe cost 120 shillings, that is, between £6 and £7. We then got 4 cabbages of noble proportions, and also 10 lemons, but I don't think the lemon-seller could count, as we seemed to get 18 rather than 10 for our money. Next on the list was a kilo of carrots, and there was great rivalry by adjacent stallholders to undercut each other's price, so we definitely did well on carrots. In spite of a gloomy forecast by Mary, it turned out that there were indeed mangoes to be had, so we got 20 of those. It all amounted to a highly diverting exercise in shopping, by English standards, and I was glad that Annie Jones had shown me over the market last time, so that I could actually guide Yoka.

After making a few other purchases for Mary, we were gasping for a cup of tea. The garden of the New Arusha Hotel was its usual colourful self, though almost empty of people. The waiter announced dolefully that there was no sugar, and Mary told me that the sugar ration for a family of eight in Tanzania is at present one pound of sugar per week. In the end, he did bring about an egg-cup full, with an air of great triumph. Another sign of the failing Tanzanian economy, I thought, was the fact that in the hotel the rolls of toilet paper had all been carefully cut in half: I'm not sure how much of a saving that actually creates, in practical terms. Mary said that rice and salt were also currently unobtainable. Tanzania produces all these commodities itself, but has to sell the whole lot to get 'hard' foreign currency.

After tea, I spent a little while sorting out and repacking my luggage, did a little writing and had a hot bath before dinner. I was intrigued by the Tanzanian bath-plug: it had a hole in it which let the water out when it shouldn't, but when one pulled the plug out completely, the water seemed to run away less fast. At least there was plenty of hot water. Dinner was served in near darkness, and it wasn't completely clear whether this was an attempt at Artistic Lighting, or simply shortage of light bulbs. Ominous signs of a band preparing to play, with very large loudspeakers pointing directly at us from not very far away, caused a great acceleration of the meal by mutual consent, and we escaped before they had played more than half of the first number. The band was called Sunset, which seemed entirely appropriate to the deep twilight of the dining room. Mary went off to read a book in bed, even though it was only 8.30. I continued to write draft text, as far as I could get. So much for getting at least to Gibb's Farm today and possibly all the way to Olduvai. Instead, the gremlins of Arusha have had a field day at our expense, mainly Mary's. Surprise, surprise.

Thursday, 23 June

Breakfast was at 7.15, as planned last night, and Mary was clearly a little surprised to find me ready on time. The car had spent the night in a locked yard, for safety, and I was sent to drive it round to the front of the hotel, which I found an interesting exercise with absolutely nil rear view because of all the luggage. Mary went meanwhile to resume her negotiations with various local officials. I worked in the peaceful atmosphere of the hotel room, after a walk round the garden to look at all the flowering trees. By 9.30, Mary had got as far as she could with her errands, and we were ready to leave. There was no petrol to be had in Arusha, of course.

The day was cloudy, but offered the promise of brighter weather to come: the vast distances were soft, and expressed in muted tones. Traffic was extremely light, as well it might be, with no petrol. Mary drove, and her driving, with only one good eye, seemed fine. Everything was very green around Arusha itself, but later there was a sudden change to dry, brown grass. There was little game to be seen on this stretch, barring one group of nine ostriches, but there were plenty of brightly coloured small birds and the occasional eagle. The next main landmark of this journey is the turn off the tarmac road down into the Rift. This section is good for baobab trees, which I always like, and it was curious to see some of them completely bare and some in full leaf: they have not got their act together, as the saying goes. Near two particularly fine baobabs, we met a bus, rather surprisingly marked Haleluya Haleluya Amen, and immediately afterwards collected a puncture, which gave me a chance to photograph the baobabs while Yoka efficiently changed the wheel.

The next stop was at Mto wa Mbu, though it turned out that there was no petrol there either. I had seen to it that, this time, I was properly equipped to visit the market, knowing what to expect, and I dived eagerly for my bag of trade goods as soon as we stopped. It turned out that I was the only customer in the whole place, and a source of great interest accordingly. I parted with two tee shirts, eight bars of soap, one hat, one baseball cap of a kind I wouldn't myself want to wear, one red-and-white striped scarf, two pairs of sunglasses with mirror-style lenses, one pocket knife with several gadgets, rather a bargain at 50 pence, I had thought, and one quartz wrist watch (£2.99). In return, I became the owner of one Maasai warrior's beadwork belt, one Maasai 'snuffbox' (that's a tubular container made of bamboo, with leather and beadwork ends, carried by means of a leather strap that goes round the neck), one Maasai woman's neck ornament of beadwork, two of the flat local baskets and one charming wooden cup. In financial terms, of course, I won easily, because I don't suppose my objects had cost more than about £10 in total, while the official inflated asking price of my purchases would have been 1500 to 1600 Tanzanian shillings, which bargaining with cash might well have reduced by about 40 per cent. Far more to the point, both sides were absolutely delighted with the deal, and the local people have no other source of such goods as I had brought, which Peter and Annie had advised me were the kind of things they would particularly like at the moment. At the end, rather sadly, really, there was even great competition for the plastic carrier bag in which I had brought the things. Yoka wandered over as a spectator during the exchange, and clearly felt I had not driven a hard enough bargain. It was interesting, however, that the Africans would remonstrate with any of their number whom they felt to be making me an inadequate offer, and whisper to me to refuse. Mary had no intention of coming anywhere near, and I expect she thought I was behaving like the worst kind of tourist, but these things are simply not tourist objects. She has never really been a collector or dedicated acquirer of artefacts of any kind, which I'm quite happy to regard as a fair and reasonable policy, so long as no one insists that I subscribe to it.

Having been unable to buy petrol at Mto wa Mbu, we siphoned into the tank the contents of a large jerry can of it brought from Nairobi, before setting off again, now up the steep side of the Rift on the road that goes to Ngorongoro, though the immediate next destination was Gibb's Farm at Karatu, to deliver messages and cheese, and to purchase coffee and lettuces, and maybe to have lunch. Across this agricultural stretch of the journey, much of the local domestic fauna seemed to be in a suicidal frame of mind, much inclined to rush cheerfully into the road almost under the wheels of the car. Yoka, whose turn it was to drive, contrived to avoid them all. Gibb's Farm proved to have been just invaded by several dormobiles' worth of tourists, so we did not in the end stay very long, and found a shady place for a picnic lunch instead, during which we watched a large flock of birds, very high up, wheeling round in unison: even Mary could not say what they were. The next stop was at a mission farm near Karatu, to buy a huge sack of red beans: this had been on the list for Arusha Market, but Yoka and I had thought the price asked there outrageous. The mission farm seemed to specialise in badly bent lorries and very grunty free-range pigs, but it had the beans too. Back on our way, we passed the remains of a beer lorry that had gone off the road a little while ago and shed its load rather excitingly, causing a certain amount of local satisfaction – a Tanzanian version, perhaps, of the events in Compton Mackenzie's *Whisky Galore*. Mary also pointed out the place where another lorry had recently overturned spectacularly, emptying and mixing inextricably its cargo of bags of cement and bags of sugar. People are now said to be building with sugary cement and putting cementy sugar in their tea, all for free.

We made our way up the great winding ascent to the rim of the Ngorongoro caldera, mainly in warm sunshine, though cloud was almost down to the level of the road when we reached the top. There were fresh-looking elephant droppings most of the way along the road, but no elephants were to be seen – indeed, no game at all – and the view down into the crater was very hazy. We made a brief stop at the post office to collect mail, and to enquire for petrol: yes, there was some here, but it so happened that the generator that worked the pumps was out of action today, so the petrol could not be got at. We left the large spare petrol jerrycan to be filled in due course and collected eventually, and pressed on along the final lap, the road down to Serengeti. For the first several miles, there were signs of the road having recently been quite well repaired, but later on it was as bad as ever. There were some fine giraffe at the bottom of the hill, near the turn off for Olduvai, also a pair of golden jackals and some very pretty bee-eaters, but little else to be seen except a few gazelle and some wildebeest and zebra, widely and thinly scattered, which had stayed behind when the main migrating herds moved on.

So we came at last to Olduvai, beautiful as ever in the early evening sunlight, with three giraffe standing like statues by the camp gate. We arrived at about 5.20 pm to an ecstatic welcome from the three Dalmatians and Brown Dog, not to mention Peter Jones, who, however, was a bit under the weather with a recurrence of malaria symptoms, for which he had just started a 14-day course of pills. Much unloading and storing of goods and trophies followed, with exchanges of news and gossip, while a very welcome pot of tea was made. Peter reported that two prides of lions were about, and had frequently been near the camp: splendid – the long saga of my attempts to see lions at Olduvai can resume, and perhaps this time I shall actually do so. In correspondence with Mary before the trip, I had been warned to expect dry weather and complete absence of mangoes and lions, and so far we have had rain and mangoes ...

Before dinner, there was time to enjoy a shower and hair wash in the excellent camp shower, with its canvas bucket hauled up on a rope, and soon afterwards we could hear both lots of lions roaring down in the Gorge, though some way off. There was an excellent dinner of roast chicken, after which Mary and I made plans for tomorrow's work on the book. We retired at about 10 pm, Mary to bed and I to write my diary first. As I write these words to conclude today, one of the prides of lions is roaring again, now much closer, down in the Gorge just below the camp, a magnificent sound. Things seem quite hopeful, *simba*-wise.

Friday, 24 June

It is in fact just six months since I left Olduvai at the end of my previous visit, although it does not seem as long as that. Kabebo, mainstay of the camp's staff, is on leave in Nairobi, but with only Mary, Peter and myself here, Kiteto, the long-serving cook, can manage well enough. He brought early morning tea today at exactly the moment when my alarm went off, at 6.30 am. On the last visit, I always used to call out '*Jambo*' when the tea arrived, and Kabebo, who brought it, always waited by the door till I got up and opened it. This time, I remembered to try '*Karibu*', which is the proper reply to a knock, actually meaning 'Welcome' or 'Come in', while '*Jambo*' is more in the line of 'How are you?', and it worked like a charm. A wonderful language, Swahili.

Since the dogs' walk and the humans' breakfast usually coincide precisely, and only Kiteto is trusted to take the dogs, the current regime is that we cook eggs and make coffee for ourselves, after he has put everything ready and set off. Today it seemed quite cool first thing, but by mid-morning it was pleasantly warm at about 80 degrees in the workroom, rising to 85 in mid-afternoon, though I was told that these figures are much higher than of late. There was bright but rather hazy sunshine for much of the day.

Things seem much the same as they were when I left but, as soon as one looks closely, it is not difficult to note some seasonal differences. The big acacia tree at the front of the camp, which was in full flower in late January, now has green seedpods all over it. The sun, which previously rose over Ngorongoro, now comes up much further to the left, left of Olmoti and even left of Lengai, which puts sunrise well out of sight of my window, and it sets quite a way to the right of Kelogi. The aloes are in flower. The adult ravens have some while ago driven off their young to find their own territories, so only two birds flew in this morning at 10.30. I noted a different population of small birds, too – many small yellow and greenish ones, rather like English greenfinches, but smaller (which I later learned were various kinds of canary), and a pair of love-birds, bright green with red fronts: they are small parrakeets, and large numbers of them are usually to be seen at Ndutu. Very few mosquitoes are in evidence, and nets are not needed at night.

Aloes in flower

Peter and Mary brought me up to date with the local news which, as one would expect, mainly concerned the animal population. A por-cupine has been active around the camp area, though it is a nocturnal creature, of course. Several snakes have been about recently: one visited this afternoon, in fact, but the camp staff only managed to cut the tip of its tail off. It was thought to have been 'only an egg-eater'. On the other hand, a *very* large snake has been seen several times, but has always escaped successfully so far. It is thought – and indeed hoped – to be a python, the alternative being a very large mamba, whose bite would certainly be fatal. Perhaps I shall get a sight of it.

While I have been away, the volcano Lengai has been somewhat active: there was no spectacular eruption, but it did produce thin clouds of fine ash, which reached as far as Olduvai. It has apparently stopped now. Several cheetah have been seen near the camp, and a striped hyaena has been in once or twice. Once a young male lion came and stood by the camp gate, roaring and seeming likely to jump over the thorn fence, which caused even Peter and Mary to bring their dinner to an abrupt end and take refuge.

The pleasant Spanish visitor, whom Hazel had brought to the border when she met me on my way home last time, had not, in Mary's view, been a success at Olduvai, and I fear he will not have enjoyed his stay very much. It turned out that he had had a bad expe-rience with a dog in childhood, and was accordingly frightened of the Dalmatians and Brown Dog when they greeted him. When the lions roared at night, he barricaded his hut door with the furniture, and was too nervous to walk outside the camp enclosure even when accompanied. On top of all that, one of the finest of the stone implements he was studying can now not be found. He is definitely out of favour. Poor man: there will be no route back, I fear, because Mary does not change her mind about her visitors, once she has made it up. I'm just one of the lucky ones, or I wouldn't be here now.

Today, I worked peacefully on the autobiography text, both writing new material from my notes and checking over the previously completed parts with Mary. As I had feared, now that she has the text before her in cold typed form, even though I had previ-ously read every word out to her, she is inclined to cut out all the little flourishes that seem to me to give it life, along with everything she regards as 'embellishments'. Well, it's her story, not mine, so I can't stop her, but I fear the simple truth is that she is killing precisely those qualities in the telling of it which would make it a success with readers, and which I am specifically here to provide. She herself is of course used to the straightforward pres-entation of archaeological data in a published report, where casual commentary and spec-ulative interpretation may indeed need to be avoided. But there's no captive fact-seeking audience of colleagues and students for this book, and she needs to give people reasons to buy the book and recommend it to others, since the whole project is supposed to be aimed at making some money for her retirement. I shall try to salvage all I can of what from my point of view is the livelier writing, but it may not be much. Goodness knows what she would do to the text of this diary, but that's mine, not hers. I did mention to her that I was keeping a diary, but she expressed no interest – as indeed I would have expected.

Towards 5.0 pm, a great thunderstorm came up across the plains – one of those solid wall-of-water jobs, and we eventually had quite a lot of rain out of it. For a while, it was actually impossible to hear oneself speak, in the main room, which has a corrugated iron roof. We even had to roll down the very efficient canvas storm screens across the open front of the building, something that happens only very rarely. When we could eventually roll them up again, we found circling outside the swallow family, whose nest is inside, built against a beam in the centre of the roof: we had inadvertently completely blocked off their usual free access. Mary was mortified that we had caused them such inconvenience. The nest is very elegant and long, built of mud, with an entrance at each end. No mess whatsoever comes down from it. An earlier nest, built in the same place by wiretails rather than swallows, had to have a blanket slung permanently under it, since it was directly over the dining table, and wiretails are distinctly messy.

There was more rain later in the evening. This is all most unusual: we checked the rainfall records Mary has kept over the years at Olduvai, and in most years June produces a nil rain measurement, though in 1982 the month showed a total of 22 mm. Today's rain gave a reading of 8 mm – I'm very surprised it wasn't a great deal more than that, but I suppose the metal roof made it sound worse than it was, and it didn't last very long. The weather had cleared up by bedtime. As I went to bed, there was a brief outbreak of rather distant lions, and some small creature appeared to be dancing about on the roof of my hut, but when I went out to see what it was, there was nothing there, of course. That was a mystery I never succeeded in solving during the previous visit. As the work on the book gets going, these long entries in the diary may well get a bit shorter, but the thing about being at Olduvai is that one simply never knows quite what will happen next and most of it seems to me worth recording.

Saturday, 25 June

Today didn't particularly seem like a Saturday but, since I left England on Monday, counting the days indicated that it must be. I heard more animal movements outside my hut door around 4.50 am, on the ground, this time, but was too sleepy to go and see if it was the porcupine.

I worked all day with Mary on what I regard as repairing needless damage done to a perfectly good draft text, but in fact this went pretty well, and she seems to have left in, for the moment at least, rather more than I had feared. I was able to make the particular changes she wanted, in ways that seemed to please her greatly and still left the text reading reasonably well, even if not quite as I had had in mind originally when writing those parts. I reminded myself again that she is fully entitled to make changes: after all, it's her book, written in the first person, and the first person is Mary, not myself. It all took quite a long time, however, as much had to be copied out by hand. The pay-off came late in the evening, when she revealed one or two items of distinctly personal information for inclusion, which she admitted she had been holding back until she had decided whether I could produce the kind of text she wanted. That struck me as a considerable landmark in the operation, and I got the impression that there might well be more such revelations to come. I hope the mood will last. We both felt that what might have been a difficult day had in fact gone extremely well.

It went rather less well for Peter, who was feeling distinctly ill again, and was now suffering stomach pains, which are definitely not a malaria symptom. Yesterday he had felt quite bright, but today he was very poorly again. There is a risk, given the symptoms, that it might be one of the forms of hepatitis, so we all looked with proper detached scientific interest to see if his eyes were yellow, which is supposed to happen with hepatitis, but they weren't. After lunch, he agreed to drive himself over to Endulen near Laetoli, to get advice from the hospital there. The Swiss doctor, Philip, who featured in my account of the first visit, was known to be away at present, doing a turn as Flying Doctor, but his wife is also a fully qualified doctor, so Peter could see her. He returned just before dark with a diagnosis of probable amoebic dysentery and a stock of prescribed pills. The next few days will prove or disprove the correctness of the diagnosis, and Mary is clearly somewhat worried about him.

Much like yesterday, the weather was bright and sunny in the morning and early afternoon, the indoor temperature reaching 84 degrees in the main camp room, where I have been sitting to work; then thunderstorms came up. This time, we only got the edge of one, with about 10 minutes' rain, though Peter met a much bigger one in the course of his trip. After the rain, I was able to walk for about half an hour out by the airstrip, it having been decided that there would be some risk of meeting lions down in the Gorge itself. Where the thousands of wildebeest had been when I last walked here, back in January, there was now only empty vastness: just me, a butterfly and an unconcerned eagle, which flew lazily to the top of an acacia tree and then allowed me to walk right up to the tree. The grass is now reduced to short, dry, yellow tufts, with bare earth between them. Scurrying pairs of plover could be seen here and there amongst the grass tufts, doubtless with nests in the shallowest of scrapes in the ground. Other pairs flew urgently overhead, screaming abuse at the eagle. There was a huge thunderstorm far out over the plains, though not moving towards us: occasional flashes of lightning came from its centre, and there was rather a cool breeze blowing from that direction. On my return to the camp, I saw a coal-black mongoose by the edge of the Gorge, and a full moon was just rising over Ngorongoro in the twilight. After dinner, Mary and I talked until 10.30 pm, which is long after her usual bedtime: by then, the moon had climbed high into the sky, and was very bright; distant lions were roaring some way down the eastern arm of the Gorge.

I was just going to bed when curious scratching noises began on the outside of the hut wall. I was determined to solve this puzzle at last, but my torch for a long while revealed nothing. Eventually I discovered two very small frogs, sitting on one of the wooden beams that hold the corrugated iron of the wall in place. They had beady eyes, and looked fully capable of making annoying scratching noises, if they felt like it. I decided to leave them to it. They did have small claws, so I suppose it certainly was them, though I doubt whether they could be responsible for all the noises I hear.

Sunday, 26 June

On Sundays, by tradition, breakfast should be a whole 15 minutes later than on weekdays, but at 5.50 am there was a tremendous bark-in by the Dalmatians, which disturbed everyone. It transpired that looking out of the window of Mary's hut, where they sleep, they had seen giraffe down by the camp gate, and were demanding to be let out to chase them off. Somehow, after that, breakfast seemed to happen at the weekday time. Shame.

I worked all the morning on transcribing the agreed corrections from yesterday into my own clean copy of the text, and making sure that Mary's copy and mine tallied exactly. After that, I continued to write new draft text, using Mary's pile of information cards and also referring to the second of the tapes which we had recorded at the end of my previous visit. The temperature again got up to 84, but this time there was a thin haze everywhere. This is understood to be smoke from bush or grass fires a long way off in western Serengeti, drifting down to us. It certainly doesn't appear to be more of the erupted thin ash from Lengai, which they had a few months ago.

In the evening, I drove with Mary a few miles down the Gorge, to hold the end of a long tape for her, so that she could check a measurement at one of the excavated sites, for the report that will eventually appear in the Olduvai monograph series volume on Beds III and IV and the Masek Beds, on which she is now at last able to do some work. Originally I completed my chapter for it no less than ten years ago, and have added to it and revised it twice since then. The Dalmatians came with us, for the ride: Sophie, who is currently much troubled by arthritis, rode in the front, with Janet and Matthew in the back. Janet was convinced that she was too fat to jump unaided into the back of the car, but eventually made it, after three refusals. Brown Dog seems to spend Sundays with his friends amongst the camp staff – or maybe he is just quietly getting on with the thesis that I am firmly convinced he must be working on: he certainly has something of the air of a serious research student, has Brown Dog. It was a nice ride, though with very little to see in the way of animals – what a contrast from January. Six ostriches, three gazelle, one hare and one dik-dik, was the total count. I was just thinking that holding one end of a tape for a few moments would do very nicely as my field work for the year, when I discovered how painful the local 'wait-a-bit' thorns are, if one is careless enough to back into a bush of them while wearing shorts. The thorns are so called because each has a barb like a fish-hook, and you can't simply pull yourself free. Mary eventually released me. This was justice, I suppose, for my remarks about Anna-Maria's torn shorts last time (26 January). What are you laughing at?

Mary cooked supper, as is traditional on Sundays. Some of the mangoes from Arusha are now ripe enough to start on, which is good news. Peter was still unwell and spent most of the day sleeping, but claimed to be a little better than yesterday.

Last thing before bedtime, I heard a curious sound of crunching and rustling down in the direction of the camp gate. I went to investigate, with a torch to supplement the bright moonlight, and found two or three giraffe browsing peacefully on the nearby acacia trees. It was a nice contented sound, and it's no coincidence that they have so frequently been standing patiently around in that area. The local acacias seem to produce their new shoots and subsequently their seed pods in succession, rather than all the trees doing so at once, so the giraffe do the rounds, and this is clearly where the current action is. No doubt that is why those three were standing by the gate when we arrived on Thursday; and there was also the incident with the dogs this morning. A big giraffe has absolutely no difficulty in stepping elegantly over the camp thorn fence: they wouldn't come in when there are people around, but I reckoned they might well in due course make for the big acacia outside my hut under cover of darkness, as its top is very green with shoots and seed pods at the moment. They are gentle creatures, with no natural enemies, but are discouraged from coming into camp (as the Dalmatians knew), because there are electric cables running between the buildings, quite high up but certainly lacking giraffe-clearance, and they would be likely to run into them. Let's hope that doesn't happen.

Monday, 27 June

I think the giraffe might indeed have been coming into the camp sometime during last night, but as luck would have it there was a loud clang from one of the petrol tanks at the critical moment – they do that occasionally, in response to temperature changes – followed by a noise of hooves. I was awake, and looked out of my window – I could dimly see in the moonlight five or six giraffe, some of them young ones, down by the gate, but couldn't tell whether they were actually inside or out. I heard no more of them.

Lions could be heard down in the Gorge at around 6.30 am, so the dogs' walk a little later had to be in the opposite direction. Their usual race back from the camp gate was won by Brown Dog by a clear couple of lengths, which earned him disapproving looks from the Dalmatians.

I researched and wrote draft text all day, mainly about Mary's dramatic find of the *Proconsul* skull on Rusinga Island in 1948. She would have been remembered for ever for that, even if she had never achieved anything else.

It was a noticeably cooler morning, even though the thermometer was actually showing 60 degrees as early as 7.15 am, at which time there was a round yellow sun rising in slight haze one side of the camp and a pale, almost transparent-looking moon the same height above the horizon in the opposite direction. Later in the day the indoor temperature did get up to the usual 84 degrees, but this time the sky remained clear and there was no sign of thunderstorms or smoke. I walked with my camera after lunch: it was hot, but not too hot, and this is not lion-time: I saw occasional butterflies, and one huge grasshopper or locust. A Maasai herd was making its way along the floor of the Gorge, in search of such grassy places as there are at the moment, a few of the cows with gently tinkling bells.

Peter Jones was feeling much better, and I showed him my trophies from the Mto wa Mbu market, of which he entirely approved. He got a Maasai of his acquaintance, who happened to come to the camp a little later, to identify the belt: it is definitely that of a warrior, and just decorative, rather than the heavier functional kind which is designed to carry a knife. It is certainly not a tourist one, either – well, I could see *that* for myself.

At sunset, hearing a distant croak somewhere high overhead, we looked up and suddenly saw huge numbers of flamingo, flying very high up in blunt V-formations, crisscrossing each other, and trying to follow air currents. It was an extraordinary sight: I took a couple of photographs, but doubt whether much will show, as the flocks were so high up and the light was fading fast. Kiteto told us that many flamingo had passed over, much lower, last night at about 1.0 am. What on earth was he doing, up at 1.0 am? Even I was asleep by then.

Later in the evening, I took a flash photograph of one of the genets, since my attempts at that on the previous visit had not come out. I waited for ages for a second shot, but the genet didn't return. It was a mild night: I stood outside in the soft warm air and listened to the insect noises for a while. No giraffe were to be seen or heard, and there were no more flamingo.

As I write these words just before turning out the light, I can hear tiny feet on the hut roof again, and an odd wolf-like howling somewhere round the back of the camp: hyaena, I suppose, unless it's a wild dog. I

Genet

must ask Peter tomorrow, as he sleeps round that side, unless whatever it is turns out to have eaten him, which I suppose might be the case. It's all happening, as they say.

Tuesday, 28 June

Hyaena and jackal were both around at the back of camp last night, according to Peter, who fortunately proved not to have been consumed by either. His improvement in health has continued. Being eaten would certainly have constituted a setback to that, we decided.

I got a lot more writing done, completing the section on Rusinga and going on some way further. Mary was clearly very happy with the result, when I read it to her, and I must say it came out quite well in the end. All this was in spite of a number of interruptions, the first of which occurred at 10.0 am, with the unexpected arrival of Patti Moehlman, who is now back at Ndutu with her beloved jackals. She brought with her a friend known as Lala, though her real name is Lois, an Australian who runs safari trips. It turned out that Lala's present set of customers were actually on their way to Olduvai from Ndutu, and she had come on ahead with Patti to get a more peaceful ride and to see Mary, whom she knows quite well. An unexpected coffee break began immediately: I never mind those. We were supposed to know that Patti was coming, it transpired, but for once the bush telegraph had failed, and no message had arrived. It was nice to see Patti again, and to learn that the jackals are currently thriving. An exchange of Serengeti and Arusha gossip followed, most of it passing way over my head. At around 11.0, they went off to meet the arriving safari vehicle, taking Peter with them to give a quick demonstration of stone-tool manufacture. I went back to my work until Peter and Patti returned in mid-afternoon, Lala and the safari party having set off for their next destination, the Ngorongoro crater. Patti, who has a standing guarantee of welcome at Olduvai, decided to stay for the night.

The next excitement was the sound of an aeroplane, somewhere low and near. Since it was a Tuesday, this could only be the Flying Doctor, who doubles as an area postman, with mail to drop, so out we all rushed. The plane came over very low with its luggage door open, the signal for an imminent mail drop, and then circled: on the next run, a single padded envelope landed neatly at our feet, the most accurate shot ever, apparently. The plane went round once more, to make sure we had received the package, and then head-ed off towards Endulen, passing quite close to a stork which happened to be circling at the same height. The mail included letters for Mary and for Peter and for Peter's wife Annie, who is due back at Olduvai shortly, plus a scribbled greeting in Swahili and English from the pilot and colleague, who are the well-known team of Phil and Phil, one Phil being the Endulen doctor, and the other Phil Matthews, the pilot.

I worked until I reached a suitable stopping point in the early evening, and then walked for a while, from a little before till a little after sunset. The giraffe were back in position near the camp gate, when I got back, the group having now increased to eight, including four young ones. They watched me a little uncertainly, ready to move off, but returned to their acacia tops when they were sure I really had turned towards the camp. Dinner was a very cheerful occasion, with Patti in good form and clearly pleased to have an evening's company, though she was also glad to retire early after a series of late nights and early starts with the jackals. After she had done so, and Peter had also retired, Mary gave me quite a lot of off-the-record personal information which, while it will certainly not appear in the book, should greatly assist my writing of some of the difficult later chapters – and no, I'm *not* going to repeat it here, because I'm not a professional enough diarist to break such confidences. I ended the day with some preparatory reading, till about 11.30 pm, for the writing that must be done tomorrow. I heard the sound of what could only be more flamingo passing over, but the moon was behind cloud, and they could not be seen.

Today was a little cooler than of late, mainly because there was a breeze. There was a smoky haze in the air again: Patti told us that most of western Serengeti is burnt black, almost up to Seronera, but the recent rainstorms have already produced shoots of new grass. This afternoon there was a small bushfire to be seen on Lemagrut, the highest and nearest of the local extinct volcanoes, on to which one looks out directly, across the Gorge, from the front of the camp. The flames moved up the mountain, but petered out when the breeze died away in the evening. Last night, incidentally, the wind got very strong and gusty for a while in the early hours, and I woke to find the door of my hut had blown wide open. I sleepily decided I had better shut it, with all those bitish creatures around, like the ones that might have been eating Peter at the back of camp: most of them could probably jump over a low thorn fence if they put their minds to it, I reckoned. Mary would be furious, if I got eaten at this stage of the project, I'm sure, and we selfless biographers always take every care to ensure our subject's happiness.

Wednesday, 29 June

Now that's a familiar-sounding date: it occurs to me that my father would have been one hundred years old today, had he made it, which seemed entirely possible less than four years ago. As things turned out, this was a fairly uneventful day, by Olduvai standards. Patti left around 8.30 am: there is a tentative arrangement for her to go to Nairobi when I return there at the end of this visit, as she needs to arrange certain permits, and it would save valuable petrol if she could hitch a lift. There were clear giraffe prints to be seen *inside* the camp compound this morning, but no one had heard them during the night.

I wrote steadily all the morning, without a break, completing two and a half thousand words or so about Mary's work on the Tanzanian rock paintings in 1951, something she has always regarded as a personal highlight. Later she approved my account with only minor amendments, so I moved on to preparatory work for the next section, which will mainly concern Leakey family life at Langata. A small flock of flamingos passed over at around 12.45 pm, or tried to: they seemed to be having great difficulty getting past the upcurrents and turbulence which the Gorge evidently causes. Mary said that it is very rare to see them on a long-distance flight by day. Eventually, they managed to find a smooth current of air, and glided off in a shallow V-formation, but apparently back in the direction from which they had come, and we lost sight of them. The strong wind that blew all day can't have been helping them much, either. Though it wasn't a cold wind, it made the day very draughty and kept the temperature down to a maximum of 77 degrees; this was the first day on which I have not changed into shorts as the heat built up and indeed a sweater was needed for some of the time.

In the late afternoon, the sky cleared so I took my walk earlier than usual to get some photographs in a strong but quite mellow light, which seemed particularly good for the areas of red sediments in the Gorge, most of which belong to Bed III. I went right down into the Gorge as far as the FLK *Zinjanthropus* site, as it wasn't the time of day for lions to be about: indeed, I saw no animals at all.

After dark I got everything set up to photograph the genets again, but the annoying little creatures for once failed to show up at their usual time.

Thursday, 30 June

Another very windy day, which was therefore mostly cool, or at least felt so. Mary even wore *two* sweaters. After breakfast, I looked to see whether there were any new giraffe footprints, and found that there certainly were: they had been right up to the tree by my hut in the night, though on the far side of it. I certainly never heard a sound of them, though the dogs did bark once or twice. Nor were there any sounds of lion in the night, for the first time: they must have moved away. Apart from the giraffe footprints, I noted two trails of prolific animal droppings, rather small and round in shape. I wondered what incontinent smaller animal had passed through the camp unknown to us, but Peter assured me that those *were* typical giraffe droppings, which are surprisingly small for such a large creature, and always very frequent. Goodness me: their digestive systems must operate like machine guns. It's amazing what one learns.

I wrote solidly all the morning again, without interruptions, and got a lot done. That sort of progress simply wouldn't have been possible in Oxford: people would have come wanting things, and the phone would have rung a great number of times. I walked early, after lunch, mainly along the edge of the Side Gorge. The group of eight giraffe were standing together, round behind camp, and watched me from a distance – reloading the intestinal artillery, maybe. There was a ninth one, an adult, standing a little way off from the others.

The sun came out as I walked, and it got quite hot – well, it did anywhere one could get out of the wind, which was only possible in a few places amongst the trees and bushes. I took a couple of photographs and returned to my writing. At about 4 pm, the small birds gave their distinctive 'snake' alarm call, which instantly produced the whole of the camp staff, who love a snake-hunt, variously armed with wooden poles, a ranging pole from the digging equipment store, a catapult, a panga and goodness knows what else. There were many birds around, who soon showed them where the snake was, but it didn't turn out to be the big one that is known to have been visiting the camp occasionally. It escaped down a shallow hole, so they dug it out and killed it: a very thin-looking green and yellow snake, about three to four feet long, which even Mary couldn't identify. I took some photographs of the hunt. The snake may have been harmless, but one could not be sure. The big snake has not been seen for at least a week, nor any of the trails it leaves, so it may have gone off elsewhere. And then again, it may not.

I finished my section of text after tea, and must have written about 5000 words today. Considering the number of words I also write each day in this diary, I reckon I have been quite productive on this trip, and it all seems to flow very easily at present. I gave the finished section to Mary to read and took a warm shower, in spite of the cold wind. At about 7.30 pm, just before dinner, we suddenly heard the sound and then almost immediately saw the lights of a car, emerging from the Gorge a few hundred yards away and heading straight for camp – one of the sights Mary dreads most, if it's unexpected, as I have mentioned before.

'Oh, no!', she groaned. 'I think I'd better feel very ill.'

But all was well: it turned out to be Annie, Peter's wife, back at last after a stay of several weeks amongst the Hadza for her research, and she was warmly welcomed by everyone. She was full of news, and her work had been going very well; she had also brought fresh vegetables and pawpaws, which came at just the right time, since supplies were dwindling. Dinner was very cheerful, with much Serengeti gossip as well as Annie's account of her work: I suppose eventually I shall get to know where all these names of people fit into the local saga, but I was soon completely lost. In the course of her work (which concerns plant foods used by hunter-gatherers, both ancient and modern), Annie has now discovered another previously unknown plant species, her second. She also brought with her a Hadza bow and arrows: these are actually for Patti, but she will show them to us tomorrow. The Hadza are nomadic hunter-gatherers, still leading an approximately traditional life, scattered over parts of Tanzania, though there are none in the immediate area of Olduvai.

The genets came back, of course, a little later on, just because I hadn't got my camera ready, what with Annie's sudden arrival. They'll be absent again next time I try, you wait and see. Earlier today, Mary briefly saw a wildcat in camp. They are known in the area, but apparently none has ever dared to come right in before. I'm sorry I wasn't there when it appeared, as I have never seen one. The wind continued to blow, right into the night. The last sound I heard was that of the windmills whirring round, generating and storing useful electricity, for the third night in succession.

Friday, 1 July

There is no obvious sign that June has passed quietly into July, but such seems to be the case, according to the calendar. When Kitetu brought the early morning tea, there were still sounds of strong wind, so it had probably continued to blow right through the night. On this visit, unlike last time, I cannot actually watch the sunrise from my window, as it takes place away to the left, beyond Lengai. At 6.30 each morning, when the tea arrives, it is light enough to see the world outside, but the colours are still flat and grey-looking. One can always tell when the sun breaks clear of the low cloud on the horizon, even though one cannot see it: first, the sides of the branches of the big acacia tree catch a golden light, but only in places, because the branches droop quite low and there are other trees between them and the sun. Next the light picks out the high slopes of Lemagrut, on the right-hand side of the window, and then gradually spreads to the rest of the landscape – but by then it is time to get up.

Everyone would be glad if the wind would stop: it is keeping the temperature down and bringing quite a lot of cloud, and it blows any loose bit of paper off the table. We prolific authors, who create quite a lot of loose written sheets, find that sort of thing rather a bore, I discovered. I was unable to dispense with wearing a thick sweater until mid-afternoon, which was curious, since by then the thermometer was at almost 80 degrees. Mary and Peter reminded each other that things would be far worse if we were at Laetoli or Kekasio, the Pliocene sites away to the south-east: the wind would be stronger and the temperature 20 degrees lower, they said.

Annie put her Hadza bow and arrows out for us to see on the flat top of the low wall at the front of the main workroom and they caused an immediate sensation amongst the local bird population: the arrows were at once mobbed by over a dozen bulbuls, the finch-sized birds with dark head and bright yellow feathers below the tail, which normally spend all their time prospecting for food in the larder, since they can easily get through the wire mesh over the window, which is an anti-genet and anti-mongoose defence rather than an anti-bulbul one. It wasn't clear whether they disliked the feathers on the arrows, or whether they were aware that some of the smaller arrows were the kind which the Hadza use against birds. I wondered whether the fletching of the arrows had perhaps been done using feathers from birds of prey, but in fact it turned out that most of them were from guinea fowl. There were also some larger hunting arrows, with broad, leaf-shaped metal tips: very interesting. The bow was much larger and heavier than I would have expected, but was a very nice object, in its elegantly functional way: no attempt at all had been made to decorate it, I noted.

At about 10 am, a Land Rover arrived, driven by John Bower, an American from Iowa University, who is known to Mary. He is at present excavating a relatively recent site amongst the Gol Kopjes, about an hour and a half's drive away to the north-west. He had looked in to pay his respects to Mary, on his way to Arusha to collect Diane Gifford, who is joining his dig for a while: I know her slightly, and have heard her give a lecture on taphonomy. John said that his team was bearing up well under the present difficulties in getting supplies, amongst which petrol poses the worst problem. Apparently the local radio has now put out a warning that there will be no petrol obtainable in Tanzania, and no diesel fuel either, for the next two to four weeks. Already at Seronera the Serengeti Research Institute has neither light nor water, because they depend on generators and pumps powered by diesel engines. There are stories that queues over a mile long for petrol developed recently in Arusha, on the mere rumour that a tanker lorry with petrol had just left Dar-es-Salaam, which is actually some 300 miles and at least 12 hours hard driving away from Arusha. When petrol does arrive, apparently, there is usually chaos, with people snatching the pump hoses away from each other to fill their own jerrycans, and spilling much of the precious liquid – smoking cigarettes while they do it, too, Mary added. Her own accumulated supply at Olduvai is holding out, but certainly she has none to give away. John Bower invited us all to drive over and visit his dig next week, and the invitation was accepted, subject to there being enough petrol to spare for the journey.

After he had left, Mary and I went through the long section written yesterday, and I made the various amendments she requested, which were not too many at all, though it took us several shots to get straight the different kinds of hyrax amongst the pet community at Langata, and she kept remembering yet more of the tricks they got up to. I then wrote on, but found it rather harder going, after yesterday's burst of rapid productivity. I was just thinking that perhaps a break was needed, when one was offered: Peter and Annie suggested that they and I might go in Peter's Land Rover to visit Shifting Sands, a remarkable crescent-shaped migrating dune of volcanic ash and dust, which Mary had once taken me to see in 1972 – always a beautiful place, whatever the time of year. It is out on the plains beyond the guides' camp and only about 5 miles away, though they are slow miles across the Gorge and over bumpy tracks. Annie was keen to take Brown Dog, knowing that he tends to get a bit brow-beaten by the other dogs for not being a Dalmatian. Old Sophie, in particular, is inclined to growl obviously rude comments at him when he passes, and Matthew also makes sure that Brown Dog is aware of his lower social status. We also took with us Omari (the mechanic from Arusha whom Peter brought to Olduvai when I was last here, who has been a great success) and Naade (I think it is spelled with two 'a's), another member of the camp staff, who seems to know a lot about Maasai things. Neither of them had ever visited Shifting Sands before. Mary carefully maintains a distance in her dealings with the camp staff, even the longest serving ones, but to Peter and Annie most of them are just close personal friends.

It was rather overcast, though with brief shafts of sunlight, and the plains were dry and brown. The trip was very enjoyable, and provided us all with a break from the camp and a couple of hours of real fresh air. We saw only a dik-dik, a hare and a solitary giraffe on the way out. Omari in particular was delighted with the dune, whose crescent shape is perfect, though he seemed to view it mainly with a builder's eye, in terms of lorry-loads of sand. Brown Dog, emancipated from the Dalmatians, tore across the grasslands and belted up and down the dune, barking joyfully and having a wonderful time. Beyond the dune, there is a low circular hill formed of the basement rock – white quartzite – up which we walked for the wide view of the empty plains, the great volcanoes beyond, and the Gorge itself, immensely impressive. Lengai, or Ol Doinyo Lengai, to give it its full Maasai name, showed clearly in the distance, its sides clad in white ash ridged by erosion channels. The light was not of the best for photography, but I took several pictures.

As we descended from the hill, the two camp ravens, who live down the Gorge in this direction, came winging slowly home from somewhere out on the plains: it was hard work for them into the wind, and maybe they were also heavy from feeding on the remains of a kill, because they had not been seen in camp all day. Peter made a detour on the way home, to show us the cliffs where the ravens nest on a ledge, in a very spectacular offshoot of the Gorge called Kestrel Korongo. This detour gave Brown Dog a chance to bark at some Maasai cattle, and he was also very pleased to find, when we got to the place, that there was a large troop of baboons, spread out over the cliff face, some climbing on the narrow ledges and some sitting on the ground at the cliff top. It was clear that Brown Dog had a substantial number of points, not necessarily connected with his thesis, which he would rather have liked to discuss with them in a free and frank manner, so he had to be locked firmly in the Land Rover for his own safety: there were just too many sheer precipices, and also baboons are notoriously fierce creatures, with extremely sharp teeth. So he said it all from a distance, and the baboons barked back at him a bit. It was definitely a big evening for Brown Dog.

We got back to camp in the last of the light, having made a brief stop at the guides' camp for the two Africans to go in search of tobacco. There were some more dik-dik in the Gorge as we drove across, with the lights coming on in camp ahead of us, and the windmills

Shifting sands with the small Engelosen volcano (centre) beyond

already in vigorous action. Revived by the trip, I was able later in the evening to finish my draft of the very long chapter, Chapter 9 as things are at the moment, to which the recently written sections belong. It may well need dividing into two chapters eventually.

During dinner, Mary reached the decision that she would travel to Nairobi, when I go back there, which will be on Monday week, taking Sophie to the vet to see if he can ease her arthritis at all for what looks increasingly likely to be the last few months of her life, she being over 13. I can remember her as the newest and youngest member of the then Dalmatian team on one of my earlier visits to Olduvai, either in 1972 or 1974. This change of plan meant a radio call to Hazel in Nairobi, which Peter achieved very efficiently, in spite of long delays caused by various stinkers, each of whom wanted to make not one but several calls in Swahili.

The others went off to bed, but I stayed on for a while, as there were bright stars to be seen in a clear and moonless sky. I wondered whether there might be a Southern Hemisphere star chart amongst the books on the camp shelves, and eventually found one, to my delight, in a not-very-recent *National Geographic* atlas of Mary's. This enabled me to identify a few of the brighter objects, and find the Southern Cross, which I had in fact seen previously in Africa, when I was in Zambia, I think: it strikes me as a rather disappointing constellation, for all its fame, since one of the stars is rather too faint for the cross-shape to be impressive. The Milky Way was very clear, and I saw two or three meteors. After 10 pm there was a growing brightness over Ngorongoro, to herald the moon's rising, though it would not be up for some while yet, so far as Olduvai was concerned.

Saturday, 2 July

The weather continued as before, with a strong wind from the south-east, though the day was mainly bright. Now, I suppose, the conditions are just what I was warned to expect: cold, dry, no lions – and the mangoes are finished, too. Ah, well.

Yesterday, Mary had been keen to start using the tape recorder again, to get more material down for me to work on but, when I set it up this morning, she claimed that her mind had gone blank, so I returned to my writing. We tried again in the evening, but with little success. Well, it was her idea, not mine, and I suppose it might have worked well, but, as it turned out, it cost us time rather than saving it.

After lunch, I photographed Annie's bow and arrows, and she showed me slides and photographs of the Hadza people with whom she has been working: very interesting. There was talk of her possibly taking me on a brief visit to them when I am next here, if time allows: now, that would be splendid, if it could be arranged. I also spent some while

The Olduvai plant, wild sisal, growing near Camp, part of Main Gorge beyond

talking with both Peter and Annie about their own research plans. Annie is to leave again tomorrow, and Peter will be away for two days, taking her to Arusha.

I walked for an hour in the evening, going westwards along the edge of the Main Gorge, then out on to the plains and back via the full length of the airstrip. It was a nice enough evening, though distinctly cool if one stood around. The landscape was utterly empty of animals, with hardly a bird to be seen either: just me and the setting sun, in all of the few hundred square miles that were visible, and a feeling that infinity was just over the horizon, doubtless also empty. If it hadn't been for the cold wind, I would certainly have taken my clothes off to stand naked for a few moments at the centre of it all and see what it felt like to be an early hominid, though there's no evidence that a real one would have been wearing glasses, or have a camera and a small pile of clothes by his feet. Anyhow, there *was* a cold wind. Some other time, perhaps.

After dark, I resumed my exploration of the Southern Hemisphere stars, and was amazed to find myself looking at the Great Bear, completely the wrong way up (of course) in the north, and not all that low down, either. I would have expected it to be well below the Tanzanian horizon: not at this time of year, evidently. Zambia, where one couldn't see it, is quite a way south of here, of course, and Swaziland and South Africa much more so. I ended the evening with a little more writing. Earlier, I had gone to see if I could see the camp porcupine, just after its usual dish of food had been put out down by its known den in the bushes, but it didn't emerge.

Sunday, 3 July

Just before 1.0 am during the night, I woke suddenly to the sound of hooves and the bark of a dog. The hoof sounds were very near, so I think they must have indicated the rapid departure of a giraffe which had been browsing on the tree right outside my hut window. There was nothing to be seen, but in the morning I certainly noted some very fresh giraffe droppings just there.

During breakfast, the four dogs suddenly got up and rushed to the camp gate, barking loudly: it turned out that a jackal was passing, on business of its own. Brown Dog, in particular, would clearly have been glad of a word with it: he has killed three jackals so far, Peter said. That soulful look evidently conceals hidden depths. Peter and Annie were not able to leave until about 9.0 am, delayed by a faulty alternator on Peter's vehicle, though it hadn't been causing trouble during the trip we made a couple of days ago to Shifting Sands. Mary and I then worked until we reached a reasonable stopping point, shortly before lunch, she expressing satisfaction with the results. As a concession to its being Sunday, I read a book and even dozed for a while afterwards. At last the wind had dropped, and there was only the occasional gust, which could be heard coming across the plains long before it actually arrived. As a result, the day was much warmer, as well as being bright: the temperature reached about 80 degrees.

When it was time to resume work, I had a very useful discussion with Mary about the nature and shape of the next sections, rather than going back to the writing, and after that took a few portrait photographs of her with Matthew, the youngest of the three

Dalmatians; remarkably, this was at her suggestion, in the hope that one of them might turn out well enough to be used as a cover photograph on the book's dust jacket. I had to change the film during the course of this operation, and subsequently had the unsettling thought that perhaps I had put the old one back in again by mistake, wound back to its start, instead of the new one, though I don't *think* I did ...).

After tea, I went for quite a long walk, it being shorts weather again, and got some proper exercise, going down the steep path into the Gorge and getting as far as two of its landmarks: the cliff of black lava thrust up by one of the faults, and the well-known feature Castle Rock that is in so many of the photographs. There were many giraffe down on the floor of the Gorge, browsing on green acacia shoots: I took some photographs of one group of 11, and then a little further on encountered a separate family of five. I saw a couple of dik-dik, too. Much fossil bone and worked stone was lying around, as usual, on the erosion surfaces.

Group of giraffe on the floor of the Gorge

Mary and I returned to talking rather than writing, over pre-supper drinks. After her third glass of whisky, she decided that perhaps I had better cook the Sunday evening meal rather than her, so I did (chops and aubergines). Plenty of useful information emerged during the conversation. Later, having the camera handy, I managed at last to photograph the genets again, and I watched their comings and goings for some while. There were two, one much more shy than the other, but it was never possible to get a picture of them both together. I trust the pictures will come out well this time, after the failure of those I took on the first trip.

Monday, 4 July

I remembered my weekly malaria pill again: is there no limit to the ruthless efficiency of this budding author? Mary and I were expecting a clear working day, but at about 10.15 a Land Rover suddenly appeared down at the camp gate. Fortunately, the driver could be seen to be waving a red scarf, which meant that it must be Patti, because that is her established personal signal to Mary not to hide or pretend to be ill – her usual reaction to unexpected visitors.

Patti was indeed not expected this time, but explained that she was the advance party for an expedition consisting of Margaret Gibb (the owner of Gibb's Farm), who had been staying at Ndutu for a few days' peace and quiet while she did her accounts for the year and was now returning to Karatu, accompanied by some Norwegian relatives of hers, namely Eva-Marie and her two children. Up to this point, so far as I was concerned, Eva-Marie had been one of these shadowy figures lurking on the edge of the whole Serengeti saga, whom people always seemed to mention when exchanging news and gossip, so I was mildly pleased to know that she really did exist: an actual person, not some abstract Serengeti concept. They had offered Patti an earlier lift towards Arusha than we would have been able to provide when I leave, so the new plan is that we will collect Patti there and take her with us to Nairobi. I expect this scheme will come unstuck in one way or another between now and then, but meanwhile the others arrived and we all had coffee together before they made their way on, Patti having transferred herself to their vehicle, leaving her own Land Rover parked in the camp, various belongings stored here and there for safe custody, and her guitar on loan to Kitetu, the camp cook, which pleased him greatly.

Various news of interest emerged over coffee. A rhino had definitely been seen at Ndutu, to general amazement and delight, though it was thought likely to be the very last one anywhere on Serengeti to have escaped the poachers. Yesterday no less than 10 lions had been roaring not far from Patti's tent, clearly visible. (Huh, I thought to myself.) Such petrol as currently exists in Tanzania is now officially reserved for the use of government vehicles and the army only. Accordingly, certain members of the army and government are said to be cheerfully selling it to all comers on the black market, their price being 300 Tanzanian shillings per gallon – that's over £16 per gallon, at the official exchange rate. I wondered who would pay such an amount, but apparently there are safari companies who have parties of tourists out in the bush and need to get them safely home at any cost.

After the unexpected interruption, Mary and I then worked more or less undisturbed till lunch: there was one minor outbreak of Maasai-at-the-camp-gate, this time demanding a cure for pneumonia, but Kitetu dealt with that and sent them off happy, I'm not quite sure how. We also worked non-stop and quite productively between lunch and tea, Mary foregoing her usual rest, and we continued after tea too, to catch up on lost time. The day turned very windy again, and cloudy, so it was quite cold. The reason for the urgency was the tentative arrangement made by John Bower, when he was here a few days ago, that he would call in today with Diane Gifford, for an evening meal and to stay the night, on their way from Arusha back to his excavation site amongst the Gol Kopjes, so we might find we got no working time later. In the event, there was no sign of them, either before, during or after the evening meal. Of course, non-arrival never surprises anyone, in East Africa, and at Olduvai there is really no way of finding out the reason for it. The most obvious one in this case is the total absence of petrol: John would not have had

enough, when he left here last Friday, to get to Arusha and to Kilimanjaro Airport and back to Olduvai, so if none could be bought he would inevitably be stuck by now. No doubt we shall hear more when Peter gets back from Arusha tomorrow, and I dare say he will end up bringing them with him. We shall see – or not, as the case may be, Tanzania being Tanzania. Whatever happens, the world will doubtless continue on its way.

Mary was in a mood to communicate further confidences, while we watched and waited after supper, and in the end we talked until after 10 pm. The genets came in and out, one of them entering at floor level, seemingly inclined to

Mary and dogs: Matthew (left), Janet (centre), Brown dog (right)

explore, instead of appearing dramatically by jumping up from outside on to the wall where their food is placed, which is what they usually do. One genet suddenly scented danger, during the course of stuffing its face with banana, and sat bolt upright and rigid, peering out into the dark, its tail all fluffed out, until whatever it was had passed by. Mary and I could see and hear nothing to indicate what the trouble was.

Tuesday, 5 July

There was the sound of jackals barking down in the Gorge during the night, and Mary said that she had also heard hyaenas. It was also discovered that the genets, however charming, had behaved abominably during the night by breaking into the banana basket and eating most of the remaining stock; opinion was that it will serve them right if Peter doesn't happen to bring any more bananas with him when he returns. In the Dalmatian world, I observed Matthew carefully burying a large dog biscuit for future use, but his fat colleague Janet also saw this, and when Matthew had gone she immediately dug it up and ate it. I could also see that Mary was becoming very worried about Sophie, who suddenly seems to be failing fast, and it might well be that she would not be able to stand the stress of a journey to Nairobi to see the vet. I suspect it is really becoming a question of how soon it would be a kindness simply to put her to sleep. Later, Mary herself said as much.

There were the sounds of a vehicle at about 11.0 am, but they were from the wrong direction for it to be Peter returning: instead, a completely unexpected large safari truck drew up at the gate, before Mary had time to escape. The driver turned out to be an old friend of hers, Dick Estes, who said that he had written to her about the visit, though in fact the letter had not come. He hoped Mary (and I) would join him and his party for lunch over at the Gorge museum, the catch being that she would have to give a talk for a few minutes to please the customers. Mary agreed, a little reluctantly, and off we went. They do a surprisingly high standard of picnic lunch on these safaris, it transpired. When we got to the museum, there was yet another well-populated safari vehicle of similar type there, though this one was red and ours was yellow. I now recalled that my sister Molly had mentioned, before I left England, the vague possibility that an acquaintance of hers, met during a holiday in Canada, might pass by Olduvai on safari while I was there this time and would ask for me if so: my only information was that she was elderly, American, quite sporting and called Mary. I had almost forgotten about it, amidst all else that had been happening, but seeing the safari trucks reminded me, and I wondered whether the red truck's party might include her, and such proved to be the case.

'How is your sister Mary?' she bellowed, obviously in a slight muddle. 'No, she's Molly and I'm Mary,' she decided after a while. 'This is my friend Ruth.'

Her friend did not deny this, so I expect she was right on that point. Anyhow, they both got to be introduced to Mary Leakey, which is what they really wanted, though the addition of another Mary to the equation seemed to confuse her further. They were nice, though I noted with surprise that they had no cameras, which seemed very strange for Americans on a safari in Tanzania. They left not long after, as their party had finished its picnic.

'Remember me to Mary,' was her parting remark. 'Let me rub you' (doing so) 'and you pass some of it on to her.'

Exit the red safari truck. The other party also seemed to be slightly muddled, after their two weeks in the wilder parts of Tanzania: and well they might be, of course. They told us that they had heard that there had been an attempt on the life of President Nyerere, only they referred to him as President Ndutu by mistake, Ndutu being where they had just come from. The attempt was believed to have failed, and the story might be no more than a rumour anyhow. Mary gave her talk, which was received with rapt attention and was followed by very predictable questions of the 'Gee, Dr Leakey, what did it feel like to discover ... ' kind, until one man asked something altogether more technical, relating to the comparative morphology of early hominid teeth, based on something he had once heard Louis Leakey say during a public lecture about 15 years earlier. He may genuinely have wanted to know the answer, or perhaps he was just trying to impress his colleagues. Either way, watching Mary's face, I could see that she had completely lost track of the question half way through his asking it, but I certainly wasn't expecting her to toss it across the room to me with an airy 'Perhaps my colleague Dr Roe from England would like to answer that one: he probably knows more about it than I do.' If I'd done something like that to her, I'd have found myself on the next bus home as a stinker. In fact, the question was not in my field at all, far from it, but by sheer chance I had been referring to a highly relevant paper only that morning, just before the safari party arrived, in the course of my preparatory reading for the next section of the autobiography.

'Well,' I said, brightly, if not downright sweetly, 'perhaps Louis Leakey was referring to the feature known as the bucco-lingual swelling, which is one of those traits which distinguishes certain Australopithecine teeth on the one hand from those of members of the genus *Homo* on the other.'

There was a stunned silence, followed by a murmur from the questioner of 'Gee, yeah, I guess that *was* the phrase he used.' I caught a look of distinct awe on Mary's face. You never know your luck, do you? I think she had about made up her mind that, while I could perhaps write a bit, I didn't really know anything useful about anything really worthwhile. The final question from the audience was also of interest:

'Dr Leakey, are you ever going to find time to write your autobiography?' Mary and I had agreed some while back that casual enquirers were not to be told at this stage that any such project was in hand, so she gave a guardedly non-committal reply.

'You could get one of those word-processor things to do it all for you,' suggested someone, helpfully.

It was on the tip of my tongue to reply that she had done just that, and that I was it, but I remained silent. Exit the yellow safari truck, with its satisfied customers: I hoped that they would remember who they were and where they were by the time their trip finally ended. Mary and I drove back to camp in silence and somewhat thoughtfully, possibly for different reasons.

At 3.30, John Bower and Diane Gifford finally made their arrival, but could stay only for a cup of tea. It turned out that vehicle repairs and then queuing for petrol had delayed them in Arusha yesterday until it was too late to start out for Olduvai, but they had at least managed to get themselves a huge drum of petrol with the help of some special official signed chit from some section of the Conservation Office, and it should be enough to last for the rest of their dig. They had heard nothing about an attempt on the life of the President. Arrangements were agreed for us to go over and visit their site on Thursday (the day after tomorrow). They also reported that Peter had still been busy getting things done in Arusha at the time when they themselves left, but that he was still hoping to reach Olduvai by the end of the day, as planned. I wouldn't bet on that, myself.

I returned to my writing, and in due course darkness fell. There was no sign of Peter by bedtime, surprise, surprise. The afternoon had been quite warm and reasonably still, but the wind quite suddenly got up again, after dark. I could hear jackals barking again, and I also thought I could hear lions somewhere a long way off, through the noise of the wind: if so, it would be the first time for a week. Opposite the camp, a small flicker of flame broke the darkness somewhere on the slopes of Lemagrut: another bush fire, no doubt.

Wednesday, 6 July

Today, my children should be off to France with their mother: I hope they will enjoy their visit. They will still be away when I get back to England. And I wonder how my builders are getting on at Fordwells, come to think of it? Meanwhile, here at Olduvai, there was a red-gold dawn to be enjoyed, two hours ahead of whatever kind of sunrise they might be getting in England today.

It was a slowish morning, with great tangles about the facts of Mary's visit to South Africa ('or did I go more than once?' she wondered), in the 1960s. We more or less sorted the story out in the end, but lost quite a lot of time in doing so. Peter returned during lunch, having had more things to do in Arusha than he had expected, though with no particular adventures. Sophie is rather better today, and seems to be moving more easily, so there is a return to the idea that she should go with us to the vet in Nairobi when I leave. We shall see.

The bulbul bird population has now reached epidemic proportions: no food is safe from them, unless it is actually in one's hand or in the refrigerator with the door firmly shut. Breakfast, in particular, was virtually a siege.

During the afternoon, I began preparatory work for what will inevitably be a difficult next chapter, since it is about the breakdown of relations between Mary and Louis in the period 1968–72. I suspect that this may take some while. After tea, I walked with Peter across the Gorge as far as the guides' camp, where he had various messages from Arusha to deliver and, as that would be a lengthy business, I returned ahead of him, diverting from the direct path here and there to look at one or two of the archaeological sites. There were no animals to be seen, though once I thought I could hear something moving in the bushes. Peter arrived back about 20 minutes after me, and had found fresh tracks of two lions along the floor of the Gorge, which certainly hadn't been there when we went over, or indeed when I returned. Well, well.

Just before and during dinner, after darkness had fallen, loud roaring began, quite close by, down in the Gorge below the camp, so Mary suggested that Peter and I should drive down in her Peugeot, to see if this time we could actually find the lions. In seconds, I had grabbed my camera and fitted the flash eagerly, pausing only to switch the 'distance' button across, on the grounds that we probably wouldn't get within 10 feet of any lions, and then we were off, under bright stars, feeling reasonably optimistic. Peter made for where the roaring had come from, down at the bottom of the Gorge, and drove very carefully and slowly along the part where there is an actual track there: nothing to be seen, and the roaring had stopped. We continued on to rocky and grassy terrain, still passable in a vehicle if you know the way, though the track has ended by that point, going as far as we could, and then turning slowly, when we could get no further. Peter then saw two distant shapes move quickly aside, and was sure they were lions, but I had been looking in a different direction and saw nothing. We waited for a while, with the engine switched off, but nothing appeared, so we started up again and set out slowly for home. Then, suddenly, I could hear roaring above the sound of the engine. Stop. Switch off. Silence. But Peter had heard something too. Lights on and start again for home. And then, quite suddenly, there they were, in the beam of the headlights: two young male lions, right ahead and coming slowly towards us: beautiful, unconcerned, even a little curious. They passed about eight yards away, and I photographed them as best I could, hoping that the focus was at least approximately right. Peter advised shutting the car window for safety, which simply hadn't occurred to me, but the young lions were so disdainful of our presence that in due course I opened it again and tried a few more pictures. We turned again and followed them gently, and as quietly as possible, about 20 yards behind, for at least quarter of an hour, and they did everything for us except roar: they rubbed noses, rolled in the dust, played for a moment, yawned, sat down, and then just watched us for a while, with eyes shining red in the headlight beams, before eventually wandering off back the way they had come. For a moment, it seemed that they might take the road that leads back up to the camp, at which point Peter and I realised we had left the gate open and would actually be driving them towards it, but fortunately they decided against it. So we drove home, happy, to a welcome cup of hot coffee.

I can hear them roaring again now, as I write, and it sounds as if they are still in much the same place where we finally left them. I wonder if any of my photos will come out? This is clearly a highlight of this entire visit, whatever there may be yet to happen. And I just wonder what it was that I thought I heard in the bushes, when I was walking home by myself, down in the Gorge, in the early evening, almost exactly where we eventually found the lions? Oh, probably a bird, I expect, or maybe just nothing at all.

Thursday, 7 July

This was the day set aside for the visit to John Bower's dig somewhere amongst the Gol Kopjes. Peter was to have come with us, but he simply had too much to get done, after his delayed return from Arusha, so in the end Mary and I went alone, with me doing the driving. Our instructions were to follow the main road to just beyond the Ndutu turning, and then to leave it and simply drive across the plains towards the kopjes, which seemed a little vague even to Mary, but off we set nevertheless, planning to be back for a late lunch, unless it seemed polite to stay and have lunch at the dig (should we actually locate it).

There was little game to be seen: just three large giraffe, a scatter of gazelle and one or two ostriches – very different from my trip along this same road back in January, during the first visit. After an hour, we turned off the road and took to the plains, having by then seen just two other vehicles, although it is now the middle of the tourist season. That was a result of the petrol shortage, of course. The surface of the grasslands is basically flat and firm, but one has to watch every moment for animal burrows or sudden erosion hollows in it. I managed to miss most of them, but sometimes one gets only a foot or two's notice, depending on the height of the grass. The Gol Kopjes, which I had often heard mentioned but never previously seen, turned out to be low granite tors, rising for no obvious reason here and there out of the grassland. There were mirages to be seen in all directions on the plains, and the shimmering heat made distances very hard to judge for driver or navigator. Besides, a perfectly good kopje for which one was making had a way of suddenly vanishing: the plains are not as flat as their vast size makes them seem, and there are sudden rises and falls which can change the appearance of the horizon in a moment. Eventually, we reached the first of these rocky outcrops, which proved to be entirely devoid of archaeologists, though there were lots of rather charming lizards basking on the warm rocks, some of them with purple bodies. We surveyed the landscape and the several other visible kopjes for signs of people, tents and so forth: there was nothing to be seen, so we set out on a rather random tour of kopjes, which seemed to be about a kilometre apart. At about the fifth, we had a puncture, so Mary was glad to have me there to change the wheel.

Rocky though the outcrops are, it proved very hard to find a suitable loose stone to use as a wheel chock, but I got one in the end. During the wheel-changing operation, I saw a distant vehicle approaching, and it eventually arrived, proving to contain a small and exclusive American safari party of two persons, plus driver. The latter knew Mary (of course) and said that he had written to her and asked if he could bring his visitors to meet her at Olduvai today, but tomorrow would do. Mary, who hadn't received the letter, was forced to agree, and the two Americans looked suitably respectful. Yes, said the driver, they had seen the archaeologists: just go past that kopje over there and straight on – I forget if he actually added, in the traditional manner, that we couldn't miss them. We followed his instructions, but could find no sign of life: when he had said 'straight on', he had perhaps forgotten that he had been travelling in a curve, but fortunately I had noticed that and so, after a couple more false shots, we did actually find the camp, and there was John Bower himself.

We inspected the dig, which seemed to be going well, though the deposit is very shallow. Then John took us back the way we had come for several kilometres to see another site he had discovered, where there is much archaeological material eroding out beside a kopje that has a great natural hollow in it filled with water, even at this dry time of the year. That looked quite a promising site. There were also some interesting artificial cup-like hollows cut into the rock surface, probably for a game, and there was no way of telling what their age might be. There were more trees at this kopje, because of the water, and quite a lot of birds, including a hornbill. We took John back to his camp: it was already 2.15, and he asked whether we wouldn't like to stay to lunch, which would be at about 3 pm, but that would have meant getting back very late, so we settled thankfully for an alternative offer of black instant coffee and a banana instead. Beside John's camp there was a tree with an eagle's nest (with sounds of young in it), while in another tree about 100 yards away lived two falcons, who were said to spend all day diving at the eagles whenever they got airborne – we watched them at it.

We eventually started for home at about 2.45, and almost immediately ground to a halt with the radiator almost empty and boiling – all that low-gear work across the hot plains, I suppose, because it had been filled before we started out. Mary produced the interesting theory that it also overheats if one is driving for a long time with the wind behind, because the engine gets less in the way of cooling air. I'd never have thought of that. We had in fact brought John Bower a large drum of fresh water, and we now had to go and beg a little of it back, which was rather a loss of face. Eventually, the journey could be restarted, and we set off, both somewhat weary by now, perhaps partly because of the late non-lunch. The plains seemed to have more and more concealed potholes, not all of which I could avoid, and Mary, while declining to drive herself, became an increasingly nervous and petulant passenger, announcing that I was failing to see the potholes because I was driving far too fast – absolutely untrue, in my perhaps not unbiased opinion. Noting the speed, I obediently slowed by 4 mph. 'There's no need to crawl,' she snapped. So I said that this was very helpful, as I now knew that 2 mph faster would be exactly right, and I kept the speedometer precisely on that figure. A frosty silence ensued, which did not, however, do much to relieve the rather oppressive heat of the mid-afternoon. It was actually a bright and beautiful day, but a long drive home lay ahead and one really couldn't take one's eye off the ground surface for a moment to look around, until we reached the road. After that, there were moderate numbers of gazelle to be seen, some of them leaping about in that very odd stiff-legged way that they have; also a few jackals, and two fine impala at Granite Falls, where even the road surface is extremely bad for a mile or two and has to be watched very closely. So at last to Olduvai, around 5.20 pm, both very glad to be back. I noted a small herd of gazelle on the airstrip, and reflected that last night's lions would doubtless be pleased about that, if they were still around.

During our absence, Sophie's condition had sharply deteriorated again, and Mary decided that she would almost certainly have to be put down tomorrow, which naturally created an air of gloom. After the somewhat sombre evening meal, I was too tired to write effectively, so read for a while and actually went to bed around 10 pm, which was very unusual, but rather needed. When I drew back my curtains, there were giraffe quietly busy at the tree immediately outside the window, having arrived absolutely silently. They declined to stay for a flash photo, however.

Friday, 8 July

Sophie was no better at all, so Peter and Mary gently put her down with a painless injection, and she was buried near the edge of the camp compound. Mary was very upset, of course, and things were not helped by her having got some dust or grit in her eye, which was very uncomfortable. She has lost many Dalmatians to death of one kind or another in her time, but the grief clearly does not get less with each new occasion, nor would I expect it to do so, knowing her as I do. All things considered, the two safari Americans we met yesterday at the Gol Kopjes could hardly have chosen a worse time to arrive, which they did at about 10 am. They were a very pleasant married couple from Dallas, Texas, evidently very wealthy, in a quiet and unassuming way. The husband had a serious and consuming interest in the whole history of human neuro-physical development and politely pressed Mary to explain human evolution to him. Not surprisingly, he got monosyllabic answers, and not very many of those: that might have happened to him anyhow, even on a less fraught occasion, but he persisted, unable to understand why she was so unforthcoming. Peter and I attempted polite conversation, but they didn't stay very long. I rather liked him, and would gladly have tried to answer his questions, but Mary very clearly only wanted them to go. They left her a large quantity of very expensive film as a gift, saying they had more than they needed, but she couldn't even raise a thank-you. I walked with them to their vehicle and tried to explain what the trouble was, but I fear they won't have enjoyed their visit much. Mary's verdict, when they had safely left, was that the husband was 'a nut', which I know very well was not the case, but once Mary has decided someone is a nut, she never changes her mind. At least he wasn't diagnosed as a stinker, but it must have been a near thing.

Nothing was going to lighten the gloomy atmosphere, and Mary retired to her hut, while I worked on by myself: it was fortunate that I had plenty of material to write up, as it was very clearly not the moment to offer text to read, or to ask new questions. Sophie, in her last weeks, used to follow Mary everywhere. The other dogs seem quite unaffected by her disappearance, though Matthew was clearly a bit puzzled at not having an extra plateful of food to finish off after his own, when they were fed. I suppose Brown Dog will come out of it quite well, as he will be on the receiving end of one-third less canine abuse, so he is unlikely to mind, and Janet's thinking doesn't seem to extend much beyond food at the moment.

The evening was more cheerful. Peter announced that he needed a goat, for which the source is the local Maasai *manyatta* (encampment), out at Kestrel Korongo near Shifting Sands. No, there's nothing odd about Peter's requiring a goat: he is leaving for Arusha again tomorrow, to meet up with Annie and various friends, and there is to be a party with roast goat, a great Kenyan and doubtless also Tanzanian delicacy. So, he needed a goat, and I was offered a ride to help collect it. Omari came too, and we went first to collect one of the Olduvai guides who actually is a Maasai, and an unusual one, in that he has recently been accepted to study archaeology at the Institute of Archaeology in London. His name is Charles, and it soon transpired that he had been anxious to meet me, because he wants a pair of jeans when I next come out to Olduvai. He requested a pair with 32 inch waist and 44 inch leg, so that there would be extra material to cut off and use: I can't believe such a combination of measurements is made, but we shall see. (Patti Moehlman later told me that 44 inches would be the total length of the outside of the leg up to the waist: well, that sounds a bit better, but I'm still doubtful). On this occasion, Charles was to act as interpreter and bargain-striker, though Peter can speak quite a lot of Maasai himself.

On arrival at the *manyatta*, we were met by an elder, accompanied by his pregnant wife, several small children, two charming puppies and several junior goats and sheep (not easily distinguishable). Various young warriors were sent for, to discuss the deal. The negotiations proceeded with much rapid Maasai and a certain amount of rather slower Swahili, Peter keeping me abreast of progress with brief English summaries. The main difference of opinion evidently concerned whether they should sell Peter the goat for cash in hand now, or for a promise of maize-meal to be brought by him from Arusha when he returned, the second option being complicated by the fact that they are due to move camp tomorrow to a place near Lake Masek, which is about 30 miles away. There was a very long discussion, punctuated by much handshaking, during which I got a chance to admire the beadwork worn by the warriors, amongst which I noted a nice neck collar, many earrings (two pairs each were worn), ankle-rings, a bead wristwatch, a belt and various other ornaments. The women had fine neck-rings and the children bead necklaces. At least 10 tee shirts' worth in all was on view, I should think. The Maasai are well known to be camera-shy (except those who have sold themselves to the tourist trade in Nairobi and will gladly pose for photographs, optimistically demanding hundreds of shillings afterwards for having done so). I knew it would be tactful to leave my camera well out of sight in the car, and accordingly could get only one surreptitious and very distant telephoto shot when we left; it was a shame not to have been able to record the scene in the *manyatta*.

Finally, the Maasai side of the negotiation decided on maize meal as payment: at present they cannot get any, and indeed are apparently not allowed by the Tanzanian government actually to purchase it. That being settled, we drove over to where the goats were – a large flock of them – taking two of the warriors with us in the Land Rover, to their delight, while another walked after us. Further long discussions ensued, with nearly a change of mind in favour of 300 shillings cash, which Peter was quite ready to pay. Then two young women appeared, carrying firewood, with more elaborate beadwork and beaded leather skirts: one also had heavy looking metal arm-rings covering almost all of her forearms. They naturally came over to join the action. Finally, a bleating white goat was selected for Peter – it looked a good 300 shillings' worth to me – and was bundled into the back of the Land Rover, where it immediately settled down cheerfully on the floor, quite unaware of its fate and as if well used to such transport, which it certainly wasn't. Off we went. We dropped Charles at the guides' camp, promising me a wide variety of Maasai decorative objects in return for his pair of jeans – which I shall certainly try and get for him – and crossed the Gorge in a fine sunset, goat and all. Only one giraffe and one dik-dik were to be seen during the whole expedition, but this was an ethnographic trip, not a zoological one, and fascinating enough.

Later, I watched again for the camp porcupine, which I still have not managed to see, until it got too dark and cold: it was evidently not inclined to dine early this evening on the food left for it. Maybe it was watching television. Those giraffe were at the tree by my hut again, last thing, but they left as soon as I opened my door.

Saturday, 9 July

At 3.30 am, the giraffe were right outside my window and woke me up, busily champing up the new green acacia seed pods again in the dark, one of them even rubbing up against the hut wall, I think. They are very persistent creatures. Do they never sleep? Is no other acacia tree in this part of Serengeti in a suitable state to be browsed? This sort of thing simply does not happen in rural West Oxfordshire. However, I was far too sleepy to care or do anything about it.

Peter left for Arusha at 8.15 am. Mary seemed much brighter today: she wrote numerous letters during the morning, while I wrote text: her letters are for posting in Nairobi, when I get there. She will still make the trip, even without Sophie, as she has other things needing to be done there. In the afternoon, I finished my draft of the difficult chapter on the rift between Mary and Louis, and gave it to her: she read it with great approval, and it seems as if I may have scored a real success, on what was certainly a very delicate subject. Time will tell, since 'great approval' doesn't always last, after a second reading. After that, we talked over the subject matter for the next chapter, which it is my target to complete as my last act on this particular trip. I went for a walk, around sunset, going down to the junction of the Main and Side Gorges, and back via the Side Gorge and the LLK Archaeological site, where Louis found the *Homo erectus* calvaria in 1960, for a change. I saw only two dik-dik, but lion could be heard in the distance not long after I got back, there not having been a sound of them yesterday or the day before. After dinner, I had more useful talk with Mary about the next piece of writing.

The giraffe having become rather a feature of my life, I made a plan to go and sit in the Land Rover that is parked not far from their favourite acacia tree, with the flash already set up on my camera, and wait for them to arrive. At 9.30, when Mary went to bed, I could hear one or more of them moving around down by the gate, so got myself in position. I had a long wait, keeping completely still, and nearly dozed off. Eventually, one of them appeared quite suddenly near the tree, as a faint silhouette, having quietly arrived after coming in over quite a different part of the camp fence from where I had expected. It just stood still for ages, checking that all was clear – which it evidently wasn't, because a Mysterious Dark Shape, which I couldn't identify in the darkness, scurried past on the ground towards the centre of the camp, stopped, turned and went back wherever it had come from. A jackal, perhaps? It was too small for a hyaena – unless perhaps it was the smaller striped hyaena, the kind I saw for the first time earlier on this visit. After that, the giraffe moved in to start feeding, so I let fly with the flash, which startled it a bit, but it only went back a few paces, so I thought I'd wait and try one more. This seemed to involve almost as long a wait again, but eventually I got a second shot of it actually feeding, and climbed out of the Land Rover. Exit giraffe, doubtless annoyed that I had fooled it by being there undetected. The whole operation turned out to have taken about an hour and twenty minutes, but I thought it had been well worth the wait – or it will have been if the photos come out. They will probably be a bit faint and distant. As for the giraffe, I hadn't the slightest doubt that it would return in due course to finish its supper, probably with a few colleagues, getting its own back by waking me up in the early hours – indeed, I think I can hear it not far off even now, as I finish writing this. It certainly seems actually true that they never sleep: Mary, whom I consulted about this, says that they just doze on their feet for an hour or so, from time to time.

Sunday, 10 July

This was my last day at Olduvai on this trip, and was always going to be a busy one, with virtually a whole chapter to get written. As on the previous visit, I thought as I got up that it seemed quite inconceivable that, in just 72 hours' time, I should be landing at Heathrow. Nothing seemed different from any other morning, and nothing seemed likely to change or even to be capable of change. The rest of the world was just as remote and unreal as ever.

Those perishing giraffe *did* come back in the night, surprise, surprise. There seemed to be two, and it was 2.44 am when I became aware of their presence. I felt just awake enough to go and peer out of the hut window: there was no moon, but I could just make out a huge giraffe silhouette, only a very few yards away, and there was a warm animal smell. I considered a photograph through the window, decided it wouldn't work and returned to bed. The giraffe noises continued, and before long I was wide awake, grimly setting up the flash on my camera. Just for once, the hut door actually opened quietly, and the giraffe were far too busy browsing to notice, so I sprang out, shooting from the hip, as it were – well, not really, but aiming the camera and focusing in the dark were entirely a matter of guesswork. I took three photos, the giraffe being in no great hurry to leave at first, but they did move off in the end, or at least I heard no more of them.

The next I knew was Kitetu's arrival with the early morning tea. He seemed to have forgotten that it was Sunday, in that he arrived actually slightly early by weekday standards, just when I could have done with the traditional extra 15 minutes. It had been rather a giraffish night, really, and they will doubtless be back tonight for one final occasion, as there are still plenty of their favourite green pods left on the tree.

I worked all day with hardly a break, and had got 12 pages of new text done by supper time, almost completing the draft of the chapter. I might still do so before the end of the day, or if not, tomorrow night in Nairobi would do – or will we be stuck in Arusha, as usual? Meanwhile, Mary sorted out all the luggage that was to go with us on the journey, and eventually it was all packed ready into the vehicle. An early start at 6.30 am has been decreed, because the plan is to go the whole way to Nairobi, collecting Patti Moehlman in Arusha about 11.0 am and seeing Peter and Annie briefly, as we pass through.

During the morning, various Maasai were to be seen, making purposefully towards the camp kitchen area, when Mary wasn't looking, for their regular but entirely unofficial Sunday lunch. Even if those we visited to collect Peter's goat did make their planned move to Masek, there are other groups nearby. It looked as if this might be a bring-your-own-goat lunch party, as two of the earlier arrivals were leading one.

During the day, Mary showed me a solifluge – a curious insect with long feelers, which featured in an incident rather earlier on in the book, and was something I had never heard of prior to writing about it then. At least I now know what they look like. Nothing else much happened, except for Brown Dog's mistaking the pile of luggage assembled by the car for a lamppost, and having to be ejected sharply to prevent disaster. Not really his fault: there aren't too many actual lampposts on the Serengeti Plains, so how was he to know?

I successfully cooked the Sunday evening meal, which was fried fillet steak. Both the genets arrived at the same time, apparently independently, and rather charmingly rubbed faces. I retired to pack up my own luggage around 9.0 pm, since the early start is serious. No sign or sound of giraffe – yet.

Monday, 11 July

We were away by 6.30 am as planned, it being dawn but not yet sunrise. Nearly one and a half hours of driving passed before we actually met another vehicle or saw another person – just as well, perhaps, because up on the top at Ngorongoro we were travelling in thick cloud, and in places visibility was down to just a very few yards. But you can't travel that long in East Africa without seeing something of interest, and nearer to the start of the journey the sights included a new-born giraffe – well, it was old enough to stand, which they do pretty quickly, but absolutely tiny, a few hours old at most – beside a particularly large adult. We also saw a nice group of eland, about ten of them, and nearby a small herd of elegant impala. But soon we had climbed out of the early morning sunshine into the cloud. There was absolutely no sign of the crater to be made out: nothing except the road itself, on which there was abundant evidence of the very recent passage of elephants, in the form of fresh droppings and torn-off branches. We might well have met them – or buffalo, which are frequently around in this part – in the middle of the road at about 10-yards' notice, but fortunately this did not happen. There was an animal, however, at one point, in the mists beside the road where the cloud was just slightly thinner. It scrambled up the bank: hyaena, I thought, and so at first did Mary, but in fact it proved to be a very beautiful lioness, apparently alone, who crouched down on top of the bank when we stopped to admire her and was a bit inclined to snarl. I had finished my film, unfortunately, but I dare say it would have been a poor picture anyhow, with the dim light and all the cloud.

At the Conservation Area checkpoint, on the way down beyond Ngorongoro and out of the cloud again, we picked up an African lady needing a lift to Arusha, who managed to find just enough room amongst the luggage in the back. There was nothing much of note between there and Arusha – well, there were a few baboons at Mto Wa Mbu, where we did not stop this time, and there were flamingo to be seen on Lake Manyara when we looked down on it from the side of the Rift. We arrived after a journey of four and three-quarter hours, not bad in those conditions.

Patti, Peter and Annie were waiting as arranged at the New Arusha Hotel, with varying degrees of hangover after their goat-roast party the night before, which had been a great success. Lala was also there, and a few others. We had coffee and exchanges of news, during the course of which Mary made two trips to the Immigration Office and eventually returned in triumph with her long-awaited new Resident's Permit. We got away after one and a half hours, which was agreed to be amazing for Arusha, taking Patti as passenger to Nairobi, precisely as planned. Indeed, Mary was actually congratulating herself aloud on getting out of Arusha unscathed, when we stopped for a picnic lunch at her usual favourite spot, which is down a little-used side road in a coffee plantation just outside the town. You'd think, after all this time, she'd have known not to say anything aloud: never underestimate Arusha. As she pulled off the road, the front of the car sank into a concealed ditch, with the bumper resting on the far side and the number plate bent flat. There was no serious damage, but it proved impossible to get the vehicle out by using the engine in reverse or by pushing, and there was no wood around to try making a ramp. I tactfully passed up the opportunity of drawing a scholarly comparison with the potholes on Serengeti near the Gol Kopjes, on which she had expressed such strong views a few days back, though the thought did cross my mind. Still, luck had not actually deserted us: within five minutes, I saw a tractor approaching in the distance, so we all waved helplessly at it – just at the moment it turned off the road, as it happened. But fortunately the driver had seen us, and he drove up. Even better, the tractor actually had a towing bar fitted, and carried a heavy chain. Its driver was a very cheerful Tanzanian, much amused by the car's predicament, and delighted to help. In another five minutes, we were out, and the tractor driver was more than happy to accept a reward of fifty Kenyan shillings, which was worth a great deal more than the same sum in Tanzanian money.

We then had the delayed picnic, and drove on to the Kenyan border. Near Longido, a fine oryx ran across the road a short distance ahead: they are not the commonest of the antelopes anywhere, and virtually unknown in this particular part, Mary and Patti thought. Rare or not, it looked just beautiful. At frequent intervals we saw vehicles that had run out of petrol, and everyone seemed to be wanting lifts – we did pick up and drop a few here and there, but there simply wasn't enough passenger space to help very much. In Arusha we had seen a long queue of vehicles at a garage that had no petrol at all and no obvious expectation of receiving any. Actual moving traffic right through Tanzania was predictably light.

Crossing the border was amazingly quick and easy on this occasion: there was no inspection of the vehicle on either side, which was probably just as well, with all the complicated regulations that now exist. Isaac, from the museum, was there on the Kenyan side, having been sent with the necessary permit for Patti: he had the air of one who had been waiting, quite contentedly, for some hours. There were no petrol problems at all, once we had crossed into Kenya: it gave a real boost to morale to be able to say 'Fill it right up'. We had a clear run in to Nairobi, in bright sunshine – there had been a little rain, earlier in the journey, between Ngorongoro and Arusha. Quite a lot of game was to be seen, on the final lap: nothing very uncommon amongst it, but this stretch is often more or less empty of animals.

We eventually reached Mary's house at Langata at around 5.0 pm: three hundred miles in eleven and a half hours, including stops, is not bad, for East Africa. Welcome hot baths for everyone followed, and the evening was relaxed and cheerful, with plans being made for shopping and other such things tomorrow. Before the end of the day, I had also written the final page of my draft of Chapter 12, thereby reaching my target for this trip, which was the death of Louis Leakey in 1972. The first time I ever came to East Africa, which was three years before that, he met me himself at the airport in the late evening and drove me to this house: next morning, we breakfasted on the verandah before he sent me off to Olduvai in his own Volvo car, with a hired driver, to meet Mary for the first time. That was certainly the first step on the path that has brought me here again today, though this is not a matter of any moment for the text I am here to produce. Writing in the first person singular for someone else enables one to maintain total invisibility, if one wishes, provided one has not been incautious enough to play a significant role in the story, and I certainly fulfil that condition. Perhaps at the end I shall be instructed to write myself into the acknowledgements, and then again, perhaps not: time will tell. The diary text is quite a different matter, of course.

Tuesday, 12 July

It was quite cool for breakfast on the verandah at about 6.30 am, but it developed later into a pleasant and not too hot day. We drove into Nairobi, and went first to the museum, meeting Richard Leakey very briefly and then going on to Hazel's office to collect mail and messages. Mary, who had insisted on doing almost all the driving yesterday, was now having a reaction of tiredness, having slept badly. Patti, by contrast, couldn't wait to 'hit the town', as she put it: more specifically, she proposed to hit the bank first, then the market, and then various other hittable institutions, having a long shopping list (or perhaps it's a hit list) for half of Serengeti as well as for herself, apparently even including some early Christmas shopping for some of her younger relatives back in the States. I had a rather shorter list, but was quite easily persuaded to act as Patti's porter – just as well, too, since her first hit involved drawing out 300 US dollars' worth of local currency (which in the event proved to be nowhere near enough), and her second was to buy three shoulder baskets, for immediate use. One could definitely tell that this was to be a serious shopping trip. So, we had a highly diverting morning, acquiring beaded belts, carved soapstone chess sets, sundry semi-precious stone necklaces, spare parts for two Land Rovers, kangas, shirts and goodness knows what else – oh, and about half of the contents of both the chemist's and confectioner's counters at Woolworth's, where Patti spent so much money that she was given a free copy of a large book of wildlife photographs by the delighted management. I think I had only contrived to buy three items from my own list by lunch time, but I had somehow not been short of things to carry. One does one's best to be of assistance – or, to put it another way, people soon realise that one is an absolute sucker.

Hazel collected us by car to go and have lunch in her office with Mary, who had been joined by Jonathan Leakey (the only one of the three sons of Louis and Mary that I had not previously met) and his wife Janet, who was fairly imminently expectant. In the best traditions of literary scholarship, I took the opportunity to check with Jonathan whether Sonia Cole had been right, in her biography of Louis (*Leakey's Luck*), when she said that Jonathan (who has been a herpetologist from an early age) had survived bites from both green and black mambas, something which Mary had hotly denied.

'Yes,' he said. 'Yes, I'm sure I told you at the time, Mother.'

I was not wholly surprised, but not very thrilled, to hear that Mary, in her tired state, was having reservations about parts of the newly completed final chapter of Part II, which I had left with her to read while Patti and I shopped. I myself had thought it was a lovely piece of text, which followed directly on from the previous chapter, dealing with one of the more difficult major topics, and it certainly contained nothing which we had not already discussed. Oh well.

A second shopping session took place during the afternoon, the heavy acquisitions of the morning having been sent back to Langata with Mary, who had decided to go home and rest for a few hours. Essentially, it was more of the same, though this time Patti also had some messages to deliver and arrangements to make, so after I had accompanied her in my porter role to a shop called Abdullah bin Abdullah (which somehow sounded a more interesting name than, say, Marks & Spencer), selling brightly coloured cotton items in what proved to be the wrong sizes, I continued on my own, being by now thoroughly familiar with the way round. I completed my own modest list of items, which were mainly presents for the children, and couldn't resist adding a few avocados and a couple of mangoes, for which I didn't really have room.

Eventually, Hazel gave us a lift out to Langata, where a badly needed cup of tea was quickly provided, and I then settled down to go through the text of the latest chapter with Mary. As I feared, she had had second thoughts about some of the passages in which she had revealed personal information, all of which we had discussed and agreed, and I had written up accordingly. For the first time, I actually began to feel a little weary, but I made the more factual of the corrections she was requiring, and we agreed to leave the other points, which I shall endeavour to defend for the text's sake, to be reconsidered in due course. We also discussed the dates for my next and last visit: it looks likely that I will travel out on 12 September, which might sound a long way off, but in fact is just eight weeks from today.

After that, as the closing event of my present visit, we went out to dinner, Mary, Hazel, Patti and myself, to a remarkable restaurant, relatively recently opened, I believe, though already very well known, called The Carnivore. It was vast, but seemed to be completely full. The system is that there is a huge central fire, over which a continuous supply of different meats and kebabs is roasted on long iron spikes: each table has little dishes of sauces and vegetables, and waiters are constantly circulating, adding as much meat, of the many different kinds available (including the meat of some game animals), as the customers think they can eat, to the large iron plates with which they have been issued. You pay a flat rate sum on your way in, and are then left to get as much value as you wish for it in terms of food consumed. I must say, it was very good, but some of the customers seemed to be consuming unbelievably large amounts of everything just on principle, and quite soon I found myself tired of watching them and thinking that it would be nice if the African population of Serengeti, much of which is meatless not from choice, could be brought here for a square meal now and again. Life in Kenya and Tanzania is really very different.

We left about 10.15 and, when I had collected my luggage, the patient Hazel kindly drove me out to the airport, in good time for check in at 11.0 pm. It looked as if the flight was not going to be too full, and that was indeed the case. The plane had quite blatantly arrived from the dreaded South Africa: I wonder why they let it land? It was on time, and the whole boarding procedure worked very smoothly. I was surprised that my case only weighed 16 kilos, in the end – ah, but they didn't think to weigh my handluggage, did they? Just as well. We took off a mere six minutes late at 00.36 or, by London time, 10.36 pm. There was a baby in good voice a few rows away, but it sounded to my experienced ear as if it was about to go clunk shortly, and so it did. The captain informed us that yester-day's temperature in London, where a heatwave was in progress, had reached 90 degrees – that's hotter than any temperature I have encountered in Africa on this trip, if so. I declined the offer of headphones for music or a film: what, at *this* time of night? I dozed off as we flew north towards Sudan and Egypt. We shall turn left at Crete, the captain said. I thought I could probably safely leave it to him.

Wednesday, 13 July

I dozed on and off, reasonably successfully, for three to four hours. The sun was up by 4.30, though it had been light for an hour before that. Perhaps that vague shape below was Crete, because we seemed to be turning left. Breakfast was served over the Alps at about 5.30: there was a certain amount of mist and cloud, but this time many summits of the Swiss and Austrian Alps were visible. Mont Blanc was said to be on the other side of the aircraft.

The flight was non-stop, and we landed at Heathrow nearly 20 minutes early, thanks to a following wind: it was evidently true about the heatwave, because ground temperature was already 66 degrees, and it was only 6.45 am. The queue at Passport Control was quite long, as more than one Jumbo jet had arrived at about the same moment, but everything else was very quick and efficient. The coach I needed to catch to Reading was already in place and waiting, and at Reading Station the Oxford train was also actually in, so I found myself at Oxford Station by 9.0 am. Things looked less parched than one might have expected, if it has really been as hot as that for some while. The taxidriver was full of mete-orological statistics, which didn't leave me much wiser, but that may have been my fault rather than his.

At 60 Banbury Road, the accumulation of mail could have been a lot worse, and everything at the Research Centre seemed to be in good order. I had fought my way through the whole pile by the end of the morning, assisted by doses of coffee. To have lunch at St Cross College, Oxford, seemed a reasonable follow up to dinner in Nairobi, Kenya, and breakfast over the Alps, though I have never yet learned to take sequences like that quite for granted. The heatwave soon proved all that it had been advertised to be, and conditions seemed much more humid in Oxford than they were anywhere I had visited in Kenya or Tanzania. After lunch, I collected more mail from the house in Hamilton Road, empty while the children and Fiona are away in France, and made for Fordwells and home. The builders had made considerable progress, but it appeared that certain prob-lems over the kitchen units were now causing delay ('as such', I shouldn't wonder). Three weeks' dust was all too clearly visible over everything, and quite a lot of furniture seemed to have got moved and needed putting back where it belonged. I delivered news and small African gifts to neighbours. The evening was enlivened by a power failure, said to be caused by a blow-out at a cable-carrying pole a mile or so away. Noises of fire engines could be heard – very unusual at Fordwells, and rather different from the evening noises at

Olduvai, I couldn't help thinking.

Power was restored by about 9.30 pm. I struggled to read more mail, and only when I got down to the dull circulars at the bottom of the pile did I finally fall asleep, sitting in my chair. Something (not a giraffe, for once) woke me with a start at 12.15 am, and for several moments I was completely unable to work out where I was, or how I had got there. Of course, the obvious solution would have been to read this diary, but somehow, at the time, I just didn't think of it.

The third visit, September to October 1983

Monday, 12 September

I was in bed by 2.45 am, with all luggage safely packed – not too bad, with so much to be done. A busy morning in Oxford followed, spent trying to catch up with essential correspondence before leaving, with many interruptions from telephone calls and from visitors arriving with packages to add to my already heavy luggage. The suitcase itself was comfortably under the weight limit, but I thought they'd better not weigh my small handcase which, for all its deceptive appearance, must be almost as heavy as the case itself. It's odd what peculiar items other people cause one to carry, that might not have high priority on one's own list. Somewhere amongst it all, a plastic waterpistol, ordered by Patti for use against the bulbuls, was tucked into one shoe and there were Land Rover engine parts in another. There was an extremely heavy box of photographic paper, which actually cost over £23 – I hoped they still wanted it. I didn't even know what other various paper packages might contain, and dreaded to think, though there was no reason to suppose there was anything actually explosive or illegal – well, probably not. The large jar of Marmite requested by Peter and Annie could best be added to a duty free bag, when I got one, like last time, I thought, and the same went for a Camembert cheese for Mary, brought during the morning by a cheerful lady called Sally Moyes, whom I hadn't previously met, but must look up when I get back. She used to live in Arusha – Heaven help her – when her then husband was a local Director for Oxfam, and she knows various members of the cast of this saga. We accordingly had coffee and exchanged gossip, which delayed things further, though pleasantly enough.

Two of the phone calls were from the publishers, Rainbird, in London, with last-minute comments on the text thus far, which their person in charge of the autobiography, Karen Goldie-Morrison, had read while on holiday, from which she had just returned. Mary is not a fan of hers, and always refers to her as 'that Goldie woman', but I find her perfectly amenable to work with. I should think the text at this stage, whatever may happen to it later, might not be bad holiday reading, and Karen certainly seemed pleased with it. The two phone calls totalled at least an hour.

I salvaged five minutes for lunch at St Cross College, and walked to the bus station to check personally on departure times for Heathrow, since I had got it wrong on both previous occasions. They seemed to have cancelled the service that goes directly to Heathrow, but there were a 3.15 and a 4.05 that would get there eventually, and I decided to aim for the first of those. More desperate letter-writing and a trip to the bank a mile and a half away in Summertown had to be achieved. By 3.05 I was as ready as I ever would be. Jack Hewlett, faithful and indefatigable caretaker of the Research Centre, kindly drove me to the bus station, as he did last time and yes, there was indeed a 3.15, so off we went, via Abingdon and what seemed to be most of Southern England, though the 3.15, being just too early to pick up school children, is actually a quick and efficient service. I contrived to finish addressing a few more letters and managed to post them when the bus stopped at Abingdon, without getting left behind. The weather was fine, without much sunshine: the first touches of early autumn were to be seen in the Thames Valley's always beautiful beech woods, but only if one looked hard. The first signs of the wheat planted in late summer could already be seen coming up in the fields. What is it about a bus entering Maidenhead that sends one to sleep? – I remember that happening to me before, on this particular route. I was wide awake again by Heathrow, however. England seemed remarkably empty of people on this September Monday, and the airport was quiet too. I acquired the essential box of cigars for Mary at the duty free shop, and added the planned items to the duty free bag. It was a mercy that the cheese brought by Sally Moyes was a properly packed

Camembert, as her original plan had been to send a quantity of Gorgonzola, which might not have been in its own box. I would doubtless find out tomorrow the validity or otherwise of my theory that Customs at the far end of a journey don't often bother to examine duty free bags.

Boarding began on time. The man at the check-in thought the plane would be pretty full, though there didn't seem to be many people in the Departure Lounge. The plane was a Tri-Star, not a 747 – somewhat smaller. A slightly forceful British Airways lady at the departure gate was telling a miscellaneous American that he certainly couldn't take more than one piece of handluggage on board because there was a weight problem, so I joined the queue for her colleague instead, who was displaying no such inhibitions. The plane as a whole didn't look very full to me, but the answer appeared to be that the tourist section was full and the rest wasn't, so everyone was either right or wrong, according to taste.

With a slightly sinking heart, I found myself next to a 5-year old Asian girl (there were lots of Asians travelling), who was charming but *very* fidgety. I suspected it was about 18 years too early to be sitting next to her on a long flight. Well, maybe 16 years. We left on time, and a gin-and-tonic seemed a good idea. My growing experience of the jet-set life reminded me that wine with the meal is now free in tourist class: the other customers didn't look as if they knew that, to judge by their drinks orders, and naturally no one was going to tell them. We made a tight turn immediately after take-off, to cross the coast near Hastings, not far, I suspect, from Rye, where I used to live, but it was already dark. Dinner was served somewhere over Italy, and that finally sent the young Asian lady out like a light. Her mother and I exchanged a wordless glance full of parental experience and international understanding. The moon, about at its first quarter, started the journey properly upright in the English manner, but could be seen to be leaning well back by the end of dinner. Weren't we all? Perhaps it too was tired after a hectic few days. By an optical illusion, it looked imminently likely to collide with the flashing wing-tip light, but then suddenly vanished from view. When I next see it, it will doubtless be flat on its back. I shall never understand the sheer geometry of this moon business. Perhaps the wing-tip really does knock it over? Enough was enough: it was time to sleep, while one could.

Tuesday, 13 September

What is the good, one asks oneself, of children going out like a light, if they are then going to toss and kick in their sleep all night, and one keeps finding their feet quite literally in one's face? So I rested rather than slept. We landed five minutes ahead of time, in pitch darkness still, there having been only a bare trace of light around the rim of the world before the descent to Nairobi began. On the ground, it seemed to be cloudy and mild. For some reason, it took ages for the luggage to reach the customs hall, although the preceding passport clearance had been quick and efficient (and no sign of worry, this time, about the presence of South African stamps in anyone's passport). I decided they must be bringing the cases round in a wheelbarrow, as so few arrived at a time. Meanwhile, another flight had landed, so a major queue built up at the customs desks, further delayed when one lady began a loud and very long argument about paying duty. That proved quite helpful, because a senior customs *bwana* – the kind that wears a smart suit – had to come and help out, to get things moving, and it was clearly beneath his dignity to make more than a token search of one's largest piece of luggage. So I was soon bearing my heavy and dubious (but ultimately completely innocent) cargo through the exit, and there was Hazel, patiently waiting.

She drove me to her own house for breakfast, because Mary's house has temporarily become Philip Leakey's campaign headquarters for the Kenya parliamentary election, due in a fortnight: Mary has fled, and is staying with Richard. She has arranged to come to Hazel's house to collect me, and we are to leave for Tanzania this very morning. That just allowed time for a reviving wash and shave and a nice breakfast, before there she was, looking well and cheerful. Some intermittent stomach troubles that had bothered her during my last visit had been diagnosed as an incipient ulcer, which was now responding well to a prescribed diet, so she was now claiming to feel very fit. With her was Kabebo, of the Olduvai camp staff, happy to be returning after having spent the last 10 weeks waiting for renewal of a permit. Off we went, leaving just after 9.15 and reaching the border at Namanga by 11.25. Everything was looking very dry: there were few animals to be seen, though there was the occasional circling eagle. Crossing the border was very easy this time, and took only 50 minutes. Following tradition, Mary declared her large and varied cargo, much of which was doubtless technically illegal for import, as 'four bags of dog biscuits and a few groceries', and by the same tradition the Tanzanian customs staff made no search of the vehicle and charged 300 shillings duty. Honour was satisfied. At the border police post, we picked up one or two local people who wanted a lift towards Arusha, and proceeded on our way as usual. For the first time in recent memory, there was actually no petrol to be had at the petrol station on the Kenyan side of the border, but fortunately we had enough spare on board in jerrycans to complete the journey. The sun came out, and the air cleared to provide a beautiful day. The only delays along the way were for fauna in the middle of the road, including a particularly stupid ostrich and some fairly professional Maasai goats.

Mary's original plan was to by-pass the main part of Arusha altogether, but she fortunately remembered in time that Omari, the mechanic, had to be collected there and that some tea was needed for the camp, so we made for the town centre after all and had a sandwich lunch at a cafe Mary occasionally uses. I took the chance to send an 'arrived safely' card home, as promised, and then we started meeting people, always a risk in Arusha, including Margaret Gibb, with whom it had been arranged that we would spend the night at Karatu, since starting as late as we did from Nairobi means not reaching Olduvai the same day. Arusha seemed to be in a staggeringly benign and helpful mood: Mary actually got some permit she needed renewed while she waited, Omari was where he should be at the arranged meeting time, the sun shone, the jacaranda trees were in spectacular bloom, the desired tea was actually available, and the shop next to where we bought it was called Happy Watch Maker, which I liked. We were on our way before 3 pm, with absolutely no disasters having occurred and Mto wa Mbu the next scheduled stop. Amazing!

In spite of valiant efforts, I found myself dozing off intermittently on the next stretch, after the rather sleepless night, but I don't think I missed anything of interest. The late afternoon became increasingly beautiful – even Mary remarked on it. At Mto wa Mbu, the market stalls were all packing up for the day, it being about 5.20, but they unpacked again fast enough when they saw me approaching with a purposeful look. There were no tourists about, so I ended up having a quick walk round and then being encouraged to stand at an empty stall while goods were paraded for my benefit by various young Tanzanians, trading rivals, but all immensely cheerful. I'm sure any local expert would have felt I did not drive a hard enough bargain, but I was well satisfied with my acquisitions: two baskets, one snuffbox, one calabash, one beadwork belt (a young warrior's) and two beadwork 'wristwatches', while the other side seemed ecstatic with its two old (real) wind-up wristwatches, two tee shirts, sundry bars of soap, one hat, two pairs of mirror sunglasses, one penknife and even the plastic duty free bag, for which, as last time, there was great competition. I have reserved a few tradeable items in my luggage, this time, since who can tell what retail opportunities may present themselves at Olduvai? While all that was going on, Mary had done a staggeringly good deal with tomatoes at the fruit stall, so everyone was happy.

On we went, up the Rift escarpment, with beautiful light below on Lake Manyara and the game park: one elephant was visible amongst the trees, with buffalo and other game dotted here and there out towards the lake, and strong pink drifts of flamingos. I took four photographs, but they will do little justice to that view. We reached Gibb's Farm around 6.20, just ahead of several vehicles carrying local African government officials, who are also spending a night there, and had to be introduced to Mary. She and I each have a comfortable hut with suite of double bedroom and shower, the windows hung with bright curtains made from local *kangas*. In spite of the lateness of the hour, trays of tea immediately arrived, and we were invited to have dinner with Margaret and her husband Per, in their own dining room, instead of in the main restaurant. Their part of the buildings has some beautiful Makonde carved wooden combs hung as wall decorations. Mary laughed herself into a state of complete helplessness at the sight of a large and comprehensively ghastly drooping candle, in an incongruous brass holder, standing on the floor, which she decided looked vaguely obscene: she is clearly much restored to health, and that is very good to see.

Afterwards, as I walked back to my hut through the garden of flowering shrubs, there was moonlight and bright stars, and the piercingly beautiful sound of two nightjars calling to each other on the wing from high up, not able to be seen. Lovely liquid musical notes – the Olduvai nightjars, which one sometimes hears, have less melodious voices. The bed was extremely comfortable.

Wednesday, 14 September

I was deeply asleep when early morning tea arrived at 7.0 am: it might have come earlier still, but Mary told me she had requested that it be delayed till then because she thought I was in need of what she regarded as 'a long lie-in' after all the travelling. After breakfast, we purchased supplies of coffee grown on the farm and plenty of fresh vegetables and some fruit for camp, including, of all things, some fresh mulberries, which apparently grow particularly well here. Then we went on our way towards Olduvai, first collecting two more members of the Olduvai camp staff from Karatu village. As on previous trips, the spectacular road climbing up from beyond Karatu to the rim of Ngorongoro crater bore abundant fresh signs of elephant, but once again we didn't actually encounter any.

At Ngorongoro village, we made a visit to the headquarters of the Conservation Unit, and found it buzzing with news of Mary's impending visit to China, and also of her plans to leave Tanzania for good shortly, both of which she believed she had kept completely secret. This is the famous 'bush telegraph' in action, again: it works effectively and swiftly, and one never seems to find out just how. The Conservation Unit had recently received supplies of both petrol and diesel fuel, and the people there were kind enough to offer Mary 100 litres of the former and 200 litres of the latter, to boost her stocks at Olduvai, which she eagerly accepted, though we had no room to carry them today. Next we went to the post office and the garage, and then Omari announced that he needed to go and have an injection at the local surgery, which he did, though no one could establish exactly why.

Once again, everything seemed to be going extraordinarily well with the journey and all the errands, but before very long Mary and I were telling each other that we should have known all along that it was too good to last, as the car's gearbox suddenly and without notice decided that it would no longer allow the engaging of either first or second gear, which are precisely the two gears one needs most on the long, rough and steeply winding descent from Ngorongoro and the Volcanic Highlands to Serengeti far below. We struggled on in third gear as best we could, with much wear on the brakes, and twice had to get out to push. The second of these occasions, while undoubtedly good exercise, was only partially successful, and we ended up with the engine stalled on a short up-slope – though the road is always ultimately descending, it does so in a very undulating manner, so there is no shortage of brief climbs too, sometimes quite steep. We were just putting rocks under the back wheels to stop the car sliding backwards, when a Land Rover appeared from the opposite direction, packed with Africans who all got out eagerly to help, but at precisely the same moment Mary suddenly succeeded in finding bottom gear and started to move forward, so they never got a proper chance to join in. There were still about six miles to go to the camp, but she dared not try changing up to second gear, since there would be no possibility whatsoever of getting across the Gorge itself without use of first. So we crept slowly and noisily along in bottom gear, with me holding the gear lever firmly in place, in case it tried to jump out again, which it certainly seemed to have a mind to do. Eventually we made it, around mid-day.

We found that Peter and Annie Jones were away for the day, having gone over to the hospital at Endulen for injections, after being in contact with a dog that had turned out to have rabies. They were also helping a Canadian television crew with some filming, no doubt at Laetoli: apparently it is shortly due to come to Olduvai. Otherwise all was well, and there was a predictably warm welcome from the dogs and from the camp staff.

We had seen very few animals on our way down from Ngorongoro (even allowing for all the noise we were making), but Kitetu reported that last Friday lions had walked right past the camp gate in the morning, just when he was about to take the dogs for their walk. Mary also told me that, during the time since my last visit, half a dozen wild dogs had taken up temporary residence in a thicket near the camp, and had been hunting the dik-diks. Wild dogs are really rather dangerous to have around. Matthew, as chief Dalmatian, had taken their presence as a gross invasion of his territory and a personal insult, and one morning had succeeded in breaking out of camp and attacking one of the wild dogs, which had just killed a dik-dik. He successfully took the dik-dik carcass away from the wild dog and drove it off, returning to the camp covered in blood, to general alarm, but fortunately it turned out that none of the blood was his own. The wild dogs appeared to have decided to move on elsewhere at that point, or at least they had not been seen recently.

Other animal news included the fact that the giraffe, who had been such persistent feeders on the camp acacia tree during the later part of my last visit, had continued their incursions after I left until they had eaten all the shoots and seed pods they could reach and had then brought down most of the electric cables in camp and wandered amiably off in search of other trees in an edible state. They had not been seen for a long while, but Kitetu said that only last night three giraffe had come right into the camp again. The word must have gone round that I was returning.

I was not too tired to begin work by mid-afternoon. Mary had prepared a lot of new information cards, which I sorted through, and we discussed the principal topics that remain to be covered and the best ways of getting everything done in the time available. This was very useful, and after dinner we talked until about 10 pm. Both the guest huts are free at the moment and should remain so while I am here, so I can use one to live in and have the other for writing, which will mean a lot less moving about of work. I went and adjusted the furniture in them accordingly. Olduvai at the moment is hot and dry by day, and at night, apparently, there is usually quite a strong wind. The temperature today reached 88 degrees indoors, so I'm not sure what it will have been out in the sun. There have been only 13 millimetres of rain since my last visit: no wonder there is little game around to be seen.

I had not supposed that Charles, the Maasai member of the Olduvai guide staff, would have forgotten the pair of jeans that he asked me to bring him on this visit. On this very first evening, a charming note from him arrived by hand of one of the camp staff – delivered to me, I noted, at a carefully chosen moment when Mary was not around to see. It was addressed 'Comrade, Leakeys camp' and read as follows:

> 14.9.83. 2.30 pm. Dear Comrade; I hope your fine. We also are fine a lot. I would like to know if you have brought me the thing (trouser). I have got three pairs of beads. But if they're not enough I will give you money, says Charles.

I sent a note back to say yes, I had brought the jeans, and I would see him when Peter got back.

I went to bed not too late, by my usual standards. There was bright moonlight, and on the hills around one could clearly see the flames of grass fires in several places – on Lemagrut, on Olmoti and on the long side of Ngorongoro. Mary had explained about the fires: the Maasai start them, entirely illegally, to make the new grass grow greener for their herds and flocks, on the hillsides where they graze them, but the fires run out of control and often destroy considerable areas of forest too. That is bad from many points of view and the Maasai do not understand that it leads to serious soil erosion and ultimately to actual loss of grazing land.

The night sounds as I went to bed included the roaring of lions, some distance off. I felt that I had hardly been away.

Thursday, 15 September

I was woken once – or was it twice? – in the night by loud roaring of lions down in the Gorge. It sounded as if there might be two lots, perhaps disputing territory. Early morning tea arrived at 6.15, revealing a minor technical problem: the trouble with the door in the hut where I am now sleeping is that it doesn't have a latch that is openable from both sides, and because of the strong wind at night I have to latch it firmly on the inside to keep it shut. That in turn means one actually has to get up and open the door either when the tea arrives, or else shortly before it is due. It's still well worthwhile, either way, of course, but surely any proper creative writer ought to be able to fix something up, when it's a question of staying in bed rather than getting up to answer a door?

I noted that the temperature was 60 degrees at 7.0 am, and it then rose to reach 90 by 1.0 pm, staying there or just above until about 5. It must have been well over 100 out in the sun. Mary and I worked with the tape recorder for an hour or more to start the day, much more successfully than on the previous visit. The key to success seems to be to let her have both the machine and the cards in her own hands, and to ask as few questions as possible, just being sure to write down a heading before she starts each bit, and then to add notes that will assist when listening to the play back. Also the fact that she is feeling much better is clearly a help. After that, I went carefully through all the cards she had written and read various other sources relevant to the chapter on Laetoli, including Don Johanson's book *Lucy*, which is certainly going to loom a bit large later on, because Mary clearly hasn't a good word to say about it or its author. She has plenty of bad ones, though, and plans to use them all. Eventually I stopped reading and began writing, though perhaps not progressing quite as rapidly as I might have done if it had been a mere 80 degrees.

After lunch, Peter and Annie arrived, though it transpired that they were only passing through on their way to Arusha, where they need to go to deal with permits and to try and establish a petrol supply of their own. I gave Peter all the mail and the odds and ends I had brought in my luggage, though we deferred the main exchange of news until Monday, when they should be back at Olduvai. Peter said they had seen two large lions yesterday, on their way to Endulen. No sooner had they left on their journey to Arusha than the vigilant Charles arrived, clearly determined not to wait any longer than necessary for his jeans, so I gave them to him. He had brought two nice beaded wrist bands, of just the kind that I think my daughter Biddy will like, newly made by the local Maasai at his request, plus a fairly simple bead-and-wire neck ornament with the usual flat triangular metal pendant, nice but unexciting. We agreed to let Peter and Annie decide, when they returned, what balance was owing for the jeans after this exchange. The jeans were a great success.

'I see you do not forget a promise,' said Charles gravely. I wonder whether he really will go to the Institute of Archaeology at London University, where he apparently has a provisional place to study Archaeology. His essays should in time make dynamic reading, to judge from yesterday's letter, but I'm not at all sure how he will manage to get the necessary funding.

The Canadian film crew arrived in a Land Rover at about 3.0 pm, but Mary dealt with them herself, and they spent the afternoon photographing the casts of the famous Laetoli hominid footprints in oblique sunlight. They arranged to return tomorrow to take shots of the Gorge and to conduct an interview with Mary, after which they will go on to the Ngorongoro Crater. The word from Peter and Annie was that everyone so far – they have been all over the place in Tanzania and also in Kenya – has found them very nice, but has thought them rather amateurish and not at all sure what their film is actually about. Mary was in full agreement with this verdict after her afternoon with them.

By a little after 6.0 pm the temperature was down towards 80 and a mild easterly wind had begun to blow, so I walked out in the general area of the airstrip and watched the sun go down. It seemed to disappear very rapidly once it actually touched the horizon: perhaps it had found some soft ground over there to sink into, which it certainly wouldn't have done where I was on the airstrip, where the remains of what had been grass crackled as I walked on it. There was not an animal to be seen in all the wide landscape, as far as the eye could reach in any direction, but that is what one would expect, as there is just nothing for them.

During the day, Omari and Yoka worked busily on Mary's car, and got all the gears functioning again. Tomorrow she will send them in it up to Ngorongoro, with empty drums to collect the petrol and diesel fuel that she was offered: that road would surely provide a rigorous test for car repair work by any mechanic in the world.

No ravens came into camp today, and they only made a brief visit to drink yesterday, so presumably the lions must be finding something to hunt, and there must be carcasses for a raven to scavenge. Small birds were numerous all day at the drinking trough: several dozen canaries and finches, and quite a few of the brightly coloured so-called lovebirds, which are actually small parrakeets. I must try and take a telephoto shot of them sometime, but it's not easy, as the trough is not often in the sunlight.

The wind gathered strength after dark. I had made a rough wedge for my door in an attempt to solve the early morning tea delivery problem, but the wind soon got too strong for the wedge to hold the door, and I had to revert to the inside latch. Ah well, back to the drawing board for that one.

Friday, 16 September

That's a familiar date: my sister Molly's birthday, back in distant England. I don't think I actually recalled that, however, when I was woken at 3.30 am by loud lion roaring somewhere nearby in the Gorge. One of the lions had a very hoarse voice, and was evidently the one known to Mary as 'Laryngitic Lion' – she had been telling me about him. Her names for animals are always simple and to the point, as in this case and also as in 'Brown Dog' or 'Roof Cat' back at Langata. Similarly, the cat at Langata that had got caught in a wire noose and was released by Mary at the cost of a scratched hand (see 20 June), has now become known as Noose Cat, and incidentally is said to be doing well. Anyhow, Laryngitic Lion is currently a regular visitor to this part of the Gorge, and was certainly in good voice on this occasion, or as good voice as a laryngitic lion can be. Two and a half hours later, I made a classic mistake over the door and the early morning tea: waking up shortly before it was due to arrive, I got sleepily out of bed to unlatch the door so that Kitetu could come in and, having done so, absent-mindedly relatched it again, thereby

Mary with film crew under big acacia tree in camp

destroying the entire strategy. Not all the *Karibus* in the world could cure that, when the tea came, so out I got again. One day I shall get it right.

I spent the day writing, and by the end of it had completed Chapter 13, subject to destruction by Mary in due course, no doubt. Meanwhile, the Canadian television film crew came and went, still very vague about what it was they actually wanted to film. I took a photograph of Mary, hemmed in by the camera and microphones, with a view of the Gorge behind, which might be quite a graphic portrayal of her in meet-the-public mode, if it comes out. The filming took up much less time than had been anticipated, and the television people are said to be paying the Olduvai Research Fund 1500 dollars for visiting, so that was good.

A man from the Tanzanian Antiquities Department also arrived, quite separately, while they were with us. He is planning a new museum at Arusha, and wanted advice about it. I didn't actually say that in my view the words 'planning' and 'Arusha' should not occur in the same sentence. It turned out that he was also hoping Mary would be able to arrange the finance for the project, which was not even a remote possibility, but apart from that he seemed to make some useful progress.

All the visitors stayed to lunch. The television people had been filming solidly in East Africa since July, and looked tired out. I made polite conversation to the only one who seemed actually conscious, and he turned out to have been at Cambridge just after the Second World War. I told him about microwear analysis and other of the more television-worthy aspects of prehistoric stone tools, and he said they had better come to Oxford and film some of it. In my experience, that is the sort of thing people frequently say but never do, even though they may mean it at the time, so I shall believe it only when it happens.

The temperature was around 90 degrees all the afternoon, but a slight breeze made it seem less hot than yesterday. In the evening, I walked down to the bottom of the Main

Gorge, keeping a sharp eye open for Laryngytic Lion and the lads, but no wildlife at all was to be seen. There was a beautiful post-sunset sky, when I climbed back up again, and darkness came quite quickly, so I went to see if the resident porcupine (which I have still not met) was about, and waited a while, but there was no sign of it. Heavy concentrations of smoke from the grass fires had built up in the distance by the evening, and after dark there were numerous points of flame to be seen on the surrounding hills, some of them occasionally flaring brightly. I counted 10 separate ones on Olmoti alone.

The positions of the stars have clearly altered a lot in the eight weeks since I was here: this time I remembered to bring a star map, but at present the moon is very bright and right overhead, so I will wait to use it.

Mary's Peugeot went up to Ngorongoro during the day, with the empty petrol drums, as planned, and returned safely with them filled, though apparently they had to stop and adjust the gears once on the journey. This was of some interest, since my own journey back in it is supposed to happen in less than a fortnight.

In the evening I found that a further Maasai bead ornament, similar to the last of the previous three, but better made, had arrived from Charles, notwithstanding the arrangement to wait until Peter had returned. There was another note: Charles's style of letter writing seems to be evolving, perhaps partly under the influence of my note to him:

```
Dear Mr Derek R, I hope you're fine this morning. The trouser you
gave me yesterday is realy fine and more interesting. I got the
other thing from the Maasai this morning. I will find more, as soon
as possible. Thanking you in advance, Charles.
```

Saturday, 17 September

There were no lions last night, so I slept undisturbed. That was probably just as well, as the working day got off to a somewhat inauspicious start. Mary needed to read right through my chapter completed yesterday, before we could begin the next session of recording, which would follow on from it. I was quite happy with it as a piece of text, and parts of it were in fact rather carefully planned to establish an order for what the rest of the book would contain, and to leave various threads for use later on, in due time. It certainly contained nothing controversial, and was simply the writing up of matters Mary and I had already fully discussed. However, almost as soon as she began to read it, she started to complain about order, accuracy and style: I'm quite happy to listen to valid criticism and useful suggestions, but after a while most of her comments struck me as destructive perversity largely for its own sake. Having had quite a lot of that in smaller doses before, I decided not to stand for it again on this scale, so I reached across, took the offending pages gently from her, and quietly tore them into small pieces, which I placed in a neat pile on the table. Since everything I write at Olduvai is in longhand, with no duplicate copies, this established as a fact the loss of several hours' writing time, and Mary knows the schedule is tight. It also led to a certain coolness, which lasted for the rest of the working day, but that was a risk one had to take. I suspect that no one has ever done that or anything like it to her before, or anyhow not for many years. In the immediate aftermath, we discussed with exaggerated politeness an alternative order for the chapter which she would find acceptable, and she started recording the next lot of information from the cards.

I spent the rest of the day rewriting the chapter in a style as featureless as grey tidal mud, which really is what she prefers, when one gets down to it, and thinking cross thoughts about distinguished ladies who are used to having everyone falling over themselves to do exactly what they want at the first sneeze, regardless of the nature or quality of the product, and speculating that such people would do better to employ ghost-writers with no original ideas, no background knowledge of the subject and a low-grade pass in O Level English. Wounded pride, of course. I later became quite absorbed in the sheer craftsmanship required to create a perfectly featureless style: flat as central Serengeti, if you obliterate the Precambrian inselbergs and drive away all the game – only that is exactly the sort of simile that has to be ruthlessly excluded, of course. So I cheered up considerably, even though my efforts will be wasted on herself, who will doubtless regard the revised text as a major improvement.

In mid-afternoon, while Mary was resting and I was writing, there was a small but rather exciting whirlwind. It was quite still and hot, when this thing started up as a circular air current near a low bush about 40 yards away, in front of the hut where I was working, with quite a noise – indeed, I thought it was a vehicle coming at first. One quite often sees small dust-devils, and sometimes larger ones, but this was different, and it ripped the top off the bush and sent tufts of grass whirling into the air, perhaps as high as 200 feet. (Just like Mary reading one of my chapters, I thought, perhaps a little uncharitably – and then again, perhaps not.) The whirlwind staggered around the camp compound, spent a little while down by the gate, and then dissipated itself on its way towards the Side Gorge. All around, meanwhile, the other trees and bushes remained quite still. It was a very odd episode, and after it was over I walked across to the bush where it had begun and found that the broken stem was around three inches across: the broken-off top was quite heavy – it hadn't managed to throw that up in the air.

At tea time, four beautiful and large giraffe walked elegantly across in front of the camp gate, with equal spaces between them, and then went searching for green shoots on the nearby acacias. Afterwards, I completed the repair of my chapter and had a very pleasing warm shower and hair wash.

I thought I would wait until Mary was on at least her second pre-dinner whisky before joining her, and when I did so was very pleasantly surprised to find a mood of benevolence and actual apology. So that enabled me to say no, no, it must have been at least partly my fault, and after all it was her life story, and who was I to impose my writing style on it or add interpretative comments in her name?, etc, etc. That was all perfectly true, apart from which it's wonderful what fringe benefits a traditional English education occasionally provides. So we got on famously, and had an orgy of mutual congratulation on having managed to get this far in the first place, in the course of which we both made our own views of the project quite clear.

'So,' I said, by way of summary, 'each side now clearly understands the other.'

'Yes,' said Mary.

'And each side will now grudgingly give an inch,' I said.

'That's just about it,' she said.

Later, in the darkness, the grass fires creeping up the side of Lemagrut were spectacular, but rather horrifying. If the patches of forest there are all destroyed, the rainfall will simply run off down the side of the mountain and be lost, instead of being held longer in the ground to make things grow, but that doesn't occur to the Maasai when they start the fires in the grassy patches lower down. One long line of fire was first a straight line, then a C-shape, then an S, and finally a V, the point towards the centre of the summit.

Sunday, 18 September

Breakfast being a whole half hour later today, to mark Sunday, I had a fabulous lie-in until 7.15 am, by which time I felt more than ready to get up. That wouldn't happen in England.

After breakfast, we began by tape-recording some additional information Mary had remembered about the Laetoli excavations. This was interrupted by the dogs' suddenly starting to bark, not this time at the usual passing Maasai, but at quite a large troop of baboons moving across in front of the camp gate, on their way from the Main Gorge to the Side Gorge. One doesn't usually see them in this area. It is as well they didn't arrive while the dogs were out on their morning walk, or there might have been a serious punch-up.

The day was pretty uneventful. I organised the notes and cards and other sources that refer to Laetoli, which is a major topic and now ready to be dealt with, and subsequently began the writing up. Charles came over to camp during the morning, not to see me, this time, but to report to Mary that someone had broken into one of the buildings by the tourist museum and had taken 130 shillings from the proceeds of sales of postcards, money which should not have been left there overnight anyhow. Mary said resignedly, fortunately not in Charles's hearing, that it would be the local Maasai who had done it, and that it happened about once a month.

In the evening, I walked out on the ground between the Main Gorge and the airstrip. I noticed many fresh burrows, which I supposed must have been made by spring hares or bat-eared foxes. Everywhere they had dug, they had brought to the surface curious round hollow concretions, something between a golf ball and a tennis ball in size, so I took one back to ask Mary what they were. Dung-beetle nests, was the answer, the next stage after the round balls that one sometimes sees the beetle pushing along or finds abandoned on the surface. The completed balls are buried, and in due course the hatching grubs – if that's the right term – break them open, below ground, when ready to emerge. The burrowing animals later bring the remains to the surface. An amazing business, natural history.

In the late afternoon, I forgot to mention, I took another set of photographs of Mary with Matthew, who really is a very handsome Dalmatian. Those I took on the last visit were quite nice, but the shadows were rather dark, and I think they would be too contrasty to reproduce well for publication, as indeed I had feared at the time. Mary is determined to have a photograph of herself with one or more of the dogs as a frontispiece or on the dust jacket, and she also announced that she is planning to dedicate the book to all her Dalmatians past and present. That will entertain the critics and reviewers, I thought: dogs, not people, in spite of there being a wide choice of the latter.

As I rather expected, I got to cook supper when the time came, following the tradition for Sundays with the staff off duty. Steak and aubergines, fried, with mashed potato. Mary decreed that the mashed potato must be light and fluffy, and she had to admit that it was. We ended the day with a discussion of how best to deal in the book with her current pet hates, Drs Don Johanson and Tim White, and the book *Lucy*, without actually being libellous, which it certainly would be, I imagine, if she included all the things she would like to say. That should be an interesting exercise. I myself have no professional involvement at all in the battle, and shall merely record; I have heard Johanson lecture, but have never actually met either him or White. I wonder if she will actually be looking for slightly more colourful writing on this occasion?

Monday, 19 September

This was a fairly solid working day, using tapes, cards, draft chapters of Mary's Laetoli monograph and a *Scientific American* article, to complete a quite long account of the five-year Laetoli project, which produced such excellent and important finds. I fitted most of it in, except Mary's account of what she calls the 'marinated mouse incident'. One day, during one of the Laetoli digging seasons, Mary, making the dressing for the lunch salad, as she always did, found that the oil wouldn't pour properly from the plastic container of it which they had been using for several days. On peering in to see why, she found that the blockage was caused by a dead mouse, which had clearly been there for a very long time ... She and Peter quietly threw the dressed salad away, and didn't tell the story for at least a week. Somehow, there was no point in the text where this episode quite fitted in, and I decided that the Laetoli story had quite enough action without it. I had completed my draft by the end of the working day, though at the cost of having no time to walk – indeed, I was still sitting there writing, when Mary arrived, changed, for her pre-dinner drink, which clearly impressed her.

Nothing much else of note occurred, for once, though no day at Olduvai ever lacks interest. I photographed the small birds at the birdbath, one of the lovebirds amongst them, during a brief break in the morning. At teatime, there was a dramatic lizard-chase out there, when a resident lizard drove off an intruder: I had no idea they could move so fast over about 20 yards of rather stony ground. A rather nice flycatcher came to share the cheese that is fed to the scrub robin from time to time, on demand, it being no less demanding than any other robin I have ever met. On this visit, it seems determined not actually to take cheese from my hand, though perfectly happy to come within two inches of it. English robins do that too, I have noted, at different times of the year. There are comparatively few of the voracious bulbuls about, just at the moment, for once: the plastic water pistol I brought with me this time was Patti's bright idea for discouraging them, but we have hardly had a chance to use it. I'm not too impressed with its effectiveness as a weapon, since after a while the water seems reluctant to leave its reservoir in the handle part, and one only gets a very few shots before having to refill to a point where it will do so.

One of Mary's tapes of information, which I was playing back in the course of writing, had numerous intermissions of dogs barking, because she happened to be recording it when that baboon troop came past the camp yesterday. The play back caused Matthew to appear at once, apparently to see what new Dalmatian had arrived to invade his territory: he barked back at the recorder, but seemed quite satisfied as soon as he heard Mary's voice also coming out of it.

Last night, the grass and bushfires seemed all to have burnt themselves out, no flames being visible on the hillsides, but today there was smoke on Lemagrut again, and this time after dark there was a great crown of fire on the highest point, and another ring of it lower down. Perhaps it looked a bit like that, only rather more so, when it was an active volcano. Having plenty of film to use up, I took a few telephoto time exposure shots in the darkness, trying out different lengths of time, with the camera propped up and held as still as I could contrive on the low wall at the front of the main building, but in the absence of a tripod and a shutter-release cable, I doubt whether anything will come out.

Peter and Annie were expected back this evening, but did not turn up, which probably means that there is no petrol available. During dinner, a vehicle light did appear away in the distance, apparently coming along the road at the point where it starts the final descent from the hills, which is about an hour's driving away, but it never reappeared, which is odd, because there is no other turning it could have taken between there and here.

Today's afternoon temperature only reached 85 degrees, and yesterday too it remained below 90. What is this – winter, or something?

Tuesday, 20 September

There was a slight panic immediately after breakfast, when Brown Dog returned alone from the dogs' walk, apparently frightened. There was no sign of the rest of the party, which had been gone a long time, so there was a general scattering of the camp staff in all directions, to go and find out who had been eaten by what. Mary and I started off in her car to lead the search, but after a few moments I saw Kabebo and the other two dogs in the distance, so a general recall was sounded. The eventual diagnosis was that Brown Dog had run off to chase a hare and had met a lion – some very fresh lion tracks were found by Kitetu quite close to the camp gate, though no one had seen the lion that made them. Perhaps it was Laryngitic Lion? One can imagine the encounter:

```
BROWN DOG (arriving at a run and applying the brakes sharply): Oh,
er, good morning, Laryngitic Lion. I hadn't intended to disturb you.
Er, um, ah, how's the throat this morning?
LARYNGITIC LION: Good morning, Brown Dog. Not too bad, thank you, as
you can perhaps see, if I open my mouth wide. I hope you've finished
your thesis? Grrrrrrrrrrrrhh!
Exit BROWN DOG, touching the ground only at 20-yard intervals.
```

But I am straying into the realms of imagination. Mary wouldn't like that.

At about 9.45 am, a party of visiting Americans arrived to see Mary, a group from Illinois State Museum, I think she said, led by an old friend, and actually here by appointment, so she went off with them until lunch time. I worked peacefully at the task of assimilating the purely technical side of the important dispute on the course of hominid evolution, between, on the one side, Mary and Richard Leakey and, on the other, the dreaded White and Johansen. There were no disturbances to my reading, beyond the arrival of some Maasai at the camp gate in search of medicines, and the dogs barking at them. Kabebo dealt with the negotiations.

After lunch, Peter and Annie arrived safely, cheerful and with petrol: they had been able to get only as far as Gibb's Farm last night. They reported that the outlook for petrol anywhere in Tanzania is bleak for at least October and November, and that the burglars in Arusha, never in short supply, apparently, are now armed with submachine-guns. Usual sort of thing, I suppose.

I wrote during the afternoon, and then checked over the Laetoli chapter with Mary, after tea, she having read the draft. The points she queried were mainly factual, and not too many in number. I asked her if she liked this piece of text: yes, she did, but not as much as the chapter I had written (some way back) about Rusinga. I put it to her that the difference was the new flat style she had requested, which she denied. Of course.

It was already nearly sunset by then, but I went out for a breath of evening air, all the same. There were certainly some clear and fresh lion paw marks on the dusty track that runs along the edge of the Side Gorge: they seemed to be heading in the opposite direction to the one in which I was walking, so no doubt they were made by Brown Dog's lion of the morning. As usual, there was nothing to be seen but the vast landscape and the evening sky, but I shall never tire of those. Darkness began to fall as I watched, and it was perhaps the moment to head back to camp, all things considered.

It was quite a change to have four people in camp again instead of just two, and there was much cheerful chatter and catching up on news. Afterwards, when the others had gone to bed, I sat down again to write a first version of the scathing comments Mary is determined to include about Johanson's popular book *Lucy*: she wants them as near libellous as possible, under a cloak of innocence. Well, I suppose I can try, and we shall see what the final version is, eventually. It was very windy outside, last thing: almost a gale.

Wednesday, 21 September

The dogs' walk at breakfast time seemed to take far longer than usual, for no particular reason, and we were just beginning to get anxious again, when they came into sight. When the sun reached a suitable position in the sky during the morning, I returned to the project of photographing Mary with Matthew, for possible use as a frontispiece or dust jacket photograph. Some of today's attempts may come out quite well, I hope, but the film at present in the camera has a slow speed, as particularly requested by the people at Rainbird, and that caused difficulty when Matthew made sudden head movements in response to sounds. This film is supposed to avoid the problems of excessive contrast in my previous attempts, though in fact I have also brought a much faster one to try when this one is finished. In the middle of the morning, Mary suddenly felt unwell, so we put off the next batch of tape-recording work until the afternoon, and she recovered after a rest. I had plenty to get on with, anyhow: quite apart from the work on the book, I had promised to read for Peter a draft of his chapter intended for the *Olduvai Gorge Beds III, IV and Masek* monograph, which Mary now has in active preparation (and about time too, in my view, since my own chapter for it was handed in no less than nine years ago).

During lunch, there was suddenly the sound of a light aeroplane flying low: the Flying Doctor, Wednesday currently being his regular day for this area, signalling that he was going to drop mail. This is always fun: I saw it during my last visit, but Annie has never watched. The system is that the plane first flies low over the camp with its light on and lug-

gage door open, and then makes a big circle over the Gorge to give people time to get ready, before coming back low to make the drop. On this occasion, down came a single package, clearly not very heavy, which landed neatly beside the big acacia tree, and off went the plane, its Red Cross symbol shining in the sunlight. The package contained mail for Mary and for Annie. One of Mary's letters was from Hazel, saying that the cost of Mary's projected trip to China had turned out to be £2800, double what had been expected. Something will have to be done to reduce that, or she simply won't be able to go.

Flying doctor about to drop mail; Mary, Peter Jones in front of camp; Side Gorge and Lemagrut and Sadiman volcanoes beyond

After the interrupted lunch, Peter and Annie were anxious to see what Maasai objects I had so far acquired, so I showed them my haul, of which they thoroughly approved. They also very kindly themselves gave me a fine flat basket – one of the Mto wa Mbu market's largest size – as a thank you for the bringing out of luggage on my three visits and the performance of various errands back in England. That was a nice surprise. I forgot to record that, one day last week, Kabebo, having waited till Mary was out of sight, suddenly brought me a very nice Maasai beadwork 'watch', and was more than happy to receive in return one of the small but actually very useful penknives I had brought. I have also brought various clothes and oddments with me this time that I thought might please the principal members of the camp staff, and had been waiting for Peter and Annie's advice on who should have what. Besides, my Swahili is simply not up to the subtleties of explaining that these are gifts, and I am not asking for anything in return – though, if anyone really wished to dispose of any local beadwork for which he might happen to have no further use, I would of course be delighted to assist. Peter promised to transmit this thought in due course, and he said that Omari had already been on to him with a similar plan from the other side. Omari, it turns out, has recently got married, and wishes to upgrade his wardrobe. Well, I did just happen to bring for disposal a little-used but outgrown light-weight summer suit, and a pair of shoes in good condition. It would certainly be hard to explain about those, when one's Swahili is limited to rudimentary greetings and the remark that two large potatoes, or three small ones, will be sufficient. *Teach Yourself Swahili* seems to set great store by an ability to comment on the size and required quantity of pota-toes, but somehow I've never yet encountered an appropriate occasion to try out my skill, and the forthcoming negotiations would not be the right time – I mean, they might think I actually wanted some potatoes. Ah, well, one day, maybe, the chance will come.

I gave Annie a packet of small, coloured beads, which I had brought from England (indeed, from Tunbridge Wells, no less), which I had thought might be of use to her in her dealings with the Hadza in the course of her research. Sadly, the present petrol situa-tion rules out any possibility of making even a brief trip with her and Peter to see a Hadza settlement, which we talked about last time I was here. That's a pity, but was really only to be expected. Annie is leaving tomorrow morning, to go back to her field work at Manyara, having spent most of the last couple of months on various travels with Peter.

Mary and I spent the rest of the afternoon working with the tape recorder, and made good progress getting down information about Mary's many visits to America, which became an important part of her life after Louis died, and have continued regularly ever since. We reached a stopping-point about 40 minutes before teatime, which was an awk-ward length of time for getting anything else substantial done, so I decided to walk then instead of later: down the road to the junction of the Main and Side Gorges, and back along the floor of the Main Gorge via the FLK area and then via the steep path directly up to camp, one of my usual routes. It was cloudy and rather humid at first, but then cleared: building up towards the rains, Mary said. The exercise was good, but there was little to be seen and I got back to the writing after tea. A little later, Annie took Brown Dog, who is a particular fan of hers, for an individual walk, but they had to turn back from the Gorge itself owing to distant lion noises in that direction. Brown Dog was clearly in favour of a safety-first policy *vis-à-vis* lions, after yesterday. By dinner time, Mary had read through my draft section on Johansen, White and *Lucy*, and approved in principle, though with the stipulation that she didn't think I had let her be nasty enough to White. Peter and Annie had been independent observers at the time of much that was described or referred to in my draft, and knew all the circumstances quite well, so conversation over dinner turned into a general discussion of whether and how to strengthen the text in the direction Mary wanted, and the tape recorder was fetched to record numerous stories of incidents that took place during the Laetoli digging seasons. I'm not sure myself how some of them could be used without distinctly lowering the tone of that chapter, but Mary is evidently determined to try. As I said earlier, I have never even met Tim White, and have nothing against him. I am fascinated by the striking contrast between all this and Mary's unyield-ing reticence over personal information when it is about herself, not to mention the ruth-less embargo on colour or liveliness in the descriptions of places and of people who have not offended her in any way. Much more thought is required over this chapter, in my view. But anyhow, it all made for a cheerful and hilarious dinner.

Thursday, 22 September

Annie left for Manyara by about 8.30 am, this time giving me only some 20 boxes of slides and one letter to take back to England. A little later, Mary and I walked over to the edge of the Gorge with the three dogs for more photographs. Having finished up the slower film first around the camp and put in the faster one, I took a dozen or so pictures, and with a little luck one or two of them may be quite good. With all the others taken over the past few days, at least there will be quite a lot to choose from.

I made steady progress with the writing as the day progressed, first adjusting the Laetoli chapter along the lines desired after last night's conversations, and then proceeding with the account of Mary's visits to America, in which there are many incidents she wants to record and a lot of people connected with them to be mentioned, none of whom I have ever myself met. I also found time to discuss with Peter his current work and the text he is preparing for the *Olduvai Beds III, IV and Masek* volume, a conversation which expanded to include all sorts of other topics.

The temperature reached 84 degrees or so during the afternoon, and there was again a build up of cloud, though it cleared away after a while. I walked from about 5.45 pm, this time across towards where I found the dung-beetle nests a few days ago. A large flight of swallows passed over. A single jackal was at the dung-beetle place, and made off in a wide circle around me to get back eventually to where I had disturbed it. It was too far away, and the light rather too dim, to be sure whether it was a golden or a silver jackal – the latter have become scarce lately, apparently, through some selective disease. I left it surrounded by a cloud of dust, digging busily – searching for dung-beetle larvae in the absence of other food, Mary suggested later. Perhaps that is why there are all those burrows there: jackals bringing the buried nests to the surface to smash open. There was a dik-dik near the camp gate when I got back there – a big evening for animals, this, by current standards. What a contrast with the visit back in January, when the migration was in full swing.

After dinner, there was a long discussion between Mary and Peter over the deteriorating situation in Tanzania, the likelihood of a major political explosion, and the increasingly obvious fact that it was time for the *mzungu* (European foreigners) to leave. They were both pessimistic over the ability of the Antiquities Department to run Olduvai well if that happened, and had gloomy visions of the camp buildings where we were sitting occupied by drunken Africans. Mary was determined that Peter and Annie, if they decided to stay on elsewhere in Tanzania while Annie completed her research, should have all the usable Olduvai furniture and equipment that was not earmarked for Margaret Gibb. It sounded to me as if she really has made up her mind to leave early in January, as she has been saying, and that Peter's departure for England in December would in fact be his own final departure from Olduvai. But human circumstances are capable of changing so rapidly, in this otherwise changeless place, that one can never be quite sure what will actually happen. The whole conversation developed because Amini Mturi, the Director of Antiquities in Tanzania, who is an old friend of Mary's, is due to visit Olduvai in a few days' time, on 26 September.

The hills earlier today became almost entirely obscured by a haze of what was presumably smoke from grass fires away to the east or northeast, though the local fires now seem all to have burned themselves out. The haze certainly disappeared when the wind dropped, suggesting that the smoke, if that's what it was, was no longer being blown down to us.

Friday, 23 September

The day was devoted almost entirely to writing, as I attempted to sort out Mary's American travels, and get them down on paper in their correct order. There was nothing particularly difficult about this, but there was certainly an awful lot of it. In the afternoon, the heat was rather oppressive, and it was more humid than usual, though the actual temperature indoors went no higher than 86. I was too busy writing to walk in the evening, and even continued after dinner, without quite finishing what turned out to be a far longer chapter than I had expected.

Such diversions as there were came accordingly from close at hand. The window of my work room looks out directly on to the birds' bath and drinking trough, which saw great activity all day, with doves, finches, bulbuls, canaries and lovebirds. Numerous small rodents and an orange-headed igama lizard were also in on the act from time to time, as were the ravens. Everyone else leaves, or withdraws to a safe distance, when the ravens arrive. It was interesting to see which of the ordinary sounds of the camp do and do not disturb the birds when they are at the trough. I took a few photographs of them, using a telephoto lens with a 2 x multiplier, since I now have the faster film in my camera. I had just succeeded in getting one shot of the lovebirds, and was about to take another, when some Maasai appeared in the distance, heading for the camp, the dogs took off to bark at them and all the birds shot up into the air in all directions.

I never found out what the saga involving the Maasai was, though it went on intermittently all the morning: something to do with a lorry that was stuck in some sand, which meant that Mary's lorry had to go and rescue it, and more particularly that two Maasai warriors got a ride in it, but I never did hear the full story.

During teatime, the bird population was augmented for a while by a very bright Hildebrand's starling, and also a scimitar-bill, a bird I hadn't seen before – about the size of a blackbird, but with a longer tail. It was dark navy-blue in colour, with a long, curved bright orange bill, and was quite an athletic customer, inclined to swing itself right round a branch. It rather gave the impression that a glass or two of Guinness might turn it into a toucan, but meanwhile its bill is narrow and round-sectioned, not broad and flat. There were more bulbuls about today, and they were inclined to make a nuisance of themselves by invading the kitchen, so after lunch Peter and I loaded up the water pistol. I shot one splendidly up the tail feathers from a range of about 12 feet, and it left in a great hurry.

It was also a day for lions, starting with loud roaring in the early hours at about 3.0 am, and they were also to be heard somewhere in the Side Gorge after it had got light, around 7.0 am. There was intermittent roaring again during dinner. No one knows what they are finding to hunt at this time of year, and there is speculation that they may start on the giraffe, which they usually leave alone, if nothing else is available. No giraffe seemed to be about today, however, so the same thought may have occurred to them.

Mary spent some time re-reading the sections of text that deal with Johanson and White, which clearly are of great importance to her. No one ever gets away with offending a Leakey. She is still dissatisfied with the existing text, but is quite unwilling to suggest a different version herself. We began to discuss this after dinner, but since she seemed in a mood to misconstrue all my own comments, which were intended to be helpful, I left her to it, after a while, and returned to the current writing, after a wander down to the camp gate in the cool moonlight to listen to the lions, who were a few hundred yards away in the Side Gorge. Loud roars punctuated by series of short grunts – a magnificent sound. I wondered whether they too were reading over some chapters of text someone had taken a lot of trouble over – it would have to be part of Brown Dog's thesis, if so, I suppose, since none of my own pages is missing. There were nice night-bird sounds, too. The moon looked to be full, or very close to it, and the hills were visible by its light for many miles.

Saturday, 24 September

There seemed to be enormous numbers of birds around at breakfast time, though nothing unusual amongst them. Also, there was the sound of Saturday. I suppose that might make a good name for a pop group, if you like that sort of thing. No, not jarring enough: this is 1983, after all. The sound that announces Saturday at Olduvai (though I don't recall it from the two previous visits) happens about the end of breakfast time, and is the distinctive metallic noise caused by the removal of the covering lids from the water-storage tanks behind the main buildings, to make possible the removal of floating dead creatures from the surface of the water.

'It must be Saturday,' said Peter, as soon as the sound began, and so indeed it was.

All things being equal, the next time that sound is heard here, I should be about one hour short of landing at Heathrow. I drew this interesting fact to the attention of those present, just in case there might be anyone who thought there was time in hand to be wasted by picking perfectly good text to pieces – not, of course that anyone would dream of such a thing, would they? Anyhow, I merely pointed out the timing, without going into such matters.

In the morning, I finished off the long chapter on the travels in America and elsewhere, and prepared a list of items to be included in the next one. This will deal with various Leakey domestic and family events over the past 10 years, which means that it will necessarily be rather a rag-bag affair. That is to be the last full-length chapter, according to present plans, and only a short conclusion will follow it. Looking at it that way, one would have to say we were making progress. Still, the way things are going, I'm not sure that looking at it that way is entirely realistic.

If the main diversions yesterday were provided by the birds, today it was the weather. We had very hot sun, which preceded a big gathering of clouds, and by around mid-day a thunderstorm was in full swing over Lemagrut, with another in the distance over Olmoti. There seemed to be a dust-storm between them, in the direction of Ngorongoro, and several dust-devils could be seen out beyond the Side Gorge. Then a great curtain of rain came up between the Gorge and the hills, and later there was a brief spell of violent wind. It always looks as if the big volcanoes rise just beyond the Gorge, however well one knows that many miles in fact lie between, and accordingly it always looks as if the rain is about to sweep across the Gorge and engulf the camp. But, as usual, it never came – all we got today was a light shower an hour or so later, long after all the rain seemed to have passed. But the wind brought a marvellous smell of distant wet earth, which I have experienced here before, and the passing of the rainstorm cleared the air and settled the dust, and brought the hills out sharply in the late afternoon light.

During the afternoon, Mary and I worked with the tape recorder on the information for the next chapter, using the list I had made. Later, I left her reading the text of the American travels chapter, and actually sounding quite pleased with it, and set off a little earlier than usual to walk, with a view to getting a bit further out on to the plains. This I achieved, walking steadily for well over an hour in all, till darkness began to gather. There was actually not a lot to be seen – three dik-dik and a large well-bleached tortoise shell the size of a Rugby football were about the best of it – but the clarity of the hills was very pleasing, and I never weary of either the beauty or the sheer scale of this landscape, with its strong evening colours fading into the softer blue distances. I passed groups of bleached and scattered bones at frequent intervals, from all the kills during the game migration, one or two of the clusters being from the very kills I saw back in January, when they were fresh. Disintegration seems to have been quite slow. Examination of the bones confirmed that most of the kills had been of wildebeest, as one would expect, but a couple of them were zebra.

At dinner, Mary confirmed that she liked the travels chapter, subject only to minor points of detail, which is a relief. With Peter's help, we also corrected some minor factual points in the Laetoli chapter.

Between my return from the walk and dinner, Kabebo came offering hot water for a shower, so I had a very nice one by torch light and emerged from it much refreshed. The spray from the canvas bag that provides the shower was turned to liquid streams of silver by my purely fortuitous positioning of the torch. I found that entrancing, but one can't waste good hot water in mere romantic contemplation, can one?

Sunday, 25 September

Once again, and this time for the last time, we have reached the big lie-in morning of the week, all of 10 minutes extra, this time, and it was also malaria pill day, which I was quite proud of remembering. The day began with a clear, bright, gently blue sky: you wouldn't think the gathering of clouds would be even a technical possibility, but I reckoned it would still happen.

Earlyish in the morning, there was suddenly the completely unexpected and therefore startling sound of a vehicle approaching the camp: a lorry, when it came into view. It turned out to belong to the Tanzanian Antiquities Department, and was bringing wood for the construction of shelves in the laboratory, something requested by Mary two years or more ago. On a *Sunday*? At *this* late stage of the Olduvai camp's history? How very odd. The lorry's crew was led by a young Tanzanian, very polite, whom Mary, in her decisive way, instantly diagnosed as being a Twit, and subsequently referred to him solely by that title, though fortunately not to his face. He was the bearer not only of timber, but also of a message that the expected Amini Mturi would be unable to come to Olduvai. Mary, who urgently needed to see him, was not pleased, and maybe that was why she decided the messenger was a Twit. Anyone who was a Twit might, of course, have got the message wrong. Anyhow, the lorry offloaded its cargo of timber and drove off: the Twit and colleagues said that they would return to construct the shelves tomorrow.

It was remarkable to see that, in the distance over beyond the Side Gorge, there were suddenly a few hundred wildebeest. Perhaps there had been more rain elsewhere than we have had here, and they were on their way to where there would be water and fresh grass to be had, but this is quite the wrong time of year for such behaviour. By the end of the day, they had gone, I don't know in which direction.

As it was the rest day for the camp staff, I decided, with Peter's help, to have a distribution of the give-away clothes I had brought with me: Mary, who would certainly not have approved, was safely out of sight. Omari was thrilled to see the suit, and didn't even want to waste time trying it on, even though I reckoned the trousers would be nearly three inches too long for him. He would be back later in the day with

View across Gorge floor in FLK area, towards camp

trade goods to clinch the deal, he said, and shortly afterwards made off purposefully towards the guides' camp, which is a source of such things. Kitetu was equally pleased with a pair of brown suede shoes and assured us that no, they were not in the least too narrow to fit. He vanished, and shortly afterwards reappeared with a nice bead watch, and a good single earring, of the kind worn by Maasai elders and warriors. I decided the denim hat I had brought would suit Kabebo particularly well, and he tried it on and went off giggling and very pleased. Peter reported that Naade, the Mbulu craftsman, who makes and mends various things for the camp, was certainly in the market for a tee shirt and a penknife, and was collecting up and himself making a few items in return.

In due course, I settled down to work, and wrote various bits of additional material to be slotted in here and there, which Mary had specifically requested. Various Maasai passed by, arriving for their traditional (if entirely unofficial) Olduvai Sunday lunch with the camp staff. One was leading a donkey – they couldn't be going to eat that, could they?

After our own lunch, Omari reappeared, with another bead watch (that's five I have acquired on this trip, all of them nice), an unusual necklace of beads and large seeds,

Snake hunt

strung on a thread made from the local sisal, and a really fine pair of earrings, including some coiled wire in their construction. I gladly passed over the suit: mutual satisfaction on both sides of the deal. Later in the day, Naade sent via Peter a necklace and pair of earrings he had himself just made, plus a small gourd calabash, which had never been used and therefore smelled of gourd rather than of Maasai. Trade seemed to be booming, and it was nice to see the Africans' genuine delight with the things I had brought them.

In the afternoon, it did indeed cloud over, as I had expected, and there was rain to be seen in much the same places as yesterday, with thunder and several sharp flashes of lightning over Lemagrut and a faint rainbow beyond Olmoti, but as usual, from it all, only the wet smell reached us at Olduvai.

At teatime, the birds in the big tree at the front of the camp suddenly gave their snake-warning, and instantly all the camp staff appeared eagerly, armed to the teeth with sticks, catapults, etc. A long search followed, amongst the stones, but nothing was found except a distinctly dead bird. The warning from the birds is hardly ever a false alarm, so there was no doubt a snake around somewhere.

After tea, Mary rather suddenly announced that she wanted to begin going right through the text from the very beginning, to make all the amendments she had noted while reading the typed-out version. My heart sank. We spent some two hours doing this, and got through about 60 pages. There were some changes of mind on factual points, and some genuinely necessary corrections, all fair enough, but also many changes that I thought completely needless, and the ruthless excision, of course, of anything expressed with a touch of colour. Yuk! – and there will be a further 100 pages' worth of similar carnage tomorrow. Myself, I would have preferred to be writing the next chapter, but Mary said she wanted to get this operation done in case Mturi did after all turn up, in spite of what the Twit had said. That was reasonable, I supposed. Ever willing to add to my linguistic knowledge, I asked Peter if there was a word for Twit in Swahili, but he thought not. A jackal walked across the front of the camp, outside the gate, exciting the dogs. At bedtime, I heard the sound of hyaenas instead of lions, for a change.

Monday, 26 September

Everyone reminded everyone else that this was election day in Nairobi, when Philip Leakey's political fate would be decided, but the results would certainly not be known before tomorrow. After breakfast, Kitetu produced for me two more single Maasai earrings, which I had not been expecting: perhaps he refused to feed the Sunday lunch guests yesterday until they had handed over some of their finery. (I saw the donkey leaving safely, incidentally, so that was a relief.)

Mary walking dogs back to camp, Side Gorge beyond, Lemagrut volcano in background

There were no wildebeest like those of yesterday visible at breakfast time, but by lunch time they were back, or possibly another lot had come. The ravens came into the camp very early, about 6.15 am, making peculiar agitated noises, and were then absent all the morning. We discovered no reason for their concern: they returned, behaving normally, in the afternoon. The Twit and his colleagues reappeared and did about two hours work on the shelves, and then pushed off in their lorry, to no one's surprise, saying they would be back: they are expected to try and spin out the job indefinitely, as they get an extra allowance for working out in the bush.

I had a four-hour non-stop session with Mary, going through the typed version of the text: lots more of what I regard as nit-picking and vandalism, and the complete deletion of some of my favourite passages. She had read through all of this already, when it was in manuscript, and was supposed to have approved it, and no changes had subsequently been made by me.

'Oh, well, it all looks different when it's typed,' she said.

I find myself beginning to lose interest in this text, now that it is so battered about: it's simply not a piece of my writing any longer. Besides, in concentrating on minute factual changes and what she regards as points of style, she is failing to take any kind of overview of the text I have produced for her with such care, and with all the cutting out of the commentary passages, she is leaving the reader less and less option to view her as a sympathetic character rather than a hard, tough operator. I have tried gently to explain this, but she does not want to listen. As the story has proceeded, on the one hand, and the moderating passages have been removed, on the other, I have found my own opinions hardening, and I can only conclude that I had better leave her to create what I fear may well be a true impression after all, instead of trying to help her use gentler or more amenable language to explain and maybe justify some of her attitudes and actions. So be it. Yet, unquestionably, there is infinitely more to Mary than that. And will people want to read this increasingly colourless stuff, when there was in fact so much more to be said, and much better ways of saying it?

When the butchery was finally finished, I began the last of the book's main chapters, and fought my way through perhaps a third of it. There seemed no point in trying to write it in a lively way, if it was all going to be killed off later. I then walked with my camera in the late afternoon light and took a few photographs of scenes I have certainly photographed before, but my current film is for prints, not slides, and I could make myself an album of prints just in case – not very likely – I should ever forget these visits. I could have prints made from some of the slides, too, for that.

After dinner, Mary expressed the opinion that I had become silent and seemed depressed this evening.

'I'm very pleased with the way the text is turning out,' she said.

'Oh, good,' I said, mildly.

Fortunately, the conversation turned to her worries over the fate of Olduvai when she leaves. I suggested raising an international outcry by expressing deep concern over this site, which is pre-eminently of international significance, with a view to raising major funding for a proper research centre and museum, possibly to be built actually at the Gorge – something Tanzania by itself would never be able to afford, for all its nationalist pride. Mary said that this had simply never occurred to her, and she would certainly think about it. I doubt that it will ever happen.

The lights of a vehicle were then seen in the distance: could that be the missing Mturi, or perhaps just the Twit and his lorry, which had never returned during working hours? It was evidently neither of these things, since the vehicle did not take the Olduvai turning. Builders, and Twits, must be the same the world over, with their vanishings and unfulfilled promises to return and get on with the work. That thought made me wonder how *my* builders were getting on, back at Fordwells.

For the first time on this visit, there was the combination of bright clear stars, and the moon not yet having risen, so I could get out my star map and see what was going on. Just as I thought: a completely different array from only two months ago: no Southern Cross, no upside down Great Bear. Cygnus was high in the northern sky, but it was very hard to find one's way around, even with the map, and to make that worse the wind became very strong: indeed, it rose to a real gale, which then lasted all night. There were no signs of rain in the vicinity today; no doubt the strong wind signifies the moving of some big low-pressure area.

Tuesday, 27 September

The camp staff have a radio in their quarters: Mary has never lowered the tone of Olduvai to the extent of having a radio for her own use. Her only link to the outside world is the

Buffalo near Ngorongoro (page 139)

radio telephone, which she uses as little as possible. Today, however, she was ready enough to ask for news of the Kenyan election, but the broadcasts from Nairobi had so far had nothing to report, except that the votes were still being counted, and that remained the situation right through the day, even when the evening meal was served. Mary was clearly at least half expecting Philip to lose, and preparing herself for that event. His main opponent on this occasion was a member of the Luo people, and she reflected gloomily that there were many Luo in the new housing estates that have sprung up around Langata. The rumour was that Philip's opponent had brought many Luo into the area specifically to vote for him, and was blatantly bribing voters in all directions.

After breakfast, I was at work by 7.30 am. I read some text for Peter Jones in connection with his own work, and then turned to my writing of the last long chapter, aiming to finish it by the end of the day. This seemed really no more than an endurance exercise:

the information to be included was straightforward enough, provided it wasn't all going to get changed or rethought. It was mainly on tape, recorded by Mary the previous Saturday afternoon, at a time when, on her own admission, she was feeling drowsy and uninspired. I am inclined to believe her, because on one occasion she had said 'chealing the steetah' instead of 'stealing the cheetah'. Today, the weather was hot and bright, with no sign of rain-clouds to be seen anywhere. After lunch I took a few 'heat-of-the-day' photographs not very far from camp, to give myself a short break.

The evening proved quite eventful, one way and another. After tea, Peter needed to walk over to the museum across the other side of the Gorge, so I went with him, and Brown Dog came too, for the walk. It was a glorious evening, and I got some good new photos: Peter showed me a path which I had not been aware of, up the steep side of the Gorge to the museum, and it offered spectacular views, not to mention much more vigorous exercise than some of my usual routes, which was good. Not having yet finished my long chapter, I returned to work when we got back to camp, to use the hour or more up to dinner time, while darkness fell. It was still warm, but had become too windy to have the hut window open, because all the papers blew about, so I left the door open for air instead, propping it with a stone as usual: I have learned that this doesn't let in a draught in the same direction as the window, so the papers stay put. Occasionally, it lets in some small bird instead, which has to be gently shepherded out, but with darkness falling all the birds had gone to bed.

I was deeply absorbed in the writing, and making good progress, with the end near, when I heard some bumps and rustlings outside the hut. I wondered whether it might be a mongoose, or even one of the genets, and whether I should go outside and look, in case I could finally solve the problem of what the creature is that I still occasionally hear brushing round my hut at night, though not nearly as frequently as on my previous visits. But I concluded that it would merely bolt as soon as I stood up, and in any case my torch was in the other hut, and I wanted to finish my paragraph. So I stayed put: it certainly didn't sound to be anything large and interesting, like a lion.

Moments later, there was an unmistakable slithering sound, and a hissing breath. Just about five feet away, a large red-brown snake was already almost half-way in through the door, forked tongue flicking. I had a split second in which to reach out and slam the door, and I thought as I did so that there must be an approximately equal chance of shutting the snake either outside or inside the hut. Fortunately it turned out to be the former: the snake turned round very fast as I moved, and made off, the door catching it a glancing blow on the tail as it vanished into the darkness. I secured the door, opened the window, and shouted 'Snake!' as loudly as I could, in the manner prescribed for such occasions. Enter African staff with torches from one side and, shortly after, Mary from the other, and then Peter.

'You should have shut it inside and then got out through the window,' said Mary, but not very seriously, when apprised of the situation,.

There followed a snake-hunt in the dark, because my description was enough for the snake to be tentatively identified as a big spitting cobra, and it was thought not likely to have gone far. And indeed, before long, it was found, lying tight along the bottom of the outside wall of the hut, more or less in the foundations, behind various rocks and a collection of herbs growing in pots and small troughs. The torch light showed the identification to be correct, and the snake to be a very big one. The men formed a half-circle round where it was, but could only prod and stab at it with their sticks in that position, and some care was necessary, as a spitting cobra emits its venom in a powerful double jet, with a fair range, usually aiming at the eyes. Next they tried pouring boiling water on it, and eventually it shot out of its hiding place and through the one gap in the half-circle available to it, hit twice in the process by Peter, and vanished into the darkness beyond the back of the hut, leaving a trail that included spots of blood. It wasn't possible to follow the trail effectively by torch light, but the search continued for a while, and various large holes were found down which the snake might have gone, but it was not seen again, and escaped, which means it may return in due course – perhaps not tonight, one felt, after its hostile reception. Peter and Mary also reminded each other that cobras tend to come in pairs ... As it is, alas, I cannot append to my diary a photograph of myself triumphantly holding a large dead cobra. On reflection, I decided that it was perhaps as well that the snake hadn't chosen exactly the same hour to arrive last Saturday, which was when I was having that nice warm shower and watching the play of the torch light on the water – a rather more vulnerable situation, one can see. Anyhow, the snake warning that the birds gave on Sunday, which came to nothing at the time, now seems less likely to have been a false alarm. And perhaps the unexplained agitation of the ravens early yesterday morning was because the snake was about. There were no birds to give a warning this evening, in the darkness.

Dinner was understandably late after all the excitement. During it, vehicle lights appeared again, and this time they did take the Gorge road. Was it Mturi? No, only the Twit and his lorry, which proceeded to grind its way noisily across the Gorge and up the road to the guides' camp. No doubt everyone there turned out to say 'Karibu, bwana Twit,' and that sort of thing, but where on earth had he been all day?

Even now, the day's events were not over. Peter had already gone to bed, and Mary and I were talking quietly, when Kabebo suddenly appeared with a torch, bringing the news that at last the radio had announced Philip Leakey's election result, and it was victory! Mary was transformed. I have never seen her so utterly delighted. She shot out of her chair, and quite literally skipped up and down for at least half a minute. Her voice rose about an octave, and she kept repeating, 'Oh, I'm so pleased!', over and over again. I thought she was actually going to take Kabebo in her arms and dance – 'I almost did,' she said afterwards.

It is certainly a famous victory, and this was a remarkable and rather privileged insight into how much her sons' achievements really mean to Mary – at the time when they happen, even more than when she is merely talking about them afterwards. Could this really be the same Mary, who would certainly be far happier if the strongest expression of pleasure in the autobiography were 'quite nice'? (That's an expression she did actually use, when describing Louis's attitude towards her on the day in Cambridge back in 1933 when he told her he wanted to marry her: 'he was quite nice to me'.)

Eventually, the excitement subsided, and after a while I was alone. The stars were bright, the sky was clear and there was no moon. So I went out and looked at the stars for a while, to end the long day. But I was careful now and again to check the ground at my feet for cobras.

Wednesday, 28 September

This was the final day at Olduvai, and I had some writing to finish and some packing up to do, but not too much of either. I did yesterday succeed in completing the last long chapter, amidst all the events of the evening. During the morning, I read some text of Peter's, and even found time to look over some of the draft text of my research student Simon Collcutt's thesis, which I had hopefully brought with me. Then in the afternoon I sat down and wrote the brief conclusion for Mary's book, actually keeping it within the four pages tentatively planned. So, at 5.50 pm I was able to inform Dr Mary Leakey that I had now finished her autobiography and was going for a walk. She was supposed to read through these last two chapters while I did that, but never got round even to beginning, with so much luggage to organise and so many instructions to leave, because her programme is to stay on in Nairobi, after taking me there, and then leave from there on the trip to China, if the plans for that work out.

It was arranged that Omari should travel with us as far as Arusha, and possibly even as far as the border at Namanga, to be on hand in case the car should break down: the trouble with the gears on the journey down here was never really properly diagnosed and cured, and we simply have not used vehicles very much during this visit, because of the shortage of petrol. Indeed, the car has probably only done a few hundred yards since then – oh, I remember now, it did go up to Ngorongoro to fetch the petrol and diesel fuel, for a test run, early on: I had forgotten that. Janet, the senior Dalmatian, will also be travelling with us: she has developed sores, and needs to see a vet. The plan is for us to leave Olduvai at 6.30 am, after a quick breakfast at 6.15.

Peter gave me various letters, etc, to take back to England, and then added a complete ostrich egg, which he had found some while ago, to keep as a souvenir of my visit. My case will clearly be a lot heavier than anticipated, because I also have the tape recorder provided by Rainbird, and all the tapes, to fit in. Ah, well.

There was another snake-hunt after lunch, in which Peter and I took part: this time it turned out to be a small thin snake, seen near the kitchen eating a lizard, which it appeared to have killed with poison, though no one knew quite what kind it was. Anyhow, we got it. There was no sign of yesterday's cobra: popular opinion was that it was still down a hole somewhere round behind my hut, probably somewhat the worse for wear.

I took my last walk over familiar ground out on the airstrip, and photographed the sunset, mainly on principle; the rest of the evening I spent packing. The growing accumulation of luggage ready to be loaded suggested that there would only just be room for my own cases in the car. I was in bed by 10.45, with everything done, having set the alarm for 5.50 am.

Thursday, 29 September

I was up comfortably in time to hear my alarm go off. Everything worked precisely on schedule, and we were actually driving through the camp gate, I noted, as the clock reached the target departure time of 6.30. Janet travelled in state and a basket in the back, while Mary, Omari and I were somewhat squashed together on the front seat. It was light, but not yet sunrise: the pale, dry grass was almost pink in the breaking dawn. There was little to be seen, and no wildebeest where we had observed them in the last two days: just two giraffe, one male ostrich and a few gazelle. There was no other traffic moving, of course. And that, I strongly suspected, might well be the last I would ever see of Olduvai. But who knows?

It was an uneventful run to Ngorongoro: we made a brief stop there for Mary to deliver a letter, while Omari and I stretched our already cramped legs. There was no mist or cloud at all at the top of the great climb this time: it was on the last trip that we met a lioness in the mist there, on the return journey. This time I had my camera with me in the front of the car, with a single photo left on the film to use up: I had saved it for the genets last night, but they never came. No lionesses, this time, either. As usual, we saw very recent traces of elephants, but no sign of the elephants themselves. What we did see was buffalo crossing the road, so I photographed them: Mary shot through a gap in the herd just as the face of the next animal appeared in the bushes.

Everything went well, suspiciously well, until we were past Karatu and getting towards the edge of the Rift. Then, quite suddenly, *bang*, followed by a noise like a tractor engine. A large rock on the road had broken the remaining exhaust bracket – one was already missing – and had comprehensively broken the exhaust with it. While in principle this was just the sort of thing for which Omari had come with us, in practice there was absolutely nothing he could do, because the repair would be a welding job for a garage.

On we went, our speed much reduced, and the noise appalling. It occurred to me that there were still 225 miles to go. Conversation was simply not possible, and everyone we met or passed turned round to see what on earth was making the noise. And so to Arusha, in five and a half hours from starting. There had been little of note to see on the way, after the buffalo, except four secretary birds, three of them together and one by itself soon afterwards. There were also various eagles circling, and a few hornbills flying. But it was far to noisy to enjoy the spectacular scenery of the Rift section of the journey as much as usual, and I had also quite rapidly established that for the middle person on the front seat, the springing in Mary's car leaves much to be desired.

Mary had various calls to make in Arusha: the police station, to collect a pass and to give packets of soapflakes to the ladies in the office there; the hotel, to use the ladies room; the office of Chimon Patel, who takes and receives messages for her. Omari, since there was nothing he could do for the vehicle, disembarked at Arusha, and he would be collected there by the faithful Hazel, Mary's Secretary, when she went down to Olduvai shortly to look after things there (especially the dogs), during Mary's absence. At Mr Patel's office, Mary learned that the missing Amini Mturi was actually in Arusha: after something of a search, we eventually found him. He explained that he was stuck for petrol, like everyone else, and they fixed a new date in November for him to visit Olduvai.

On we went, after all that: it was less cramped now, with Omari gone, but not a scrap less noisy. On the way out of Arusha, a policeman stopped the car, not surprisingly, and informed Mary that she must not drive it any further but get it mended at 2.0 pm, when the garages reopened.

'Yes, Officer,' she said brightly, and on we went.

We had a very brief picnic lunch at Mary's usual stopping place amongst the coffee plantations, and this time she was careful to stop short of the ditch into which we had sub-

Tanzanian/Kenya border, Longido Mountain (Tanzania) in distance

sided rather spectacularly last time. Janet was glad of another stretch and, being a dog of philosophical outlook and unfailing appetite, clearly thought that lunch was the best thing that had happened since breakfast. She could be right, I thought.

After lunch I took over the driving, to give Mary a break, for the stretch from Arusha to the Border. The long straight stretches of this road had minimal traffic: it was quite hard to keep awake, it being the hottest part of the day. There were the usual two places where one has to stop and sign a book at a police checkpoint: everyone knows Mary, of course, and everyone had heard about the Kenyan election and Philip's triumph (as they had in Arusha, too) so everyone wished to congratulate her. Janet also drew admirers at every stop: Dalmatians are a rare sight in most parts of East Africa, but this is a journey she has made before. The back of the vehicle was so full of luggage (and Janet), that for once we did not give any lifts; possibly the obviously very sick engine also deterred some who might otherwise have asked for a ride.

It was nearly 3.0 pm already, when we reached the border: there were no difficulties in crossing, but many more outbreaks of congratulations for Mary. On the Kenyan side, Janet rapidly acquired a new fan club of silently amazed Maasai. On we went, some 50 minutes after reaching the border, all formalities completed and the tank blissfully refilled with petrol. By now we were both deafened, somewhat dizzy and distinctly headachy from the ceaseless noise, but there was nothing that could be done about it. We shared the remaining 90 miles of driving, and made just one break to give Janet a stretch. I saw one group of impala by the roadside, and near Nairobi watched an immensely long passenger train starting off on its 400 mile run to Mombasa and the coast.

By the time we had reached the outskirts of Nairobi, my own headache had become a full-scale migraine. We were stopped again on the edge of the town by the local police for the faulty exhaust. Kenyan cars have their owners' name written on the side, if they are used for institutional purposes, so the policeman could read Mary's name for himself.

'You are Mrs Leakey, mother of Philip Leakey? Please give him our congratulations. Are you not very proud? Yes, you are free to go.'

Marvellous, isn't it?

It had been decided that I would stay in a hotel, since Mary's house had been Philip's campaign headquarters, and she was sure things would still be in full swing and doubted whether she would even find a bed there herself tonight. So she took me to the New Stanley, which I had liked when I stayed there during the January visit. Yes, they had a free room. Before we parted, I arranged with Mary to meet her at the museum next morning at about 10 am, if we were both still alive.

The state I was in by now, from the noise, the dazzling low sun on the final stage of the journey, and Mary's cigar smoke thrown in as an extra, might possibly yield, I decided, to only one treatment that I could think of: four Paracetamol tablets and a sleep, which I hoped would only be short. This remedy I applied at 6.46 pm and woke, feeling very much better, at exactly 9.46. It seemed time to go in search of a hot meal in the Thorn Tree restaurant. The head waiter was amazed that I chose the pavement section at this hour, rather than sitting indoors.

'Will you not be cold? Oh, I see, from England. I hope to go to England myself, one day ...'

After that, a bath, and a comfortable bed for a lot more sleep. You can batter us literary types to pieces, but you cannot destroy our spirit, so I found myself reflecting, as I drifted off to sleep, on the irony that the loss of an exhaust should make one feel totally exhausted. But we made it.

Friday, 30 September

Breakfast at 8.15 seemed almost wickedly late, instead of the usual 7.0 am or earlier. I sorted out my luggage after yesterday's journey, as best I could, having in mind that I proposed to do some more shopping in town at some stage. I paid the hotel bill, and put the luggage into the cloak-room store, in the care of the same cheerful porter whom I remembered from my last visit. In due course I walked up to the museum, which took about 25 minutes: I was there by 10 minutes past the appointed hour of 10 o'clock and found, as I had expected, that Mary had not yet arrived. Nor had Hazel, so that gave me a chance to make ready the parts of the manuscript that still needed to be dealt with.

In due course Mary and Hazel arrived together, plus Janet, who had already made her visit to the vet and been given anti-biotics, and was in her usual equable mood. Mary claimed to be very tired after yesterday, and indeed she had every right to be. When she eventually reached Langata, she had found her house the centre of a massive celebration party, at the end of which all the guests were sent home drunk in lorries, she said. Her own bedroom had been kept clear for her.

Our list of things to be done numbered six items, but in the event only one proved possible to achieve, which was the photocopying of the last two chapters and one other section, to be left for Mary to read in detail when time allowed, so that I could take the original copy back to England with me. Everything else received a negative reply. Had she brought from Langata, as promised, the envelope of photographs which I was supposed to be taking to the publishers in London? No. Would it be possible for us to see Richard Leakey, as planned, so that the three of us could discuss the section about Johanson and White that means so much to Mary? No: he was out at the airport, and harassed. Could Mary and Hazel perhaps now find three items of minor missing information that Mary had said would be in the office? No, no and no. Bearing in mind the disastrous results that seem to ensue when Mary reads text of mine while tired, I carefully did not suggest that she should at least look at my four-page conclusion. It emerged that she had decided, since yesterday, to go to Jonathan Leakey's place at Lake Baringo for a weekend's rest and relaxation, and would be leaving this afternoon. After a while, it seemed to me that the only role expected of me was to pass over the photocopied chapters and get lost, so these things I did, after Hazel had kindly established for me that there was a bus to the airport from the city centre every hour on the hour. I don't think the goodbyes between the weary subject and ghost-writer of the autobiography could have been described as either effusive or long drawn out, but there it was: for the moment, at least, I had done what I had been hired to do, and was now clearly surplus to requirements.

Perfectly happy with this situation, I decided next to walk the few yards to Robert Soper's office to see if he was in, we having made a somewhat tentative arrangement, when he passed through England and visited me during August, to have lunch together today if both free. He was actually out, but expected back shortly. Oh – I forgot to mention that when Hazel arrived she had very kindly brought me two nice hunting arrows made by the Kenyan Kamba people, which she thought my son Nick might like. I had admired them at her house on the outward journey: they had been collected by her own children when young, and she had said she was simply longing to get rid of them to a caring home. She had remembered, this morning, when setting out. This is merely worth mentioning because, when Robert Soper did arrive, and did prove to be free for lunch, he suggested we should go on his motorbike, and of the really rather few times when I have ridden on the pillion seat of a motorbike, this was the only one when I had done so clutching two Kamba arrows, with possibly poisoned tips, and two and a half chapters of original auto-biography manuscript. As general guidance, I should warn others who may find them-selves in this situation that one really requires four hands, as two are essential for holding on to the parcel-carrier bit. But we got there.

Robert and I enjoyed some sandwiches and beer and a catch-up of news. With luck, he would also be free for at least a farewell drink and possibly for supper, before I caught the 9 o'clock airport bus. He then took me on the motorbike to the city centre, and this was accordingly the second time I had ridden on the pillion seat of a motorbike clutching 2 K.a (with p.p.t) and $2\frac{1}{2}$ c. of o.a.m. The next occasion might be some way off, I thought.

I called first at the Kenya Air Lines office to establish where the bus left from, and immediately found that Hazel's information had been incomplete: while entirely true so far as it went, it had omitted to mention that the last bus to the airport left at 8.0, calling a little earlier than that at the hotel, and there wasn't a 9.0 one. Since Robert and I had just arranged to meet at 7.30, I now had to write him a note and take it back up the hill to his office, hoping he would get it, as he had mentioned having meetings to attend in the afternoon. He had in fact offered me a lift to the airport as an alternative to the bus, but I hadn't wanted to put him to that much trouble. So I said in my note that either it must be a very quick drink, or else yes please to the lift after all, and I would need to know by 7.30, or else I would have to catch the bus for safety.

I then went shopping, mainly in the market, and acquired five of the nice local baskets, the floppy ones with the shoulder-length straps that are so good for shopping, one soapstone chess set and board, two beaded belts for my children (made for sale to tourists, but of Maasai manufacture and very attractive for what they are), two small soapstone figures and finally one perfectly good wash-and-wear safari suit offered at the amazingly cheap price of £12.50, whereas most of the shops are asking double that. I also found a reasonably scholarly booklet about the Maasai with some quite nice coloured pictures. Not a bad haul for my final Nairobi shopping spree. I could see no way that my luggage would not be overweight, this time, but concluded that they ought not to object too much at Nairobi airport, in view of my boosting the Kenyan economy so notably.

I went back to the hotel, and extracted my luggage from the cloakroom store to repack the cases. The larger case would only just close after much skilled negotiation, and I guessed it must weigh comfortably over the permitted 20 kilos by itself. The heaviest stuff I actually put in the smaller carry-on bag, which they don't usually bother to weigh, but I had ceased caring anyhow, by the time the repacking was all done. The cheerful porter was much amused by the whole procedure. A well-earned (in my view) pot of tea followed, it being already about 5.50 pm and some of us a bit foot-weary. Prices at the New Stanley seem very reasonable: a generous pot of tea in the comfort of the hotel lounge-bar cost only 6 Kenyan shillings (about 30 pence in English money). It was curious that it was served with hot boiled milk, but I would have drunk it happily in any form. I passed the time writing up yesterday for this diary, and then moved at around 7.0 to the Thorn Tree to watch for Robert, as arranged in my note, over a glass of beer. At 7.26, in the nick of time, he arrived, complete with his car, so we were indeed able to have supper together after which he kindly took me out to the airport. Definitely not a motorbike ride, with that amount of luggage, even in Kenya.

There were no problems with the luggage weight after all: I noted that my large case weighed in at 21.50 kg, but no one bothered about that, and the smaller one was not weighed. The large one actually felt heavier than the scale showed, to me, and I hoped it wouldn't burst open. I reckoned it probably wouldn't bring the plane down, since the latter was a 747 coming from Johannesburg. In fact, the check in was only just opening when I got there, and I was virtually first through it. After that, I whiled away the time bringing this diary up to date to this point, and reading through some of the earlier entries.

Take-off was just slightly late, and it looked as if every seat would be full, especially after a great late influx of American safari parties into the departure lounge, their members much taken up with excitedly showing each other their latest acquired souvenirs, which were all classified as either 'darling' or 'cute'. I resisted the temptation to join in with my Olduvai Maasai beadwork or Kamba arrows, which probably wouldn't have qualified as either. I reflected rather tiredly, and quite unnecessarily, that the tour parties, whose members were determinedly gregarious, were showing some classic aspects of hominid group behaviour, and I noted their usual apparently psychological need to be actually queued up at the departure gate well before the flight's departure was announced, in spite of all having been assigned seat numbers. There was also an interesting display of group insecurity when the wrong gate number was inadvertently mentioned in the departure announcement. Airports are usually good value for studying human behaviour, not all of it totally irrelevant to the theorising of palaeoanthropologists. Nevertheless, it was clearly high time I went home.

At last we were all aboard the plane. The man in the next seat to me arrived with two large, smoothly polished, carved wooden animals of the kind I actually like least, but it's all a matter of taste and there's no reason why he shouldn't like them best. There seemed to be a sharp bump at the moment of take-off, actually enough to bring at least one of the emergency oxygen masks dangling down in the middle section of the seating. Perhaps my case *was* too much for the plane after all, and had just burst? I noted that none of the customers immediately grabbed the mask when it appeared, placing it over the face and continuing to breathe normally, as instructed in the demonstration just held for our benefit. The air hostess had read out most carefully that we were to do this if a mask appeared in front of us: either the passengers are highly intelligent, or else they had simply not been listening. I then put my watch back two hours, for London time, in line with another announcement, but slightly suspiciously, because I only had to put it forward one hour on the way out, and British Summer Time lasts, surely, until late October. Just as everyone was settling down to sleep, drinks were suddenly brought round, which caused an instant general revival. A film was shown after that, but I couldn't see anyone at all watching it. Sleep was all one wanted.

Saturday, 1 October

I dozed quite successfully for a few hours. The first signs of dawn seemed to be at about 4.30 am. Orange juice arrived at about 5.15, followed by breakfast over the Alps. Only one or two summits could be seen, poking through the clouds as silhouettes, though there was one very spiky one that I thought looked likely to be the Matterhorn. The sun broke the horizon at 6.18: well, it did up where we were, but not down there. Back at Olduvai, there would be the sound of the Saturday clearing of the water tanks, and here I was, almost ready to start the descent to Heathrow, just as I had told them a somewhat hectic week ago.

We landed only five minutes late at 7.10, to find thick cloud and the weather slightly inclined to drizzle, but the temperature quite mild at around 60 degrees. There were enormous queues for the poor Americans and Kenyans at the immigration desks, but there seemed to be very few travellers with British passports arriving, so I shot through with no delay at all, and the luggage appeared for collection very quickly, unlike the delay at Nairobi on the way out. My case seemed quite safe and sound, after all.

What has gone wrong with the Customs Green Channel or, alternatively, with me? That is the second time in succession – I don't think I mentioned the previous one in last trip's diary – that I have been picked out in a random check for questioning after entering the Green nothing-to-declare Channel: inspection of camera ('very nice, Sir, did you take it out with you?') and so forth. All my luggage each time was entirely legal and pretty well documented with receipts, and Customs would have been welcome to search it, though they didn't bother, but I am puzzled, possessing (or so people tell me) the useful assets of an honest face and an air of sublime innocence. Indeed, I am one of those safe and helpful-looking people to whom the inevitable pair of Japanese tourists at any tourist beauty spot in any country, having taken the ritual pictures of each other, will eagerly hand their expensive camera for the further shot that must include both of them. So, what has changed? Have I reached a suspicious age, now I am past 45? Is it travelling alone, and arriving in London with no duty free bag? Have the cares and uncertainties of life as Mary's ghost-writer suddenly given me the look of a world-weary international crook? That might be the answer, I suppose. It started after I got myself two new suitcases – is it something to do with those? Or is it just sheer statistical chance? Anyhow, on this occasion, as last time, it merely caused a few minutes' delay, and I still caught a very convenient coach to Reading Railway Station. It got there at 8.35, and by good luck the alleged 8.36 to Oxford from Platform 7 didn't actually leave till 8.41, so I caught that too, and was at Oxford Station by 9.25. There was no queue at the taxi rank, so I got rapidly to 60 Banbury Road, where I found my research student John Dumont already well into his day's work in the laboratory, and much mail waiting to be dealt with.

Steady light English rain was falling, and autumn did not seem to have made much progress during my absence in important things like changing the colours of the leaves. How very nice it was to be back. Autobiography? What autobiography? And which of these two worlds, Olduvai and Oxford, is the real one? Neither, maybe.

AFTERMATH
AND
EPILOGUE

Rift valley and Lake Manyara (page 118)

My return to Oxford took place just before the beginning of term, and indeed the beginning of the new academic year, which is always a busy period. The final rushed and tired conversations with Mary in Nairobi had not been helpful with regard to what was to happen next, and I needed her comments on the final unread sections of the autobiography before I could get much further, though immediately she would be away in China and there was no point in sending a letter to Africa. My own task, according to the contract, was to submit the finished typescript by the end of December, and to help in the selection of illustrations and writing captions for them. Eternal optimist that I am, I saw no reason why any of that should be difficult to achieve, and it was presumably what Rainbird also wanted. At least the typing of the existing version of what I had written during the third visit could begin, while I was waiting for Mary to contact me.

One pleasant piece of news was awaiting me amongst the accumulated mail at Oxford when I got back: the university had approved the award to me of a Senior Doctorate, the degree of DLitt. This is something one achieves by submitting a collection of substantial publications – books and major papers – written over the years, and these are considered by two senior external assessors, whose names are not revealed to the candidate. It is quite an important landmark in an academic career, and I was perhaps on the young side to reach it, though not dramatically so. To be honest, with all that had been happening during the year, I had not given any recent thought at all to the progress of the assessment, having submitted the necessary written work several months previously, so the letter from the Chairman of the Faculty Board was a complete surprise when I opened it. Because the degree was the same one that Oxford had given to Mary a couple of years earlier *honoris causa*, one of my first thoughts was that it might amuse her to hear that her ghost-writer had actually earned access to the same title, so I added the news as a PS when I eventually wrote to her on 16 November, having still not heard a word from her by then, and thinking that time was running short:

> Dear Mary,
> I don't know quite what became of our parting arrangement that someone would let me know whether or not you were passing through England on the way back from China, even if the answer was negative, but no news of any kind has reached me and October has now long passed into November. I hope you *did* get to China and had an enjoyable and fruitful and not too tiring visit. There was also an arrangement that you would collect up at least the black-and-white photos we sorted last summer, if not a selection of slides too, and send them by Richard or by courier, as Rainbird's were keen for a preliminary look; nothing has come. Incidentally, if this is still to be done, don't forget to pencil on the back the names of people and places so that captions can be written. There was a further arrangement that, if you didn't come, you would at least send me comments on the last chapter (not read by the time I left) and the last-but-one, read only quickly and not discussed between us. There was also talk of the typescript being read by Richard and/or Meave and/or Hazel; in particular, you wanted Richard's comments on the parts concerning Johanson and White in the Laetoli chapter. Anyhow, you were quite tired enough after the journey from Olduvai and the post-election party to have forgotten all these tentative arrangements and even my existence, so I'm only partly surprised to have heard nothing. But I hope all is well.
> Meanwhile, deadlines approach, so I am sending you a copy of the typed text as produced during my September visit. Of this you had already a manuscript photocopy made on my last morning. The only addition is several lines about Hazel, as requested, and everything else is as you have already read it, incorporating your requested changes and deletions. A copy of your corrections to the previous

section has gone to Rainbird's and, as you wrote in the corrections
on your own copy, I am not sending that again – I have followed your
wishes scrupulously, even when against my better judgement.
I do *hope* there won't be too many more changes to the part I now
send, when you now read it in typescript, though I quite realise
that new points may occur to you. Whatever they are, you must spell
them out to me carefully and fully by *post*, as it now appears that
we will not be meeting again before I send the text in to Rainbird's
at the end of December – unless, that is, you are visiting England
on some other trip before the end of the year.
As requested, I am also sending copies of this last section to
Gertrude, Thurstan and Mary Fagg. I will also send a copy *now* to
Rainbird's, telling them that there will be some amendments to follow when I have heard from you, but they'd better have it now so
that they can work out lengths and so forth for the whole book,
which I calculate at 135–140,000 words. They will no doubt impose
their own editing on us in due course. So far as I can make out,
from now on it will be Jasmine dealing with the text, not Goldie, so
that may please you.
*The text has gone in a separate packet to Nairobi, today, by air
mail.* Copies of *this* letter are going to Nairobi *and* Ngorongoro.
Please send me your comments and amendments to pp 243–347 as soon as
you possibly can: I don't know when the typescript will come into
your hands, but if you could aim to send your reply within a week
... It's not *that* long to read, and you've seen it all already. I
recall that Peter and Annie are due to fly to England on Dec 12, but
with luck you'll have received and dealt with it some while before
then.
I hope all goes well, and would be very interested to hear all your
news since I left – China, the future of Olduvai, the dogs, everything.

Best wishes, Derek.

P.S. You might be amused or appalled to hear that your ghost-writer
now has a D.Litt. No doubt it was earned by numerous purple passages
in works you never got a chance to tone down ...!

There was an ominous lack of any response to this letter, and I could not get any
information from Rainbird either, beyond the fact that Mary was said to be working at
Nairobi on the text I had sent her. Some more informative, though not very encouraging,
news came in a letter from John Williams, the solicitor whom I had visited in London in
connection with the contract, and to whom I was required to send statements of expenses
for eventual refund by 'the Company' after each trip. We were thus in regular touch: he
was always very helpful, and took a genuine interest in my visits to East Africa and the
progress of the book. A letter from him dated 6 December 1983 included the following:

> I received a telephone call from Richard [Leakey] yesterday, during
> which he told me that his mother was working on the typescript which
> you had sent to her and hoped to finish this before the year end. In
> the meantime, it seems that we do have a period of grace from
> Rainbird under the original Contract and at Richard's request I am
> advising them that Mary will be in London during January when she
> hopes to let them have the last part of the draft. Richard also men-
> tioned that she had some additions to make to the earlier part and
> no doubt she will be discussing these with Rainbird and yourself
> during her visit.

I'm sure he meant sincerely the 'no doubt' in the last line, but I wasn't so sure, myself.
Mary eventually wrote me a letter dated 8 December, but sent it to a wrong address and a

wrong postcode, which seems extraordinary, after more than 10 years' correspondence – though, to be fair, I did myself miscopy the PO Box number of her Nairobi office address when I sent her the typed text after my first visit, delaying its arrival. I do not think this double error of Mary's was a deliberate delaying tactic: if she had wanted to cause further delay, it seems to me far more likely that she would simply not have written at all. The upshot, however, was that I only received the letter on 29 December, and when it did arrive, it merely confirmed my worst fears. Two things were unusual: first, unlike almost all Mary's other letters to me, it was typed and second, it had been a very long while since I had had one from her signed 'Yours sincerely'.

```
Dear Derek,
I have not replied sooner to your letter because there have been a
number of distractions since my return from China – flu and my
Olduvai Land Rover was stolen. Anyway, everything is now back under
control again.
I have decided to rewrite parts of the typescript and put things
into my own words where I am concerned. This has taken me some time
but it's going very well and I will personally hand over the final
typescript to Rainbird myself in early January. John Williams will
be in touch with Rainbird over this but I am sure there are no dif-
ficulties. I will also do the captions for the photographs myself
and I will spend the time with Jasmine on this in January.
I really do appreciate all that you have done and I know that I
could not have got to this point with the book without your help.
Having got so far, I can see the end in sight and hence my decision
to take over, as it were, in the final stages.
I am assured by Richard that John Williams has the necessary
instructions to conclude any payments due to you and this should now
be dealt with on the basis that you have submitted your copy to the
'company' as required under clause 6.
Best wishes,
Yours sincerely,
Mary.
```

I saw no particular point in replying to Mary, but I sent copies of her letter to Rainbird and to John Williams, saying that I was not at all happy with this turn of events and had considerable misgivings over the likely end-product, without wishing to prejudge it. In the letter to John Williams, I wrote:

```
I disapprove entirely of this arrangement, which seems to me to
treat Clause 4 of the Contract in a somewhat cavalier fashion and in
doing so also to make it impossible for me to fulfil Clause 5 ...
And if I am to take Mrs Leakey's word for it, Clause 6 appears to be
irrelevant or fulfilled, according to taste.
In the preliminary discussions, I indicated that I was quite pre-
pared to produce this text without a formal contract, but Mrs Leakey
preferred that there should be one. Why does she now, as it seems to
me, operate outside its terms? Or, in more direct language,
generally speaking, yuk.
Best wishes for a happy New Year ...
```

Not in the least to my surprise, Mary did not contact me during her January visit to London, during which she evidently finalised the text with Rainbird to her satisfaction, and the simple fact is that I never saw any part of the main text again, before it was eventually published, in early October 1984. It was probably as well for the sanity of all concerned – if 'sanity' is an appropriate term in all cases – that the publishers did not send me the proofs to correct, as the contract required.

There was just a little contact with Rainbird over those months, which even resulted in my seeing two snippets of the final text, which I had not myself written. In the first instance, they telephoned me, out of the blue, to say that it had been decided that there should be a glossary of technical terms, and would I care to cast an eye over it, since they were having difficulty in contacting Mary? One particularly troublesome word, they said, was 'baulk', and were they right in defining it as a piece of timber, which seemed odd in the context? I enquired, perhaps a little acidly, whether they could tell me any valid reason why, after the way in which they had so far treated my agreed role in preparing the final text, I should not simply tell them to get lost? I don't usually say things like that, and the effect whenever I do is always dramatic – I really ought to train myself to do it more often. The honeyed tone of the lady at the other end of the line changed instantly to a petulant whine, which made me wonder just how happy the publishers actually were with the way things had gone since December (though I never found out). I gave her to understand that she could post me the glossary text if she wished, and I might or might not look at it. It arrived the next day, and of course I gave it a total overhaul, which included crossing out 'a piece of timber' as the definition of 'baulk' and substituting 'an unexcavated strip between two excavation trenches, left to record in section the deposits removed' (which, as I well knew, was exactly what it meant in the particular context, the word having been used only once in the book). I even drew some helpful rough sketches, to make clear why I had adjusted some of the other definitions, mainly those of stone tool types, and so forth. The glossary definitions were clearly not Mary's work, and I was not going to have someone else adding to whatever other disasters might already have happened. I sent the annotated typescript back by return of post, having made a photocopy. No note of thanks came, but I hadn't really expected one. Mary had always placed publishers, as a general category, high on her list of stinkers: at this juncture, all things considered, it seemed to me clearly no business of a ghost-writer to question her judgement.

The other brief contact followed shortly afterwards: I remembered that the contract stated that 'Dr Roe should receive printed in all copies of all editions of the work an acknowledgement in a form to be mutually agreed between him, the Company and Mary Leakey for his contribution to the work'. No one had contacted me on that topic, and the proofs were by now in the final stages, so out of curiosity and perhaps to fan any flames there might be, I sent a brief note pointing out that I ought to see and approve the acknowledgement. A photocopy of the relevant lines of the page proofs arrived with a compliments slip, but with no request for comments or amendments. The total acknowledgements ran to 20 lines, and the last seven of these were all for me:

```
And most of all my thanks are due to Derek Roe, who undertook the
daunting task of helping me get the whole story down on paper. With
the possibility in mind that one day my life story might be written,
I had - over the past several years - taken to jotting down memories
as they came to me. The result was a sizeable pack of index cards
arranged in no particular order. From these, Derek has helped me
piece together the full story of my personal and professional life.
```

Well, I suppose one can't complain about that, as far as it goes, though if the whole business had really been as simple as it sounds there, I wonder how I have managed to draw the story of it out to such a length. At least Mary's acknowledgement is far more succinct than the one I included, at her request, in my own four-page draft for the conclusion, written in an hour or two of the afternoon of the last day I ever spent at Olduvai, 28 September 1983. She had instructed me to include an acknowledgement to myself in it, so I did, at least partly with tongue in cheek, and certainly not expecting to get away with many of the words I was putting into her mouth, even though they were firmly based on our conversations. It was just something for her to work on, undoubtedly reflecting my mood of the moment: rather than drafting a formal acknowledgement for the front of the book, I just let it grow naturally out of a passage in the conclusion about Mary's writing up of various projects in the 1980s, something which had been taking up much of her time since the Laetoli dig ended. In the event, she changed my ending of the story entirely and the last few pages of the draft text were simply never used. That was perfectly fair, though in fact we never discussed my draft conclusion at all, owing to the rather fraught ending to my last visit, which the diary has described. Had my own 'acknowledgement' survived, this is how it would have read, following directly on from a paragraph that had Mary referring to her work on the Laetoli volume and her book about the Tanzanian rock art.

I had always intended, perhaps without really having thought deeply enough about it, to write a book about Olduvai and my work there at a fairly popular level. In 1979, Collins published the result of that plan, my book *Olduvai Gorge: My Search for Early Man*, but I was not very pleased with it. If the truth be told, and as anyone who has read it may well have guessed, I got thoroughly bored with it about one third of the way through and by the end it had become as drily technical as the kind of writing I am much more used to for journal articles, where it is appropriate, but had been trying to avoid. And that brings us to the present book, which has been written wholly in 1983.

When I was asked to write an autobiography – Richard was the first to suggest it – I knew I would need help, if it were not to go the same way as the little *Olduvai Gorge* book I have just mentioned, and indeed if it were to get finished at all. After much thought I chose as my assistant an English colleague, Derek Roe, who agreed to take on the task. I have known Derek since he first visited me at Olduvai in 1969, and he has been several more times to the Gorge since then. He is a lecturer in Prehistoric Archaeology at Oxford University, specialising in the Lower Palaeolithic, and during the 1970s he undertook a long study for me of certain aspects of the Acheulean handaxes and cleavers of Olduvai, which will be published in my Beds III, IV and Masek monograph. He knew enough about my life and work and East Africa to have a head start over some professional journalist – with whom I am sure I should rapidly have fallen out – and it seemed to me that I could rely on him to order my jumbled memories into clear and readable prose, something I could never do for myself. I also remembered him as possessing an above-average quantity of both tact and patience, which I rightly guessed would both be necessary, and he has a certain reputation for completing tasks once undertaken. So it seems to have proved: without him, this book would not exist, and in the end I have told far more about myself and my life than I ever expected.

But in no sense is this book to be thought of as the product of a ghost-writer. Neither Derek nor I regard it in that light. Derek did not only have the enormous task of turning my memories into a long connected account, working from notes I had jotted down on index cards, and any other information he could coax out of me with the aid of a tape recorder, backed by his existing knowledge – a task which, incidentally, he achieved in three visits to Olduvai during 1983, totalling only ten weeks. Having completed that, he had to undergo the anguish, for a creative writer, of seeing me turn his words into mine, cutting out subtle links, cherished passages and turns of phrase which I knew I could never myself have used. I can sympathise with his rather sombre remark made during this process that if Shakespeare had had me go over his text, the *Collected Works* would be a very slim volume, confined to brief factual statements and minimal comments on possibly controversial details. Very likely.

```
Left to himself, Derek would have made this book more lively and
entertaining reading, but then, as he of course understood, it would
not have been my own story, told in my own way, which is what I
wanted. So I have retained full control over both contents and lan-
guage, and I think it is important to make this clear. In this
respect, and I hope in many others, this book will differ from those
which are ostensibly by one person but actually written by someone
different and uninvolved...
```

Reading over the two acknowledgements, I think I like my own effort better, but it was always likely to prove a classic example of the non-starter. So, in what eventually appeared, I got an actual expression of gratitude, which I had forgotten to include in my own version, but the readers were deprived of a broad hint regarding the way things actually were. Certainly, neither version constitutes the agreed acknowledgement to which the contract referred.

I have no record of the actual date when *Disclosing the Past* was published, but sometime in October 1984 I received two free copies, rather than the six that were supposed to be sent to me. That was the first time I saw the title of the book, something which Mary and I had often discussed without ever thinking of one we both liked. It struck me as very good, and I don't know who suggested it. Mary had vetoed my suggestion of *Mary, Mary, Quite Contrary* or just *Quite Contrary*; she had rather liked *My Own Way*, which I took from a remark she once made in one of the late evening conversations, actually referring to herself in the late 1920s: 'All I ever wanted to do was to have my own way and boss people about'. But I think *Disclosing the Past* is better than any of those. Otherwise, I looked to see what pictures had been used, but I simply did not have the heart to check the final text in any detail against my own typescript. As for the pictures, I already knew that none of those I had taken with such care was included, because in late September 1984 Rainbird had sent the whole lot back with a compliments slip, thanking me for the loan of them. When I received the package, I chose a few slides of Mary and the dogs at Olduvai and sent them to her to keep, because she had been enthusiastic over their taking, and had been determined to have a picture of herself with Dalmatians either on the cover of the book or as the frontispiece. This had evidently been overruled, though I noted that she had got away with her dedication of the book 'To the Dalmatians, past and present, who have so greatly enriched my life with their companionship, intelligence and loyalty'. In my letter enclosing the slides, I regretted that none of the pictures had been used, and sent my apologies to the dogs, especially Matthew, for all their time we had wasted. In her reply (29 September), Mary wrote: 'Very many thanks for sending the slides. Like you, I think that two would have been suitable for the jacket and preferable to the picture selected, but the people at Rainbird became increasingly unreasonable as time went on.' The last few words were rather revealing, I thought, but one does not know who was giving whom a hard time. This brief exchange is a very rare instance of any comments at all about the autobiography passing between Mary and myself, verbally or in correspondence, subsequent to her 'taking over', after I had completed the typescript. Following her visit to the publishers in London in January 1984, her mind had simply moved on to other things, in particular the need to get on with volume 5 of the *Olduvai Gorge* monograph series. Since I had contributed a long chapter to that, she still needed to correspond with me. Accordingly, the next letter I received from her after the one of 8 December in which she had announced her takeover, is dated 1 March 1984: characteristically, it simply goes straight to the point and stays there:

```
Dear Derek,
The next obstacle to be surmounted is the Beds III-IV volume. I know
you are very busy, but I would be grateful if you could let me have
```

```
the amended version of your contribution fairly soon. As I remember,
there were not too many changes to be made, only those concerning
the order in which the sites are discussed.
I am writing to Paul Callow by this mail because I really must get
things moving on the volume and cannot get my part written without
your contributions.
  By good fortune, a girl who worked with me at Laetoli is able to
come here in June and tackle the mosaic and contoured plan of the
pits.
Best wishes,
Yours sincerely, Mary.
```

Not a word about the surmounting of the previous 'obstacle'. Only once (in a letter dated 10 May 1984) did I take an opportunity provided by the correspondence about the Beds III, IV and Masek volume to express directly to Mary any thoughts about the autobiography. The context was a question of where I should send Mary some new computer-generated versions of certain tables and diagrams for Volume 5:

```
I assume you want everything mailed to you in Nairobi (airmail of
course), or will you or Richard be passing through in a few weeks'
time so that we can avoid risking the mail? Last time you told me
anything at all about your movements you were envisaging a trip to
the States to attend a conference or symposium in the spring, but I
have heard no more, just as I have heard no more of the autobiogra-
phy since I submitted my original version of the text. No, come to
think of it, that's not quite true: I received a cheque 3 or 4
months late, so I assume some version no one will risk showing me is
proceeding towards publication. And at the usual nil notice the pub-
lishers wanted some glossary they had devised checked. I suppose the
best entry was 'baulk:? a piece of timber'. Oh well, I suppose one
has to learn the hard way not to get involved with these projects. I
trust the eventual outcome, if any, will please and delight your-
self...
```

I neither expected nor received a reply. There was a risk that comments of this kind would get me added to the list of stinkers, I knew, and I did ask one visitor who came to Oxford from Nairobi – I think it was Barbara Isaac – whether Mary was now referring to me as such, but apparently the worst she had said was 'Derek is impossible'.

I have no idea at all how well the book did after publication, or how much of the projected sum it brought Mary. I saw a few reviews, which varied from lukewarm to favourable, and the reviewers picked out from the text precisely the incidents I had predicted to her. Those of her old friends in England who had read the final draft version all told me that they regretted – but were not surprised by – both the cuts in the published version and the way things had ended. I received the final contracted payment from 'the Company' only about a month late, thanks to the kind efforts of Mr Williams, and that concluded the whole episode.

This would be a sour note on which to end. It was, after all, Mary's book, and I was undoubtedly exceeding my role by trying to protect her against herself and add touches of colour to the text when she genuinely preferred black and white. Having used that form of words, I can't resist a specific example. I was writing (sometime during my second visit) about the three-month period in 1951, when she and Louis were working together on the Tanzanian rock paintings which she loved so much, during what she described to me as a particular happy period of their long partnership. On one occasion a small whirlwind struck the place where Mary was working and a tent nearby, where the drawings already completed were stored, sending many of them spinning up into the air. Describing the incident, I wrote 'It is an odd and not wholly pleasing sensation, watching the fruits of several days' work being ripped into large pieces and sent spiralling up into a hot blue African sky, to drift gently down over an area of some square miles.'

When I read this aloud to her later the same day, our usual method of procedure, she interrupted at once.

'Stop, stop!'

'What's wrong with that, Mary? Isn't that what happened?'

'You can't say "hot blue". Blue is a cold colour.'

It was the daughter of Erskine Nicol Junior and granddaughter of Erskine Nicol Senior speaking, but I did not feel inclined to yield.

'Mary,' I said. 'I too was once taught to paint, by a really rather good painter, and I am aware of "warm" and "cold" colours. But it seems to me that in Africa, of all places, you can very definitely have a "hot blue" sky.'

Mary considered this for a split second.

'Well, anyhow,' she said, 'it was grey.'

I rather doubted that at the time, and in the end we merely deleted the word 'hot'. I see that in the published version 'blue African sky' has survived.

No, I am not going to end on a sour note, just because I hated what happened to my beautiful text. Mary was to live another 12 years after publication of *Disclosing the Past*, and I was to work with her again before the end, with more pleasing results. What do you think – shall we allow ourselves the luxury of a short Epilogue?

Mary returned to working on *Olduvai Gorge*, Volume 5, in 1984, while the autobiography was in the press, and she had also by then left the Gorge and moved back to Langata in Nairobi, to the old Leakey family home. I myself have no first-hand knowledge of her life at this time. She mentions in her re-written closing pages of *Disclosing the past* that another of the Dalmatians died in 1984 – Janet, our placid companion on that noisy journey from Olduvai to Nairobi, with the broken exhaust, at the end of my third and final visit. Matthew and Brown Dog were with her in Nairobi – I hope Brown Dog's thesis did not depend on residence in Serengeti, or that he had at least got all the fieldwork side of his research done before he left. Brown Dog is clearly one of the minor heroes of this book, behaving throughout with quiet consistency and wisely playing a restrained role: I'm sorry I cannot tell you how he fared after retiring from the academic scene.

Over the next few years, Mary continued to travel from time to time to America, passing through England, but both Gertrude Caton-Thompson and Dorothy de Navarro died in the late 1980s, and her connection with Court Farm at Broadway ended. If she came to Oxford at all, it was to visit Catherine (Mary) Fagg. Catherine also went out to Kenya to visit Mary more than once, and they travelled together in East Africa and in Zimbabwe. I thus saw Mary very rarely, though we had a sporadic correspondence as and when necessary about the progress of *Olduvai Gorge*, Volume 5: some of the contributors proved quite extraordinarily slow in producing or revising chapters that were expected from them, and I found myself becoming increasingly involved in editorial and advisory work, to help maintain the momentum.

So things continued until early in 1990, when I suddenly received a phone call from Jessica Kuper, who was Mary's chief contact at Cambridge University Press, (CUP), the publisher of the volume, in which she told me that Mary was finding herself unable to write a closing overview chapter for it, and had suggested that I might take on the task. She was evidently a bit wary about asking me herself, and wanted Jessica to test my reaction to the idea before doing so. In principle, I was of course delighted to write such a chapter, which would be an interesting task, and one which I felt competent to undertake, if they would send me the text of the volume to work with, but the memories of what had happened to the last text I wrote for Mary were fresh enough to leave me somewhat suspicious, and I gave Jessica a somewhat guarded yes to pass on to Mary, asking for clarification on whether she wanted me to edit a text of hers, send material for a joint contribution or write the whole thing myself. Jessica's subsequent letter and my reply are perhaps worth quoting.

Jessica Kuper to Derek Roe, 27 February 1990

> Mary Leakey wrote to me this morning. She is delighted that you are willing to 'take a hand in the bothersome last chapter', an excellent idea, because she feels stale and uninspired and is unlikely to make a good job of it.
>
> She mentioned that your ghosting of her autobiography caused problems between the two of you, because she insisted on editing your script, etc. She wants you to confine yourself to a résumé of facts, and not elaborate on your own interpretations and theories. I'm not sure what this is all about, but it's best that I tell you exactly what she wants in order to avoid trouble! I suggest a maximum length of 4,000 words, although you may want to keep it a lot shorter.
>
> I'm having the manuscript copied, and will post it on to you soon. Do, please, let me know if you agree to this; and I suppose it would be best for you to communicate with her via me.

Reading now my reply of 6 March to Jessica, I'm quite surprised by its intensity, but

Mary's words had evidently opened up old wounds, even after six years. I didn't even know Jessica very well, but must have regarded her as likely to prove a sympathetic ear, apart from wishing to warn her of possible difficulties. These things make the letter of sufficient interest to quote.

> I'd better give you what help I can with Mary's last chapter, start-
> ing by writing a draft text of it. It will be the end of April, I'm
> afraid, before I'm clear of other commitments (with deadlines
> attached), but send me the copy text whenever you're ready.
> I'm afraid Mary's comments fill me with foreboding. Do please estab-
> lish, if you can, whether this chapter is to be under her name, my
> name or both our names. If it's the first of those, I suppose her
> comment is fair enough in its way; but if all she envisages is a
> summary of the preceding chapters, a sort of extended abstract of
> the book, then 4,000 words may be excessive. It would seem appropri-
> ate to me that the chapter should draw the other contributions
> together, and that is to some extent an act of interpretation. I
> have no 'theories of my own' to put forward! Oh well, we shall see.
> As for the autobiography, I was called in to extract the story from
> Mary, who was not enthusiastic about telling it, but needed the
> financial rewards, and my brief was to produce as bright and lively
> a text as I could, but elegantly written rather than in the manner
> of popular journalism. We worked hard at it, and it went very well.
> From the first draft, Mary removed everything she regarded as 'pur-
> ple passages' (which might mean a whole paragraph or a single adjec-
> tive), and that I expected. We still ended up with a lively and
> accurate text, which I could look at with pleasure, and she seemed
> agreed on it and happy with it. But as soon as the final version was
> typed and delivered, she set about adjusting it to what she regarded
> as a suitable degree of restraint, and, in my view, destroyed it.
> All the colours turned grey. I had agreed to handle the proofs for
> her and deal with the captions for the photos, but they never sent
> me the proofs - she came to England (without bothering to tell me)
> and worked on them with the publishers. Well, it was her
> autobiography, and written in the first person singular, so all that
> was perfectly fair. But she did no service to the book's success, or
> to the image of her that the final version she made presented - and
> that is not only my opinion, because various people have read *my*
> typescript. So, I felt somewhat miffed at the destruction of a minor
> masterpiece of prose (given the difficult circumstances of writing
> it) and at the way the destruction was achieved. But that's what
> ghost-writers are for, I suppose...
> These things I tell you merely to warn you that the very simple mat-
> ter of writing this final chapter for you may not go as easily as it
> should. I'll do you a lovely, clear, elegant text, factual and
> uncontroversial - and somehow, to some extent, it will get savaged.
> I hope I'm wrong!

I'm delighted to say that indeed I *was* wrong. In due course a copy of the text chapters reached me and I read through everything. I then wrote the kind of concluding chapter that it seemed to me the book required, and the result was in the hands of CUP by early August 1990. They lost no time in sending a copy to Mary, and she wrote to me from Nairobi on 15 September:

> Dear Derek,
> Jessica Kuper sent me a copy of your tail-piece for the Olduvai vol-
> ume. I am *indeed* grateful to you for writing it. My chief criticism
> is that you have been over-laudatory, in fact, I have no other to
> make. A minor point is relating the Olduvai Acheulean to
> Olorgesailie. This site is now well-dated and could be correlated as

```
far as such things are possible.
I visited Olduvai last week. It is a depressing sight and now the
scene of battle between members of the Antiquities Dept, the
Ngorongoro Conservation Authority etc. with Johanson secretly adding
fuel to the flames. It is good to know that the Gorge is inex-
haustible, no matter how much damage may be caused to sites now
exposed.
Catherine Fagg is in Kenya and came on a rock-painting safari with
me. It was a great success in spite of being 100 per cent female.
I hope to see you again, Derek, perhaps at the end of Oct. when I'll
be in England briefly.
Many thanks again –
Yours ever, Mary.
```

In due course I sent a final version of the chapter to CUP, and wondered when I might expect to see proofs of my two chapters ready to correct. I had a vague feeling that my part in the volume's long history was not yet completed, but I wasn't really expecting the bombshell that arrived in the form of a card from Jessica Kuper, and a letter from Mary. The proofs were at last ready in the early days of January 1993, and the plan was to send out to the various contributors proofs of their own chapters, with a master set for the whole volume going to Mary, to whom the contributors were to return their own correct-ed sections. The idea of having to deal with the master set, with all its complicated tables and diagrams, had evidently proved just too much for Mary.

This is not as unreasonable as it might sound. To be fair, the whole nature of this vol-ume had altered drastically since Mary first began to assemble the text for it around 1974. If other contributors had responded rapidly at that time, the book might well have made it to publication within two or three years of that date, say around 1977, but Laetoli inter-vened, and now, nearly two decades on from 1974, the whole nature of Palaeolithic archaeology had altered profoundly, the 'computer revolution' being one of the main causes of that. Various extra chapters had been added to Volume 5 that were not originally contemplated. The kinds of data that now had to be presented, and the way in which they needed to be analysed, were in many cases remote from Mary's own personal interest in the study of the distant past, and from the brilliant contributions she had made over the years in discovery and excavation. That is not to say that she had not in her many publi-cations analysed and interpreted her own finds, systematically and with great insight, but in doing so she had not involved herself directly with such things as computers or sophis-ticated techniques of statistical analysis. If others saw fit to use them on Olduvai material, well and good – just as the actual obtaining of potassium-argon dates or palaeomagnetic polarity readings was something for specialists to do, she having commissioned the work and the results being entirely welcome. I can well believe that the thought of being per-sonally responsible for the accuracy of the proofs of the whole volume would simply have appalled the Mary of 1993.

So, what cast-iron idiot might there be around, to provide an escape route, compe-tent enough to undertake the task and stupid enough to be talked into doing so? I don't suppose that was really how she expressed it to herself, but in any case the question could only have one answer, and here is her letter of 27 January 1993 to me. It went straight to the point, as usual. I really must find out how people do this straight-to-the-point stuff.

```
Dear Derek,
You will surely be shocked and alarmed when you get this letter and
I feel rather awkward about writing it. However, you may recollect
that many years ago you generously offered to check the proofs of
Olduvai vol 5. The time has now arrived and I wonder whether the
```

```
offer still holds good? You will receive proofs of your own contri-
bution to the volume, in any case, but could I impose on your good
nature and ask for more proof-reading? I would be most grateful.
I have been out of action with malaria contracted at the coast over
Xmas and am only now getting back into some sort of shape.
You will have received warning letters from the C.U.P. If you would
consider my request, could you please get in touch with Jayne
Matthews at the C.U.P.? I would be exceedingly grateful for your
help, Derek.
With all good wishes,
Hopefully, Mary.
```

It was getting on for 20 years since I had handed in my report on the handaxes and cleavers for this volume to Mary, and I had invested a very substantial amount of time and effort of an editorial or advisory nature on other sections since then, not to mention writing the conclusion, so I was never really going to refuse the task of seeing it through to the winning-post, but it was a major undertaking, which had appeared without warning, at a time when things were particularly busy on other fronts, and I felt entitled to play a little bit hard to get. I indicated earlier that, while the story of the autobiography and the story of the highly technical and academic Volume 5 were quite separate things, for me they had inevitably become closely linked. My letter to Jessica Kuper about writing the final chapter, quoted above, shows that: here we go again, I thought. Before long my reply was on its way to Mary; the third paragraph will explain, incidentally, her reference to my offer some years earlier about the proofs.

```
8 February 1993
Dear Mary,
Thank you for your letter. Sorry to hear about the malaria and hope
you are fully on the mend.
Yes, well, I can see how your request might cause a feeling of awk-
wardness. On the other hand, I cannot conjure up a vision of you
actually feeling the slightest qualms about trying it on. But I
could be wrong, I suppose.
The deal we struck in 1972 (or just possibly 1974) involved my com-
ing to Olduvai during the game migration to correct the proofs for
you, and being rewarded with a series of agreed minor adventures,
like a trip to the Embagai crater, plus a constant supply of man-
goes. I'd have been delighted to go through with that, and we might
both have enjoyed it, as well as dealing efficiently with the
proofs. 'The time has now come', she says. Even I don't regard your
side of the bargain as possible.
I'll talk to C.U.P. and see what, if anything, can be arranged. You
probably won't believe me if I tell you how busy things are here. In
the 8 weeks of last term, I reckon I got a total of six hours, well
scattered, to devote to writing and research. Of my immediate col-
leagues, one has taken early retirement (and there's a delay on
filling the post) and the other is on sabbatical leave. Not surpris-
ingly, I've inherited some extra teaching and students, and I'm on
about 14 committees internally and around a dozen externally. Just
at the moment, I'm reading a student's draft thesis text until
around 1.0 am each morning, with another thesis waiting to be exam-
ined. Still no secretarial assistance. A new undergraduate course in
Archaeology began this year ... And so it goes on.
Well, it will depend very much on the exact timing of the page-
proofs. I'll do what I can, and won't even yield to the strong temp-
tation to put back into this text all the nice things that somehow
mysteriously vanished from the text of Disclosing the Past. Over the
past few years I've had a lot to do with this volume, since it
reached the C.U.P.'s hands, and I don't propose to desert it now: I
```

```
feel more like a co-author than a contributor, rightly or wrongly.
So, leave me to work things out somehow with C.U.P.
The things I do for you, Mary ... how can anyone go on being such a
sucker? Make the most of it - there aren't any others like me
around, I suspect. I can imagine this letter now being tossed aside,
after a quick read: oh, good, he's going to do it. Why does the
stinker take so long to say so?
Get well soon. I hope all the family are in good form, and that you
are finding plenty of things to enjoy.
Best wishes, Derek.
Shall I put a copy of this letter in as an Appendix? It's full of
historical interest, really.
```

I sent a copy of this to Jessica Kuper at CUP to let her know that I would help out. I was really not expecting either her, or indeed Mary, to take seriously my remark about being a co-author of the volume, but both did. Jessica, after expressing the view that Mary might be finding many things to enjoy, but that my letter would not be one of them, took up the point and said she would like to put it to Mary that I be a co-author: had I had as much to do with the actual fieldwork and the interpretation of it as Mary had? Would I regard my role as equal to hers? I really didn't want anyone to suppose that I thought any such thing, and I set out the facts as I saw them in my reply (15 February 1993):

```
I wouldn't want to push a request to be co-author of the Olduvai
volume very far. Indeed, I think 'co-author' would be wrong: if any-
thing, I would be a co-editor. Mary herself is author of around two-
thirds (at a guess) of the volume, and editor of the rest, in that
she has arranged the other contributions and read and approved the
final versions. Even she isn't therefore really the author of the
volume to be published, and my degree of authorship is a great deal
smaller than hers.
I think my role in actually helping to achieve publication has been
significant, but that's another matter, and anyhow all you good peo-
ple at the Press have really achieved that. As I said to you on the
phone, it's not my custom or wish to have my name attached to work
that is not fairly mine (rather an old-fashioned view, I fear!).
Mary was working at Olduvai before I was born, and has spent a very
large part of her long life there, achieving brilliant results with
the expert assistance of very many people, working essentially under
her direction. I made a number of visits between 1969 and 1983 to do
the work that led to my specialist chapter in this volume. Because
of our long, if intermittent, working partnership, and my own par-
ticular field of knowledge and experience, it was to me that Mary
turned for her final overview chapter (which a real 'author' would
have been expected to write herself), and I was very happy to supply
it. I'm not sure where else it would have come from. I never took
part in any of the Olduvai fieldwork. The story of the whole busi-
ness of the writing of Mary's autobiography is really something
quite separate from all of this, linked only by the respective roles
of Mary and myself, and it is doubtless that episode which leaves me
most dissatisfied and colours my view of the present request. For
the autobiography, I was indeed a hired ghost-writer and liable to
exorcism.
I hope this clarifies the background for you. I make no conditions
at all concerning the proof-correcting, which I will do to the best
of my ability, for the volume's sake. If Mary decides for herself
that it would be appropriate for my name to appear with hers as a
co-editor, fine; but no pressure should be applied to her, and I do
not think it likely. If you do decide to raise the point with her,
it should be as C.U.P.'s idea rather than mine. In any case, I'd
guess it's far too late, from the production point of view.
Long live the wicked witch of the South. Mary won't be fretting over
```

```
my letter, I think: once she has worked out from it that she hasn't
got to do the proofs herself, she won't reread it. 'Stinker', inci-
dentally, is her own regular term for anyone held in disesteem ...
Just now, along with the word 'impossible', it's probably being
applied to the willing stand-in proof-reader ...
```

When Mary replied to my letter, she did so in far more contrite terms than I had expected, and told me things I had not known about her health:

```
P.O. Box 15028
Nairobi,
Kenya
24/2/93
Dear Derek,
If I was embarrassed to write my first letter, I am even more so now
and am fully aware that I have traded on your good nature. I am
deeply grateful and only took the liberty of asking you when I
realised that I could not deal adequately with the proofs myself.
For your ears, I'm no longer the robust woman of Olduvai days. I had
heart trouble a year ago and am on pills for evermore. Two bouts of
malaria within a few months did me no good and have addled what was
left of my brain. I knew I was incapable of doing the proofs ade-
quately, hence my letter requesting further help from you. I tell
you all this hoping you will realise that it was not sheer laziness
or aversion to proof-reading that prompted me to write.
So much for my troubles and forgive the account outlined above.
You have my deepest gratitude and if you wish to be a co-author,
please insert yourself in that role. I have also suggested to
Jessica Kuper that the book should include a note by me expressing
my thanks and letting readers know the major part you have played in
its production.
The family is well but none of them are doing too well matrimonial-
ly. No doubt the various situations will be resolved in the end.
Thank you, Derek, once more. I have seldom felt such real gratitude
before - not to mention guilt.
Yours ever, Mary.
```

I suppose a detached observer, comparing my letters quoted in this concluding section with those at the start of the book, could be forgiven for thinking that a somewhat waspish note had begun to creep in, whether or not there had been provocation to account for it. Perhaps my reply to this letter from Mary, which is the last letter to be quoted, will show that the gentler style of 10 years earlier had not actually been lost.

```
11 March 1993
Dear Mary,
Many thanks for your letter.
I'm so sorry to hear you are feeling a bit infirm - or perhaps I
should say somewhat more gracile than robust. I quite understand
that you can't cope with the proofs. Don't worry about it at all -
leave them to me, and I'll see that everything gets done, one way or
another. I'll do the very best I can for you. I can check your own
chapters against the original text, the only risk being that if any-
thing was wrong but apparently makes sense, I shall not be aware of
it in the way that you might have been - well, at the time you wrote
it, anyhow, though perhaps not after the malaria. Anyhow, like I
say, leave it to me.
I have to make a brief visit to the U.S.A., March 18-April 2nd, and
C.U.P. will have the proofs awaiting my return - or so they say.
I'll get straight on with them.
It's nice of you to say I can be a co-author if I wish. I'm not sure
```

```
that I should feel quite comfortable about it unless I thought it
was something you actually wanted, and I don't see why it should be.
After all, you were working at Olduvai before I was actually born(!)
and the work on Beds III, IV and Masek has been very much your oper-
ation. I've certainly done quite a lot in an editorial and advisory
capacity with the volume for C.U.P., and am about to do more. It may
indeed be true that without my efforts it wouldn't actually have
appeared. But co-authorship seems a bit different. Would it really
be fair that people should refer to Leakey and Roe 1993 rather than
Leakey 1993? A great honour for me, no doubt, but I like to earn
them. Pardon my old-fashioned attitudes - well, I think you share
them, really.
I've been working long hours on the closing chapter of the East
Turkana volume, writing what Glynn Isaac should have lived to write.
Very interesting and instructive, too, but not easy to get finished
in odd hours, mainly between midnight and 2.0 am. Still, it's writ-
ten, and only needs typing.
I keep hearing vague rumours of a conference in Arusha this summer
in your honour, but no-one has sent me any details, nor have I seen
an announcement. Is it true? We used to have adventures in Arusha,
didn't we, every time we tried to pass through? I hope the malaria
and pills haven't destroyed all your memories of such things.
Get well soon, Mary. There's lots for you to do yet, even if proofs
are not on the list.
Best wishes,
Love, Derek.
```

Little remains to tell. The publishers did their best to qualify as stinkers by sending the proofs to Mary in Kenya instead of to me, after all the careful arrangements, so there was a long delay before I eventually had them in my hands. When I did, there was a great deal requiring to be sorted out, in the case of some chapters to the extent of revised proofs having to be produced, but eventually it all got done. One set of errors was rather charming, and bears out my comment about Mary's lack of acquaintance with statistics: she had painstakingly listed certain classes of stone artefacts, level by level, giving for each the ranges of measurements for a given dimension, and the average value. The only problem was that in some 16 cases the average figure lay outside the range of measurements. For example: Site WK East C, complete lava end-struck flakes, breadth: range, 38 to 26 mm. Average breadth, 21 mm. Fortunately, during my checking of the proofs, Mary was briefly in Oxford, and I was able to consult her on points that I could not solve myself.

'You can't have an average figure that lies outside the range of the actual measurements, Mary,' I said. 'It simply isn't possible.'

'Why ever not?' she asked, indignantly. I explained, and she reluctantly agreed, after we had been over it two or three times.

'But we can't do anything about it,' she added. 'The termites ate all the papers that had those measurements on them.'

The other proof-correcting problems were more routine, and eventually everything was done, and an index was completed and checked by me. I had left to CUP the matter of co-authorship, merely pointing out, when I returned the final proofs, that if they really did add my name to Mary's on the title page and dust jacket, one or two points in Mary's Introduction would require minor adjustment, and a brief explanation of my actual role would be needed (as suggested by Mary herself). In the end, the book appeared (in 1994) as by MD Leakey with DA Roe, but the adjustments to the Introduction were not made, and the explanatory note was not added, so readers may well have been a bit confused as to what my name was doing there in Mary's book. One really needs to stand over publishers right to the moment when the printing press begins to roll, or whatever the equivalent process now is, or the latent stinker characteristics will emerge, the moment one's back is turned. But overall, the volume was beautifully produced and a considerable success, well received by the reviewers. It was a fitting final major publication for Mary, and at last she could feel that the definitive reporting of her 50 years of work at Olduvai was complete.

Mary was in Oxford again just once, to visit Catherine Fagg, during 1995, and I went round one afternoon to see her and just chat. She was not in the best of health, but very much her old self, and enjoying her visit. I took my copy of *Olduvai Gorge*, Volume 5, with me, and asked her to sign it. On the title page she wrote:

```
To Derek with love and great gratitude for coming to my rescue -
Mary. Oxford 1995
```

Now, there's an altogether happier note on which to end, and perhaps some kind of a wheel had turned full circle. It was in fact the last time I saw Mary, who died in Nairobi on 9 December the following year.

1 People

The following brief notes are not intended as proper or comprehensive portrait summaries of anyone: their purpose is just to identify for the reader some of the characters who flit in and out of the saga of events which the diary and its framing chapters record. I cannot even vouch for the complete accuracy of the information given, in some cases, and I hope that any of those listed who may read this and find errors will forgive me for them. For many of the names, people not independently known to me, I had no sources to check, and often I am simply recording here briefly what I was told or given to understand at the time about visitors who turned up at Olduvai, or other people who played a relevant role, major or minor, at the time or even long before. If what I was told was wrong or incomplete, that may be of interest in itself, but I certainly hope that there are not too many errors which are misunderstandings of my own.

I am very grateful to Ray Inskeep and to Sarah Milliken for checking over the whole text of the Glossary for me and for making a number of very helpful suggestions. Where a word is in bold in the main text of an entry it indicates that a glossary entry exists for that word.

Amini **MTURI**, *see* **MTURI**, Amini.

BARTON, Nick. Research student of Derek Roe at Oxford at the time when the diary was written, working on British Later **Upper Palaeolithic** archaeology; subsequently a professional colleague as teacher and researcher in **Palaeolithic** Archaeology, first at the University of Wales College, Lampeter, and afterwards at Oxford Brookes University.

BOWER, John. American archaeologist, and friend of Mary Leakey, who in 1983 was conducting fieldwork on Serengeti in the **Gol Kopjes** region.

BROWN DOG. Abandoned Maasai dog who attached himself to the camp at Olduvai and was made an honorary Dalmatian by Mary Leakey, an appointment which the genuine Dalmatians viewed with mixed feelings. His colour was actually a pale buff rather than a deep brown (photographs on pages 46 and 100).

CALLOW, Paul. Cambridge archaeologist, like Derek Roe an undergraduate and graduate student of the late Charles **McBurney**, though a few years later. Expert in computing, and one of the contributors to *Olduvai Gorge*, Volume 5.

CATON-THOMPSON, Gertrude. Distinguished Cambridge archaeologist and intrepid fieldworker, born in 1888, so well into her nineties by the time the diary was written. She had introduced Mary to Louis Leakey and was a major influence on her entry into archaeology in the late 1920s and early 1930s. She remained an important friend of Mary's for the rest of her own very long life, and lived latterly with Toty and Dorothy de Navarro (*see* **Navarro**) at Court Farm, Broadway, Worcestershire, where Mary regularly visited her. She died in 1985.

CHARLES. English-speaking **Maasai** member of the guide staff at Olduvai Gorge, who at the time when the diary was written was hoping to study archaeology at London University.

CLARK, J Desmond. The doyen of African archaeologists, still actively working right up to the time of his death, aged 85, in 2002. He was a friend of Mary Leakey from at least the 1940s. Desmond was the excavator of numerous important **Palaeolithic** sites, during his long and immensely productive career, and did important work in the Near East and in China, as well as in Africa. Stone artefacts excavated by him at **Kalambo Falls**, Zambia, were the reason for Derek Roe's first visit to Africa and his first meeting with Mary Leakey.

COLLCUTT, Simon. Research student of Derek Roe at Oxford during the events described in the diary, working on cave sedimentology. He later founded and directed Oxford Archaeological Associates Ltd, one of the first of the archaeological consultancy companies.

CURTIS, Garniss. American expert on **chronometric dating** techniques, especially Potassium-Argon, based at the University of California at Berkeley. His laboratory dated samples from many early African sites, including Olduvai Gorge.

DANGERFIELD, Graham. Zoologist, who had been a contemporary of Derek Roe at St Edward's School, Oxford in the 1950s, and was unexpectedly encountered in Arusha during the first of the three visits in 1983.

DAVIDSON, Mary, *see* **FAGG**, Mary Catherine.

DAY, Michael and Mickey. Close friends of Mary Leakey, whose house in Hampstead, London, she regarded as 'a second home'. Michael, for many years Professor of Anatomy at London University, is also an authority on early **hominid** fossils, and studied the finds from Olduvai Gorge, at Mary Leakey's request. Mickey, his wife, is a busy medical practitioner.

de **NAVARRO**, *see* **NAVARRO**.

DOVE, George. For many years, owner of the Ndutu Safari Lodge, and Mary Leakey's nearest Serengeti friend and neighbour; previously a well-known white hunter and a long-term Tanzanian resident. He built the main workroom at the camp for Mary in 1974, after she had moved permanently to Olduvai. George's waxed moustaches were famous.

DUMONT, John. American research student of Derek Roe at Oxford, present there at the time when the diary was written, working on the microwear analysis of British and Irish stone artefacts of the Mesolithic period.

EVERNDEN, Jack. Geophysicist from the University of California at Berkeley, who worked on the Potassium-Argon dating of samples from Olduvai Gorge in the 1960s.

FAGAN, Brian. Professor of Anthropology at the University of California at Santa Barbara, and author of many books on prehistory and archaeology. When first met by Derek Roe, he was an undergraduate at Cambridge University, one year ahead of Derek on the Archaeology & Anthropology degree course. He subsequently did fieldwork in Africa, starting in Northern Rhodesia (Zambia) when J Desmond **Clark** was based there as Keeper of Prehistory in the Rhodes-Livingstone Museum.

FAGG, Bernard, *see* **FAGG**, Mary Catherine.

FAGG, Mary Catherine (*née* Davidson). Close friend of Mary Leakey's from the latter's early days with Louis in Nairobi. In 1942 she married Bernard Fagg: he was an African archaeologist and later became Curator of the Pitt Rivers Museum in Oxford, a post which made him *ex officio* Head of the Department of Ethnology and Prehistory at Oxford University, when Derek Roe was appointed as University Lecturer in Prehistoric Archaeology there in 1965. Mary Catherine Fagg was always known to Mary Leakey as 'Mary', her preferred first name, but Bernard encouraged the use of Catherine, to avoid the confusion between two Marys. In Oxford, everyone seemed to know her as Catherine Fagg.

GIBB, Margaret. Owner of Gibb's Farm at Karatu, Tanzania, and counted by Mary Leakey not merely as a close friend but a near neighbour, even though actually living a couple of hours' drive from Olduvai. Gibb was her first husband's surname: after his death, she married Per Kullander.

GIFFORD, Diane (afterwards Diane **GIFFORD-GONZALES**). American anthropologist with particular research interests in site-formation, **taphonomy** and faunal remains, who had worked in Africa; in 1983, she was carrying out fieldwork with John **Bower** at the **Gol Kopjes** on Serengeti. She is now at the University of California at Santa Cruz.

GOLDSMITH, John. British writer, whom Derek Roe had met casually in London some years earlier, when John was about to publish his first novel, *Mrs Mount, Ascendant.* He was re-encountered unexpectedly in Arusha during the first of the three visits described in the diary.

GOODWIN, AJ. John Goodwin was a South African archaeologist of major importance, author of many important books and papers from the early 1920s till his death in 1959. He welcomed and helped Mary Leakey on her very first visit to Africa in 1935.

HAY, Dick (properly, Richard L). American geologist, who worked on many occasions with Mary Leakey at Olduvai, contributing the definitive account of the geology of the Gorge and its archaeological sites. He was a regular visitor and close personal friend. He has continued to work at Olduvai from time to time in the years since Mary's death.

HEWLETT, Jack. The caretaker at the Donald Baden-Powell Quaternary Research Centre, 60 Banbury Road, Derek Roe's base at Oxford University, at the time when the diary was written.

INSKEEP, Ray. An immediate colleague of Derek Roe at Oxford, at the time when the diary was written, Ray then being Senior Assistant Curator of the Pitt Rivers Museum and University Lecturer in African Archaeology. He was previously for many years Head of the Department of Archaeology at the University of Cape Town, and before that had briefly taught Derek Roe during Derek's undergraduate days at Cambridge University.

ISAAC, Barbara. Wife of Glynn **Isaac**, who worked at his side throughout his professional career. After Glynn's death, while herself working in the Peabody Museum at Harvard University, she ensured the completion of various things he had left unfinished, most notably seeing through to publication his great volume on the archaeology of **Koobi Fora**.

ISAAC, Glynn. Distinguished archaeologist of the **Palaeolithic** (Professor at the University of California at Berkeley and subsequently at Harvard University), who worked especially in Africa (he was born in South Africa) up to his untimely death in 1985 aged only 47. He worked closely with several members of the Leakey family in East Africa. Previously he was an undergraduate contemporary and close friend of Derek Roe at Cambridge University, where they were at the same college (Peterhouse) and attended lectures and classes given by Charles **McBurney** together. Both were subsequently research students under McBurney's supervision.

JANET. Senior female member of Mary Leakey's team of Dalmatians, at the time when the diary was written (photograph, page 100).

JOHANSON, Don. American anthropologist, leader of various highly successful field expeditions in Ethiopia, where many major discoveries of **hominid** fossils were made from the 1970s onwards, including '**Lucy**'. A major conflict developed between Johanson and Tim **White**, on the one side, and Mary and Richard **Leakey**, on the other.

JONES, Annie (*née* Vincent). She had married Peter **Jones** shortly before the diary begins. Born and brought up in Australia, she became a graduate student in America, working under the supervision of Glynn **Isaac**, and during 1983 was still engaged on doctoral research, for which she was carrying out fieldwork in Tanzania, not far from Olduvai Gorge, working *inter alia* with the **Hadza**.

JONES, Peter. Mary Leakey's Research Assistant at Olduvai Gorge, when the diary was written, a post which he had held for several years by 1983. He had become one of the best experimental stone knappers (*see* **knapping**) in the world, and was a major contributor to the fieldwork and various other aspects of the research at both Olduvai and **Laetoli**. His father, Schuyler Jones, was then an ethnologist and anthropologist working at Oxford University in the same Department as Derek Roe (by 1983 he was Head of it and Curator of the Pitt Rivers Museum). Peter's early interest (as a young schoolboy) in flint artefacts caused his father to introduce him to Derek, who encouraged him and helped to start him off on various paths that were to become important to him. Later, he studied for one year at Oxford under Derek's supervision, successfully completing a Master's Degree course in Prehistoric Archaeology. (Photographs including Peter, pages 65 and 128).

KABEBO. A principal member of Mary Leakey's camp staff at the time when the diary was being written. He was a brother of Kamoya Kimeu – the latter became internationally famous as the leader of Richard **Leakey's** 'Hominid Gang', a well-organised and highly skilled team of African finders of **hominid** fossils during the field survey of several major research areas.

KATTWINKEL, Otto. German naturalist and entomologist, who discovered Olduvai Gorge by chance during a visit to Serengeti, then in German East Africa, in 1911. He reported the existence of the Gorge, and the presence of fossil animal bones there, to Professor Hans **Reck** in Berlin.

KEILLER, Alexander (1889–1955). Member of the Scottish Keiller family, famous for the manufacture of marmalade and confectionery, and a wealthy landowner. In the 1920s he developed a passionate interest in archaeology, especially that of Wiltshire and Wessex: while he remained an amateur, he became a member of the archaeological establishment, especially during the 1930s. He used his great wealth to preserve archaeological sites by purchasing the land on which they were situated, especially around Avebury, and he organised and paid for the excavation of several important sites, including Windmill Hill, where Mary Leakey first experienced excavation, under the guidance of Dorothy **Liddell**, who was Keiller's sister-in-law, and WEV **Young**, whom Keiller employed. Keiller lived for many years at Avebury Manor, and established the Avebury Museum and the Morven Institute of Archaeological Research.

KITETU. The excellent cook at Olduvai, at the time when the diary was written, a long-serving senior member of Mary Leakey's camp staff.

LEAKEY, Jonathan. Eldest of the three sons of Louis and Mary Leakey. Herpetologist (from an early age), and owner of a safari camp at **Lake Baringo**. He had worked with his parents at Olduvai, where he personally discovered the original *Homo habilis* fossil.

LEAKEY, Meave (*née* Epps). (Second) wife of Richard **Leakey**. Zoologist and palaeontologist (*see* **Palaeontology**), who worked with him in the field from 1969 onwards. Later she herself, as Head of the National Museum of Kenya's Palaeontology Department, directed very important work on the west side of **Lake Turkana** in northern Kenya, where various important early **hominid** fossils were found.

LEAKEY, Philip. Youngest of the three sons of Louis and Mary Leakey. He became the first white member of the Kenyan Parliament, in which he subsequently rose to ministerial rank.

LEAKEY, Richard. Second of the three sons of Louis and Mary Leakey, who had a distinguished career as an archaeologist and human palaeontologist (*see* **palaeontology**), followed by an equally high-profile one in Kenyan politics and in wildlife conservation. At the time when the diary was written he was, among other things, Director of the National Museum of Kenya in Nairobi.

LIDDELL, Dorothy. British archaeologist, specialising in the **Neolithic** period, with whom Mary Leakey had her first experiences of archaeological field-work, and training in excavation techniques, at Windmill Hill (Avebury, Wiltshire) and **Hembury** (Devon). She was the sister-in-law of Alexander **Keiller**, and when Mary first met her was excavating for him on land that he owned.

McBURNEY, Charles BM (1914–1979). The principal teacher of **Palaeolithic** Archaeology at Cambridge University from the 1950s till his sadly early death, as Lecturer, Reader and later Professor. Amongst his students were the author of this book and several others mentioned in it (*see* Glynn **Isaac**, Paul **Callow** and Robert **Soper**). McBurney was the excavator of several important Palaeolithic sites of various ages, in North Africa, Europe and the Near East, and the author of several books and many important papers. He is remembered by many generations of Cambridge archaeology students for his wonderful combination of distinguished scholarship, great personal charm and kindness, hilarious absent-mindedness, and a highly distinctive voice. He did visit Olduvai once, with his wife Anne:

Mary Leakey enjoyed their company, but her main memory of Charles was that he persisted in differing from her own views on certain aspects of **Oldowan** stone tool typology, even late in the evening. Charles's account of the exchange was rather different, and dwelt rather pointedly on what he perceived as the inadvisability of asking Mary scholarly questions in the late evening.

MATTHEW. Leader of Mary Leakey's team of Dalmatians at the time when the diary was written (photographs pages 1 and 100).

MAY, Jeffrey and Brenda. Long-standing friends of Derek Roe, and regular visitors to Oxford: in 1983 Jeffrey was a university lecturer and researcher at Nottingham University, working mainly in later prehistoric archaeology; his wife Brenda is a pianist and teacher of music (also at Nottingham University).

MERRICK, Harry. Archaeologist working at the National Museum of Kenya in Nairobi. Joan, his wife, also worked at the museum.

MOEHLMAN, Patti. Regular visitor to Serengeti from Yale University, to study animal behaviour, particularly of jackals. Based at **Lake Ndutu**, she was one of Mary Leakey's nearest neighbours, and a close personal friend.

MOYES, Sally. Former resident of Arusha, Tanzania, where she and her husband worked for Oxfam for a couple of years; acquaintance of the Leakeys and of Peter and Annie **Jones**. By the time when the diary was being written, she was living near Oxford. Subsequently she worked at Oxfordshire **Palaeolithic** and **Pleistocene** sites with Dr Katharine Scott's team, which was based at the Donald Baden-Powell Quaternary Research Centre, Derek Roe's base in Oxford.

MTURI, Amini. Director of Antiquities in Tanzania during Mary Leakey's later years at Olduvai and accordingly one of her main official contacts with the Tanzanian Government, but also a personal friend and the excavator in the 1970s of a **Lower Palaeolithic** site at **Lake Ndutu**, which yielded stone artefacts and an important **hominid** fossil skull.

NAADE. Craftsman member of the Olduvai camp staff, who could make or fix many things. He was of the **Mbulu** people.

NAVARRO, Jose (always known as Toty) and Dorothy de. Toty was a distinguished archaeologist, an expert in later European prehistory, formerly teaching at Cambridge University, and Dorothy was his wife. Gertrude **Caton-Thompson** lived with them in their fine Cotswold house, Court Farm, at Broadway, Worcestershire, where Mary Leakey was a regular visitor when in England. Toty de Navarro had died in 1979, before the diary was written.

NORTON-GRIFFITHS, Mike. Wildlife researcher, based in Nairobi during the 1970s and 1980s, who was a friend of the Leakey family. His work sometimes took him to Serengeti and thus to Olduvai.

OMARI. Motor mechanic, working at a garage in Arusha until enlisted by Peter **Jones** in

1983 as a member of the Olduvai staff.

POTGIETER, Hazel. Mary Leakey's efficient and indefatigable secretary in Nairobi, during the period in which the diary was written, and also a valued personal friend. She lived in Nairobi and her office was in the National Museum complex of buildings.

RECK, Hans. German Professor of Geology, who first visited Olduvai Gorge in 1913 to follow up the report he had received from the discoverer of the site, Otto **Kattwinkel**. Louis Leakey invited him to join his own first expedition to Olduvai in 1931.

SHAW, C Thurstan. Friend of Mary Leakey since 1930, when she met him (then a schoolboy) at the excavation of the **Hembury Neolithic** site in Devonshire. He became a distinguished archaeologist in Africa, working especially in Nigeria, where he was Professor and Head of the Archaeology Department at Ibadan University.

SOPER, Robert. Friend and undergraduate contemporary (1958–1961) of Derek Roe at Cambridge University, where they both studied **Palaeolithic** archaeology under Charles **McBurney**. Robert subsequently became an archaeologist in Africa, working in several different countries, mainly Nigeria, Kenya and Zimbabwe. At the time when the diary was written, Robert was based in Nairobi at the University.

SOPHIE. Junior member of Mary Leakey's Dalmatian team at the time of the writing of the diary, though as a Dalmatian she outranked **Brown Dog**. She died during the third of the three visits to Olduvai which the diary records.

WHEELER, Sir Mortimer (REM Wheeler). A senior figure in British Archaeology after the Second World War who, apart from important fieldwork and contributions to the methodology of excavation, was one of the first archaeologists to become a television star, as early as the 1950s, via the popular panel game *Animal, Vegetable, Mineral?*, which was chaired by Glyn Daniel, of Cambridge University. Wheeler died in 1976.

WHITE, Tim. American archaeologist and palaeoanthropologist, with a long record of important research and discovery in the earlier **Palaeolithic** of Africa. He had worked with Richard **Leakey** and Mary Leakey while a graduate student at the University of Michigan, but later became a bitter rival of both, a situation which was still continuing at the time when the diary was being written. He worked in Ethiopia with Don **Johanson**, and subsequently with J Desmond **Clark** and others. Now at the University of California at Berkeley.

WILLIAMS, John. Solicitor, working with the firm of Turner Kenneth Brown, whose offices were at Grays Inn, London: he handled the contractual and legal side of Derek Roe's involvement with Mary Leakey's autobiography.

YOKA. A Kenyan driver, who joined the Olduvai staff in 1983.

YOUNG, William EV. Excavations foreman working with Dorothy **Liddell** for Alexander **Keiller** on archaeological sites in Wiltshire in the 1920s, and also present at the **Hembury** excavations which Dorothy Liddell directed in the early 1930s. Mary Leakey first learned excavation techniques under his guidance and had a high regard for the quality of his work.

2 Places, peoples and things

In this section, I have not sought to create formal definitions of the items listed, so much as to give a general explanation of each and to indicate any particular points of interest about the use of that particular word or term in the context of this book and the region of East Africa in which the story is set. The latter aim is my only excuse for making some of the entries much longer than they need to be, and a little rambling in places.

ACHEULEAN. Name of the main **handaxe**-using tradition of the **Lower Palaeolithic** period, after Saint-Acheul, Amiens, France, where important finds were made during the nineteenth century. The Acheulean is long-lived in time (starting at least 1.6 million years ago and lasting till after 200,000 years ago), and is also widely distributed in space: Africa, India, western Asia and much of Europe.

ALLUVIAL DEPOSITS, ALLUVIUM. Sediments deposited by rivers on their flood plains, on valley floors. Such sediments are often fine-grained sands or loams, but their range also includes gravels.

AUSTRALOPITHECUS. Literally, 'southern ape': an early **hominid** genus found in various parts of Africa, and divisible into many species, the earliest of which were present before 4.0 million years ago. This means that it appeared before the genus *Homo*, not at present known before about 2.5 million years ago. The latest Australopithecine species did not become extinct until about 1.0 million years ago, so *Australopithecus* and *Homo* are contemporary over a long period of time.

AUSTRALOPITHECUS (ZINJANTHROPUS) BOISEI. This is the correct full name for the **robust** Australopithecine **hominid** usually referred to as 'Zinjanthropus' or 'Zinj' and occasionally as 'Nutcracker Man'. The original find was made by Mary Leakey at Olduvai Gorge site FLK I, in 1959 (*see* **FLK**), and was initially claimed by Louis Leakey to represent a new genus, which he named *Zinjanthropus*. Colleagues did not agree, and it was eventually formally reclassified as an Australopithecine. A still later designation is ***Paranthropus*** *boisei*.

BASEMENT ROCKS. The oldest (solid) rocks in a given area. Those in the Olduvai region are of **Precambrian** age, which means that they were originally formed when the earth's crust solidified. Ancient basement rocks may often be subsequently altered by processes such as heat or pressure, in which case they are referred to as 'metamorphic': this is the case with the basement rocks in the vicinity of Olduvai. *See also* **Inselberg** and **Quartzite**.

BAULK. An unexcavated strip deliberately left between two excavation trenches, to provide access and a record of the sequence of deposits and to enable section drawings to be made.

BK. Bell's Korongo. One of the archaeological sites at Olduvai Gorge, situated in the Side Gorge, having particularly good exposures of Bed II and important Oldowan sites. It was discovered in 1935 and named after Peter Bell, a zoologist on that year's expedition. For the naming of sites at Olduvai, *see* ***Korongo***.

BOVID. General term for a member of the animal family *Bovidae*, whether belonging to an extinct or surviving species: bovids include wild oxen, buffalo, bison and domestic cattle. Thus a bone or tooth could be described as 'bovid' if the family attribution was clear, but the precise genus or species could not be determined.

CALICO HILLS. An area in Southern California where Louis Leakey claimed that sites of early **Palaeolithic** age existed. Others, including Mary Leakey, strongly disagreed with his judgement. An international conference was held in 1970 to evaluate the evidence.

CALVARIA. The top part of a **hominid** skull, the skull cap, more or less domed according to the human type concerned.

CHERT. A highly siliceous very fine-grained (cryptocrystalline) rock, much favoured by early toolmakers if available, since it fractures in a predictable manner to produce extremely sharp edges. Flint is a form of chert. Chert nodules became available at Olduvai for a brief period during the formation of Bed II. *See also* **MNK**.

CHRONOMETRIC DATING. A measurement of time, that is, the assigning of an actual age in years to something, as opposed to 'relative dating', which merely places things in their correct chronological order, without stating an actual age. There are many scientific techniques which can yield chronometric dates, the potassium-argon, fission-track and radiocarbon methods being examples. Very generally and loosely speaking, such dating methods often depend on something within the sample that is being studied being subject to decay or alteration, at a known, constant and measurable rate. If the quantity originally present can be determined, then the amount of loss or change that has taken place is directly related to the amount of time that has passed. Volcanic rocks, formed under conditions of great heat and subsequently cooling, offer good material for some of the methods.

CLEAVER. A large cutting tool of stone, belonging to the **Acheulean** tradition, characterised by an axe-like cutting edge, set transversely or obliquely. In Africa, cleavers are almost always made on large, specially struck flakes.

CORYNDON MUSEUM. Properly, The Coryndon Memorial Museum, later renamed and expanded as the National Museum of Kenya, after Independence. The Coryndon Museum was founded as a memorial to a very popular governor, Sir Robert Coryndon, who died in office in 1927. It was the main museum in Nairobi, with important collections related to natural history and to archaeology.

DEVELOPED OLDOWAN/OLDUVAN. A later version of the original **Oldowan** stone tool industry, characterised by a rather wider range of artefact types. At Olduvai Gorge, it first appears in the Middle division of Bed II. Mary Leakey identified three stages of it, Developed Oldowan A, B and C, the last present only at the top of Bed IV.

EARLY (or **EARLIER**) **STONE AGE**. Often abbreviated to ESA. Equivalent to **Lower Palaeolithic**. In much of the African continent, the preferred terminology divides earlier Prehistory into ESA, MSA (**Middle Stone Age**) and LSA (**Late** or **Later Stone Age**).

EAST TURKANA/EAST RUDOLF. The large archaeological research area on the east side of **Lake Turkana**, a Rift Valley lake in northern Kenya, formerly called Lake Rudolf.

Richard **Leakey** and Glynn **Isaac** were working in the **Koobi Fora** area of **East Turkana**, at the time when the diary was written. Because the renaming of the lake, after the Turkana people who inhabit the region, did not take place until the 1970s, some of the earlier research reports refer to 'East Rudolf'.

ENCAENIA. Annual summer academic festival at Oxford University, held in late June, for the giving of honorary degrees and the commemoration of the university's benefactors. After the degree ceremony, a formal lunch for distinguished guests and a large garden party for the entire academic staff of the university take place later the same day, with full academic dress worn. Mary Leakey received her Oxford Honorary DLitt degree at Encaenia in 1980 and suffered all these experiences, as she would probably have put it.

ENGELOSEN. A small volcano, about 8 km distant from the Olduvai camp, which was the sole source of one particular fine-grained, green-coloured **lava**, a **phonolite**, used as a tool-making rock, though not very commonly: some of the finer **Acheulean handaxes** were made from it at certain of the sites in Bed IV. The name means 'the hill that stands alone' in the **Maasai** language, and the spelling Engelosin is occasionally found in the literature relating to Olduvai (photograph, page 97).

FLK. Frida Leakey Korongo (photograph page 133). Discovered in 1931, and named by Louis Leakey in honour of his (first) wife. Situated in the Main Gorge, close to the junction with the Side Gorge, this is perhaps the most important of all the archaeological localities at Olduvai, with sites at many different stratigraphic levels, including the find-spots of the type-specimens of both *Australopithecus (Zinjanthropus) boisei* and *Homo habilis*. For the naming of sites and areas at Olduvai, *see* **Korongo**.

GOL KOPJES. An area of scattered, small tor-like hills and **inselbergs** of **basement** metamorphic rock, including granite, on the Serengeti Plains west of Olduvai. Kopje (in Dutch) or Koppie (in Afrikaans) is a general name for a small hill, particularly in South Africa. The dispositions of the rock units at some of the kopjes have created usable shelters, and archaeological sites of late Prehistoric age are associated with some of them.

GRACILE. Descriptive term for early **hominid** skeletal morphology, implying relatively slender and light bones or overall forms, as opposed to those which are 'robust'. The Australopithecines, in particular, are divided into a gracile and a robust line: it is possible that the *Homo* line emerges from the former, while the latter (*see also* **Paranthropus**) becomes extinct around 1.0 million years ago.

HADZA. One of the few surviving African peoples whose economy is still based on hunting and gathering. Their homeland is near Lake Eyasi in northern Tanzania, not far from Olduvai, and their numbers are low.

HANDAXES. Large, bifacially-worked cutting tools of stone, the hallmark of the **Acheulean** people, often of flattened 'tear-drop', almond or oval shape. They were first made in East Africa around 1.5 million years ago, or a little earlier, but the Acheuleans subsequently reached large areas of the **Old World**, as far east as India and as far north as Britain, and handaxes are found wherever they went, made from whatever suitable rocks were available locally. They may have been used for many different tasks, but one of those was certainly the butchery of animal carcasses. It was the study of handaxes that first took

Derek Roe to Africa (illustration page 32).

HEMBURY. An important prehistoric site in Devonshire, England, on the Blackdown Hills near Honiton, with an **Iron Age** hill fort and a **Neolithic** causewayed camp. Mary Leakey first learned many of her excavation skills here under the tutelage of Dorothy **Liddell**, working as one of the latter's field assistants in 1930–1932 and 1934.

HOMINID. A member of the family *Hominidae*, which includes all living, recent and ancient forms of humans. It is therefore a good general term to apply to fossil human remains, without prejudice to their subsequent assignation to genus and species. Hominids are not limited to the various forms of *Homo*, since the Australopithecines and certain other genera also qualify. 'Hominoid' is a far broader term, because it denotes a member of the super-family *Hominoidea*, which includes all the apes as well as all the humans. It therefore also includes the important and elusive 'latest common ancestor' stage, just before the ape and human lines finally became separate at the level of family: *Pongidae* for the apes and *Hominidae* for the humans.

HOMO ERECTUS. An important form of early human which first appeared sometime between 2.0 and 1.5 million years ago, its members being substantially larger in stature and in brain size than preceding **hominid** types. There are also younger examples of *erectus* of Middle **Pleistocene** age and probable survival of the species in the Far East until well into the Upper Pleistocene, later than 100,000 years ago and possibly even later than 50,000. At the time of writing, there is controversy over the relationship between *Homo ergaster* and *Homo erectus*, but *erectus* is known from East Africa, North Africa, the Far East (Indonesia and China), and possibly Europe. *Homo erectus* was a toolmaker from the start, and the species certainly plays an important role in the initial spread of humans over much of the **Old World**.

HOMO ERGASTER. It is still debated whether *Homo ergaster* is genuinely a separate **hominid** species or merely a variant, probably early, within **Homo erectus**. While *ergaster* is generally agreed to be of tropical African origin, some see *erectus* as developing only after humans first reached eastern Asia, subsequently spreading from there to other areas (including Africa). This view would make *ergaster* the immediate ancestor of *erectus*. *Homo ergaster*, typified by the famous 'Nariokotome Boy' skeleton, c 1.6 million years old, found on the west side of **Lake Turkana**, was certainly a traveller, since the hominid fossils from Dmanisi in the Republic of Georgia are also attributed to this species. *Homo ergaster*, who was certainly a toolmaker, probably first appeared around 1.8 million years ago: the species is physically more advanced than the preceding hominid forms.

HOMO HABILIS. Early hominid species first found at Olduvai Gorge, at site FLK NN in Bed I in 1960 (*see also* **FLK**). The remains, dating from about 1.75 million years ago, indicated that *habilis* had a larger brain, greater manual dexterity (hence the name) and smaller cheek-teeth than the Australopithecines then known in East Africa, and also full upright walking. *Homo habilis* was therefore believed to be the first toolmaker and the earliest member of *Homo*. Subsequent discoveries have shown that both tool-making and bipedalism extend much further back in time, and the status of *Homo habilis* is currently under review, though the name is still loosely applied by some writers to any remains of *Homo* that are earlier than **Homo erectus** or **Homo ergaster**. At present, no certain examples of *Homo habilis* are known outside Africa.

HOMO SAPIENS. A **hominid** species which emerges during the Middle **Pleistocene** after the general evolutionary stage dominated by ***Homo erectus*** and ***Homo ergaster***. The early *sapiens* forms still have some archaic features, but from this stock modern humans (*Homo sapiens sapiens*) eventually emerged, probably in southern Africa. Many aspects of *Homo sapiens* in the broad sense are still debated or poorly understood – for example, whether the Neanderthal people are a sub-species within *Homo sapiens* or a separate species, *Homo neanderthalensis*, but these things are of marginal relevance to the subject matter of this book. However, there are some rather fragmentary *Homo sapiens* remains from the younger levels at Olduvai (Masek and Ndutu Beds) and also the important skulls from the Upper Ngaloba Beds at **Laetoli** and **Lake Ndutu** have been attributed to archaic *Homo sapiens*.

HYRAX HILL. A small rocky hill in the Rift Valley near Nakuru, north of Nairobi, close to the shore of Lake Nakuru. Mary Leakey excavated here in 1937–1938 and uncovered important **Neolithic** and **Iron Age** levels, the former including dwelling structures and a cemetery. Some of the remains have been preserved and can be visited today. The hill got its name from the large population of rock-hyraxes which lived there.

INSELBERG. From German words meaning 'island mountain': an isolated small steep-sided hill of **basement rock**, shaped by erosion and left standing above a flatter surface of later sediments or eroded bedrock. Inselbergs are often found in arid or semi-arid regions, and there are many in the vicinity of Olduvai Gorge, formed of such rocks as **quartzite**, granite or gneiss.

IRON AGE. The youngest of the original divisions of the 'Three Age System' (Stone, Bronze and Iron Ages) according to which Prehistory was classified in Europe from early in the nineteenth century, the introduction of ironworking being perceived as a significant technological advance. Attempts to apply the Three Age System to the remote past of other areas of the world have not always proved particularly useful. 'Iron Age' is still used as an archaeological period label in Africa, but the distribution of ironworking and the date and significance of its introduction is very variable in different parts of the continent. **Late Stone Age** communities survive until very recent times in some areas and 'Iron Age' includes the ancestors of extant African communities, prior to the introduction of written records. The term Bronze Age has no general relevance in Africa.

KADA GONA. An **Early Stone Age** site in the Rift Valley in northern Ethiopia, in the Hadar region of the Awash River Valley, within the Afar depression, some 300 km northeast of Addis Ababa. The site is actually in the valley of the Gona River, a tributary of the Awash: the artefacts are of **Oldowan** character in the broad sense, and the sediments which contain them have been dated from 2.5 to 2.6 million years ago. At the time of writing, these are the earliest known stone artefacts.

KALAMBO FALLS. A spectacular waterfall situated right on the Zambia–Tanzania border, near Mbala, a short distance from the southern end of one of the larger Rift Valley lakes, Lake Tanganyika. Nearby, excavations by Desmond **Clark** in the 1950s and 1960s revealed a highly important prehistoric sequence with various stages of **Earlier**, **Middle**, and **Later Stone Age** and **Iron Age** occupation. Clark's invitation to Derek Roe to study some of the Kalambo Falls Earlier Stone Age artefacts began the chain of events which led *inter alia* to those described in the diary.

KAMBA. A Bantu people of Kenya, whose main homeland is the Kamba Hills near Machakos, southeast of Nairobi. They are a farming people, growing maize and various fruit and vegetable crops, and also raising cattle. They also have traditional skills in hunting and fighting, and are known for their craftmanship. Mary Leakey particularly chose Kamba for her camp staff at Olduvai.

KIKUYU. A Bantu people of Kenya, and easily the largest of the Kenyan peoples. They dominate the African population of the capital, Nairobi. The Kikuyu are traditionally a farming people, settled agriculturists who raise some livestock, but in recent times they have proved very versatile, and many Kikuyu have entered various professions and been very active in Kenyan politics. Born in 1903, Louis Leakey grew up among the Kikuyu at Kabete, some 10 miles from Nairobi, where his father was a missionary: he was accepted from the start as a white member of the Kikuyu people, and was formally initiated as a warrior and a full member at the age of 13.

KNAPPING. The process of working stone, especially fine-grained or siliceous rocks such as flint, mainly by direct percussion (though indirect percussion and pressure may also be used), in particular to make tools. In more recent times, flint-knappers have manufactured gunflints and sometimes shaped blocks of flint for use as building material. Apart from the finished products, the knapping process yields easily recognisable 'knapping debris'. A 'knapping floor' is an area where stoneworking took place and 'experimental knapping' is the practical replication of prehistoric stone tools by those studying them, using the same materials and techniques as the original workers, as a guide to understanding lithic material recovered in the field.

KOOBI FORA. Locality on the East side of **Lake Turkana** in northern Kenya which gave its name to a highly important and productive **Earlier Stone Age** research area, also referred to as the East Turkana Research Area. Having established the potential of the area in 1967, Richard **Leakey** directed the work there from 1969 into the early 1980s, with Glynn **Isaac** in charge of the archaeology. Many archaeological sites and many **hominid** fossils were found. The Koobi Fora Spit is a low-lying but prominent sandy peninsula jutting out about a mile into the lake, and it was here that the expedition's permanent base camp was established by Richard Leakey in 1969.

KOPJE, *see* **Gol Kopjes**.

KORONGO. Swahili word for a gully, used in the naming of many of the archaeological sites at Olduvai Gorge. In these names, *Korongo* is abbreviated to K, with the initials of some person or persons connected with the site's discovery added: *see* **FLK**, **MLK**, **MNK**, etc. The sides of the Gorge are steep and cliff-like, broken only by the *korongos*, which are created by erosion and may be steep-sided or more gently sloping. It is in the actual sides of the Gorge, or in the erosion features, that the tell-tale traces of archaeological material are usually first found: most of the sites are therefore designated K for *Korongo* or C for Cliff.

LAETOLI. A very important Tanzanian site, some 45 km south of Olduvai, where **Pliocene hominid** fossils were found, and also the famous hominid footprint trails, preserved (together with many animal footprints) in volcanic ash dated to 3.68 million years ago. The existence of Laetoli had been known since the 1930s, but the main discoveries there were made during Mary Leakey's excavations of 1975–1980. The deposits represent a very long period of time, and there are important **Pleistocene** levels as well as those of **Pliocene** age. The Laetoli faunal remains are also of great importance. Owing to an error, the name Laetoli is incorrectly rendered as Laetolil in some of the older literature.

LAKE BARINGO. A Rift Valley lake in the Eastern Rift, situated north of Nakuru in Central Kenya. Various important **Early Stone Age** sites are known in the Baringo Basin, and a number of **hominid** fossils have also been found there. Jonathan **Leakey** owned a safari camp on an island in the lake, which was one of Mary's favourite places for relaxation.

LAKE NDUTU. Lake on the Serengeti Plains, some 30 km southwest of Olduvai. A **hominid** fossil skull, perhaps an archaic *Homo sapiens* form was discovered here, with associated stone artefacts, in 1973 by Amini **Mturi**. There is a safari camp at Lake Ndutu, which was for many years owned and run by George **Dove**.

LAKE TURKANA. A large and important Rift Valley lake of the Eastern Rift, mainly in northern Kenya, but with the Ethiopian border at its northern end, where the Omo River drains into it. It was formerly known as Lake Rudolf. The whole Turkana basin is of outstanding importance for the finds of **hominid** fossils and early archaeological sites, of late **Pliocene** and early **Pleistocene** age, made in the research areas which border the lake, particularly those known as **East Turkana** (*see also* **Koobi Fora**), West Turkana, and the Omo Valley and Delta.

LATER (or **LATE**) **STONE AGE**. In the nomenclature for the divisions of the **Palaeolithic** period used in Africa south of the Sahara, this is the youngest of the three stages, usually abbreviated to LSA. It begins at different dates in different areas, but in many cases somewhat before 20,000 years ago. The LSA people were advanced hunter-gatherers, exploiting various local resources. Unlike the European **Upper Palaeolithic**, with which it is often compared, the LSA continues well into the Holocene (our present interglacial period), and indeed in some places until quite recent times. Only in a very few areas can some LSA peoples, late in the period, be regarded as possessing a farming economy rather than a hunter-gatherer one but the Rift Valley in East Africa does have examples of this (*see also* **Neolithic, Hyrax Hill, Njoro River Cave**).

LAVA. Molten material extruded by a volcano, which subsequently cools to form a solid rock. Such rocks vary greatly in colour and texture, according to their constituents, but some of the finer-grained, more homogeneous ones offered excellent raw material for tool manufacture: at Olduvai and some of the other sites mentioned, these include various forms of basalt, trachyandesite and green **phonolite**, for example. Lava flows can also be used for **chronometric dating**.

LLK. Louis Leakey Korongo, an important site in Bed II at Olduvai Gorge, in the Side Gorge not far from the junction with the Main Gorge. Here Louis Leakey found a **hominid** fossil **calvaria** in December 1960, which became Olduvai Hominid 9 in the catalogue of hominid finds from the Gorge. It is widely regarded as belonging to *Homo erectus*, though it was initially named as *Homo leakeyi* in Louis's honour. For the naming of sites and areas at Olduvai, *see* ***Korongo***.

LOWER PALAEOLITHIC. The oldest of the formal divisions of the **Palaeolithic** period, which begins with the first traces of human activity, or more literally with the first traces of stone tool manufacture (currently recognised as occurring c 2.6 million years ago in East Africa – *see* **Kada Gona**). The period formally ends when the **Middle Palaeolithic** period starts, but that too is not synchronous in all regions. For the purposes of a glossary definition, 200,000 years ago would perhaps be an acceptable notional date for the end of the Lower Palaeolithic, but should not be taken too literally. The Lower Palaeolithic period sees the emergence of the earliest humans, and their physical evolution up to the appearance in some regions of first archaic forms of *Homo sapiens*. It also sees the first spread of humans over the majority of the **Old World**. In technological terms, it principally involves the **Oldowan** and **Acheulean** tool making traditions. Lower Palaeolithic is the equivalent of **Earlier Stone Age**, the latter term being more commonly used in East and southern Africa.

LUCY. The informal name given to a remarkable 40 per cent complete Australopithecine skeleton (*afarensis*), found in November 1974 by Don **Johanson** and BT Gray, a member of the research team, in the Hadar region of northern Ethiopia. The fossil is about 3.1 million years old. The name Lucy was chosen because a Beatles song *Lucy in the Sky with Diamonds* was being played in the expedition's camp when the new find was brought there.

LUO. A Nilotic people, whose home area is in western Kenya and adjacent parts of Tanzania, along the shores of Lake Victoria, with the town of Kisumu as their capital. Their traditional economy depended on agriculture and fishing. In recent times, many Luo have become successful scientists and doctors.

MAASAI (also spelt **MASAI**). Ubiquitous semi-nomadic, pastoral people of East Africa, especially Kenya and Tanzania, of whom there were several groups in the region of Olduvai Gorge. The Maasai are Nilo-Hamitic, and their society is structured around the male age-grades: boy, junior and senior warrior, junior and senior elder. Their whole lives are intimately bound up with the herding of cattle, in the largest possible numbers, though they keep other livestock. Their clothing, weaponry and finery (featuring especially beadwork and coiled wire) give them a colourful and highly distinctive appearance.

MASEK BEDS. One of the major stratigraphic divisions of the Olduvai Gorge sedimentary sequence, following directly after Bed IV. The deposits date from c 1.0 to 0.4 million years ago and consist largely of volcanic ash and the gravels and sands of stream channels. At **FLK**, close to the camp at Olduvai, a fine **Acheulean** industry with white **quartzite handaxes** was excavated in the Masek Beds, which have also yielded some fragmentary **hominid** fossil material, tentatively attributed to *Homo sapiens*.

MBULU. A northern Tanzanian people, also called Iraqw, now reduced to small numbers. Traditionally agriculturists, they are believed to be a remnant of the area's original indigenous population. Their dwellings, partly excavated below ground level, with low mud walls and flat roofs, were a distinctive feature of their settlements.

MIDDLE PALAEOLITHIC. The second of the three divisions of the **Palaeolithic** period in the terminology used particularly in Europe and much of Asia. It is characterised by certain changes in knapping technology, with **handaxes** and **cleavers** largely replaced by various smaller kinds of tools made on flakes which were specially struck for the purpose and were of predetermined size and shape. In Europe, the Middle Palaeolithic sees the emergence of the Neanderthal people and ends when they are replaced by modern humans, but the situation is rather different in some other regions and the timing of a Middle Palaeolithic stage, where one exists, is variable. Overall dates of from c 200,000 to c 30,000 years ago might be suggested for the period as a whole. In the terminology used in eastern and southern Africa, **Middle Stone Age** is the approximate equivalent to Middle Palaeolithic, but there are important differences.

MIDDLE STONE AGE. The second of the three divisions of the Stone Age as defined in Africa (mainly south of the Sahara), usually abbreviated to MSA. It is an approximate equivalent to the **Middle Palaeolithic** of Europe and Asia, but has great variety and different overall significance; it also involves different **hominid** types. As in Europe and Asia, the classic stone tool types of the Early Stone Age are largely replaced by well-made flake tools on specially struck flakes, but in Africa there are other technological advances during the MSA, such as the intermittent appearance of 'microlithic' forms – small tools made on fine blades – and various distinctive projectile points of stone and bone, such as do not appear in Eurasia before the start of the **Upper Palaeolithic**. During the MSA of southern Africa, humans of physically modern type (*Homo sapiens sapiens*) emerge, and there are various important changes in human social and economic behaviour, though the relationship between these events is by no means clear. A rough overall time-range might be from c 200,000 to 20,000 years ago, but with great local variability.

MIOCENE. A unit of the geological timescale, being an epoch of the Tertiary era, within which it immediately precedes the **Pliocene**. In round figures, the Miocene begins about 23 million years ago and ends about 5 million years ago. All this is well before the time of the first humans, but there are important hominoid (*see Hominid*) fossils of Miocene age in various parts of Africa and Eurasia, the earliest apes being among them. From the 1930s to the 1950s, Louis and Mary Leakey were heavily involved with work on Miocene fossils, particularly at **Rusinga Island** in Lake Victoria. There were also major geological events during the Miocene that established the basic geography of the continents with which we are familiar, and contributed profoundly to the shaping of landscape on a continental scale.

MLK. Mary Leakey Korongo, one of the named localities in the Main Gorge at Olduvai Gorge, where there are important archaeological sites in Bed II, including occurrences of early **Acheulean** tools. Louis Leakey named this *Korongo* in honour of his wife, which Mary had been for many years by the time when she first discovered it in the early 1950s (*see* **MNK**). For the naming of Olduvai sites, *see also **Korongo***.

MNK. Mary Nicol Korongo, one of the important named archaeological localities in the Side Gorge at Olduvai. **Hominid** fossils, an occupation surface with many stone artefacts and a place where **chert** nodules had been systematically exploited as a 'factory site', were all among the discoveries here. Though much of the excavation at MNK was done in the 1960s, the first finds were made in 1935, before the marriage of Louis and Mary Leakey, so, when Louis named the area in honour of Mary, he used the initials of her maiden name. For the naming of sites at Olduvai, *see **Korongo***.

NAABI HILL. A rocky hill some 12 miles or so west of the Main Gorge, and north of the main road from Ngorongoro to Seronera, which crosses the Gorge at Granite Falls.

Though not very high, it is a prominent landmark in an otherwise rather featureless area of the Serengeti Plains.

NAIBOR SOIT. A prominent **inselberg** of **basement rock**, situated just across the Main Gorge from the Olduvai camp, not far from the junction between the Main and Side Gorges. The name comes from the **Maasai** words for white stone. Its rocks are metamorphic and mainly white in colour: coarse-grained **quartzite** and quartz. They were much used for toolmaking, although not easy to work, probably because their source was close at hand: a high proportion of the main Olduvai archaeological sites are within two or three miles of Naibor Soit.

NAISIUSIU BEDS. The youngest of the main stratigraphic divisions in the Olduvai Gorge geological sequence, dating from c 25,000 to 15,000 years ago. The sediments consist largely of wind-blown material and, since they were deposited after the Gorge had been formed, can be found at the top of the Gorge's side walls, above the **Ndutu Beds** and also at the bottom of the Gorge, beside the present-day seasonal stream. They contain a little archaeological material of **Later Stone Age** date.

NAIVASHA RAILWAY ROCK SHELTER. An archaeological site of **Late Stone Age** date in Central Kenya, in the Rift Valley northwest of Nairobi, excavated by Mary Leakey in 1939–1940. The excavation was a rescue operation, where deposits were due to be destroyed when a railway line was realigned at Naivasha, near the lake of the same name. Enormous numbers of stone artefacts were recovered – over two million, including waste fragments.

NDUTU BEDS. Second youngest of the major stratigraphic units in the Olduvai Gorge geological sequence, situated between the **Masek Beds** below them and the **Naisiusiu Beds** above. The deposits are mainly wind-blown ash and sand, and their age is likely to be between 400,000 and 75,000 years. They contain a small amount of **Middle Stone Age** archaeological material, and one fragmentary **hominid** fossil, attributed to *Homo sapiens*.

NEOLITHIC. The New Stone Age, youngest subdivision of the 'Stone Age' unit of the original nineteenth-century European classification of the prehistoric past, the 'Three Age System'. The main technological innovation which distinguished the 'New' Stone Age from its predecessors in 'lithic' terms was the ground or polished stone axe, and to this the first appearance of pottery could be added. More importantly, the Neolithic came to be recognised as the period in which farming was introduced, that is, hunter-gatherer economies gave way to food-producing ones, with consequential social changes of great importance. In Africa south of the Sahara, the term Neolithic is certainly used in a few places to refer to early farming, pottery-using people, who are of **Later Stone Age** rather than **Iron Age** status. The Rift Valley in parts of East Africa is one such area. In many other parts of southern Africa, the earliest farmers were already using iron.

NEW WORLD. In Palaeolithic Archaeology, this term would most often imply the Americas, but might also be used to refer to Australasia and the Pacific islands. Its significance relates to the spread of humans (eventually) into lands beyond the natural boundaries of the vast landmass that includes all of Africa, Europe and Asia, and hence into the 'New World'.

NJORO RIVER CAVE. Archaeological site near Nakuru in the Rift Valley in Central Kenya, excavated by Mary Leakey in 1937–1938. It yielded a very important **Neolithic** cemetery, dating from the first millennium BC, the burials often accompanied by elaborate, beautiful and fragile grave goods, which Mary was able to recover with a high degree of precision and success. This always remained one of her favourite excavations, notwithstanding all her later spectacular achievements.

OLDOWAN. Name originally given by Louis Leakey in 1933 to the simple early stone tool industry represented at Olduvai Gorge in Bed I and the base of Bed II, taken from the name of the Gorge as then spelt (*see* Oldoway). The tools consist of flakes, whether plain or retouched, and various flaked cobble forms – choppers, polyhedrons, and so forth (illustration page 31). True **handaxes** and **cleavers** only appeared later, as part of the **Acheulean** tradition of toolmaking. After work on the Bed II sites, Mary Leakey introduced the term '**Developed Oldowan**' for the more advanced stages of the Oldowan toolmaking tradition, which was a long-lasting one. When it was discovered that there were simple stone artefact industries in East Africa at sites much older than Olduvai (such as **Kada Gona**), use of the term Oldowan, in a broad sense, was extended to include them.

OLDOWAY, OLDUVAI. In the early days of research at the Gorge, and when Louis Leakey first became aware of it in the late 1920s, its name was anglicised to Oldoway, and he spelt it accordingly in his earlier books and articles, but by the 1940s the proper spelling, Olduvai, which is in the **Maasai** language and means 'the place of the wild sisal', had come into general use. However, the stone tool industry of the earlier levels had already been named **Oldowan**, using the old spelling, and this has been retained. I myself used to write it 'Olduvan', and Mary Leakey once told me she thought this was a good idea, and proposed to adopt it, but she never did, and indeed the formal rules of nomenclature make 'Oldowan' technically correct.

OLD WORLD. For Palaeolithic archaeologists, this term denotes the huge landmass of Africa, Europe and Asia, over which it was possible for early humans to spread without crossing a major sea barrier. They began their migrations as early as c 1.8 million years ago, but did not (according to knowledge at the time of writing) reach any of the lands beyond until well into the **Upper Pleistocene**, and some of them only right at the end of that period or even after it. Hence the sense of 'Old' and 'New' worlds.

OLORGESAILIE. Important and prolific Kenyan **Earlier Stone Age Acheulean** site, or indeed complex of sites, on the shores of a former lake, in the Eastern Rift Valley, some 40 km southwest of Nairobi. It was discovered in 1942 during a wartime leave weekend visit by Louis and Mary Leakey, with Mary Catherine **Fagg** and Ferucio Menengetti (an Italian prisoner of war who had been given work at the **Coryndon Museum**). The Leakeys excavated at Olorgesailie intermittently between 1943 and 1947, and subsequently, at their invitation, Glynn **Isaac** carried out major excavations there in the 1960s in the course of his doctoral research. Others, notably Richard Potts, have worked there since. The site has long been preserved as a tourist attraction, and some of the spectacular accumulations of stone tools can be viewed by visitors, much as they were discovered.

PALAEOLITHIC. From Greek words, meaning 'old stone': the oldest of the main divisions of the Stone Age, which was itself the oldest unit of the nineteenth-century European classification of the prehistoric period, the 'Three Age System'. The Palaeolithic period is subdivided into 'Lower', 'Middle' and 'Upper' Palaeolithic sections.

PALAEONTOLOGY. The study of extinct creatures, with regard to their relationships and order of development. The term is most often applied to the study of extinct animals via fossil remains. Human Palaeontology is concerned with the study of early humans and their immediate ancestors, with hominid fossils a special interest.

PARANTHROPUS. Alternative generic name for the robust australopithecines: use of genus names has been somewhat variable during the last fifty years or so of research by human palaeontologists (*see* Palaeontology), as new finds have contributed to the whole jigsaw puzzle of hominid evolution. In fact, in this case, whether one refers, for example, to a given fossil as *Australopithecus aethiopicus* or *Paranthropus aethiopicus* is (or should be) of considerable importance with regard to one's whole view of how some of the key hominid fossils relate to each other, and therefore ultimately to one's overall interpretation of human ancestry and evolution. Lacking specialised knowledge, mere archaeologists of the Palaeolithic try to follow the arguments and spend a lot of time wishing the human palaeontologists would reach general agreement and stick to it, but no doubt the latter are driven equally to despair by archaeologists' changes of interpretation or redating of finds. Anyhow, *Paranthropus* seems to be in favour at the moment (2002), and who am I to suggest that it is perhaps a relief that the paranthropines became extinct about a million years ago, leaving the *Homo* line to continue alone?

PHONOLITE. A form of lava within the trachyte group, distinguished by its particular mineral composition, and named, I was told by Mary Leakey, from the clear ringing sound when a block of it is struck. At Olduvai, the phonolites, which are green in colour and very fine grained, were prized as toolmaking rocks by those who knew where to find them: they are easy to work; and a flake of phonolite has a fine, sharp edge. The best phonolite came from Engelosen.

PLEISTOCENE. The first geological division (epoch) of the Quaternary Era (in which we live at the present time), the second division being the still-continuing Holocene. The Pleistocene period begins some 2.0–1.8 million years ago, and is subdivided into Lower Pleistocene (ending c 0.78 million years ago), Middle Pleistocene (ending c 130,000 years ago) and Upper Pleistocene (ending c 10,000 years ago). The Pleistocene period is characterised by a great sequence of climatic fluctuations, colder and warmer periods, which in the higher latitudes take the form of glaciations (the 'ice ages' in popular language) and intervening interglacials (though in fact important periods of warmer and colder temperatures can now be traced well back into pre-Pleistocene time: *see* Pliocene). The Holocene, often referred to as the 'postglacial' period, is no more than another interglacial, which will eventually come to an end.

PLIOCENE. The youngest division (epoch) of the Tertiary era, with approximate round-figure dates of 5.0–2.0 million years ago. It was a period of deteriorating temperatures, and there is no very clear climatic break (as had long been supposed) between the end of the Pliocene and the start of the Pleistocene. During the last three to four decades (this is written in 2002), it has become clear that early humans (and even the genus *Homo*) were present well before the end of the Pliocene, which had previously been regarded as a 'pre-human' epoch. The oldest stone artefacts, and therefore the beginning of the Palaeolithic period, are of fully Pliocene age, at c 2.6 million years ago (*see* Kada Gona). Indeed, the dating for upright walking immediate ancestors of the first humans – to use a deliberately vague term – seems likely to go back to the very beginning of the Pliocene, at least.

PRECAMBRIAN. The immensely long geological period to which the oldest rocks belong, formed when the Earth's crust first became consolidated. Its duration was at least 4,000 million years. In the Olduvai area, the **inselbergs** were mainly of Precambrian rocks, often altered by metamorphic processes (*see also* **Basement Rocks**).

PROCONSUL. A genus of early **Miocene** hominoid creatures (*see* **Hominid**), dating from c 20 to 17 million years ago, well represented in Western Kenya and Uganda including at **Rusinga Island** in Lake Victoria, where Mary Leakey found a fine *Proconsul* specimen in 1948. *Proconsul*, an arboreal quadruped, is considerably older than the first true African apes, and there are at present too many gaps in the evidence for it to be assigned a precise ancestral position on the evolutionary line leading either to any of the modern apes that we know, or to the earliest humans.

QUARTZITE. Rocks of many different textures and colours are classed as quartzite. Mostly, they were originally formed as sandy sediments, the grains being mainly of quartz, which became cemented and consolidated, though sometimes they may subsequently have been altered by one or other metamorphic process (*see* **Basement Rocks**). The Olduvai quartzites, which are what concerns us here, are metamorphic; they are predominantly white but occasionally pale green or brown, and are of **Precambrian** origin, with very large individual quartz crystals and much mica. They were used as toolmaking rock throughout the archaeological sequence: though hard to work, being inclined to shatter, they were capable of yielding sharp cutting edges, and they were easily available. **Naibor Soit** seems to have been the principal source for the Olduvai toolmakers, though a less coarse-grained quartzite from another **inselberg**, Kelogi, was also used.

ROBUST. A term used in describing early **hominid** skeletal morphology, to indicate heavier bones or overall form, as opposed to 'graceful'. Accordingly, one may refer to a robust or gracile line of development, or divide a genus (for example, *Australopithecus*) into robust and gracile groups. See also *Paranthropus*.

RUSINGA ISLAND. An island in the Western Kenya part of Lake Victoria, where there are important deposits of **Miocene** age, which have yielded large numbers of well-preserved fossils of many different animals and of hominoids (*see* **Hominid**) at what might loosely be called the ape–ancestor stage, dating from c 20 to 17 million years ago. Louis Leakey worked on these deposits from early in his career, and Mary Leakey first went there in 1942. In 1948, at Kathwanga on the west side of the island, she found part of a skull of the hominoid *Proconsul*, the first such find ever made, and of great importance. Continued work thereafter on Rusinga Island and at sites on the adjacent mainland meant that this area became something of a holiday home for the Leakey family for several years, during the childhood of the three sons of Louis and Mary. The population of Rusinga Island consisted mainly of **Luo** people.

TANZANIAN ANTIQUITIES DEPARTMENT. A branch of the Tanzanian Government with official reponsibility for supervising the work at Olduvai, amongst other archaeological sites, at the time when the diary was written. Amini **Mturi** was Mary Leakey's chief contact there. Mary had a formal duty to report to the department, which itself was also in theory a source of facilities, equipment or help she might need, but the remoteness of Olduvai and the economic difficulties that then faced Tanzania meant that actual liaison was rather infrequent.

TAPHONOMY. Study of the processes by which things become buried (from the Greek words *taphos*, tomb or grave, and *nomos*, law). The term was first used in **Palaeontology** to denote the study of how plant and animal remains become fossilised, but its meaning for archaeologists has broadened to cover study of how archaeological material of any kind has become incorporated into the deposit in which it is found, and what may have happened to it during that whole process (which may have had several stages) to leave it in the state and position it has at the time of discovery. One who specialises in such studies is called a taphonomist.

TUFF. Ash ejected by a volcano, which has settled and subsequently become consolidated and turned into rock. It is usually fine-grained, with particles not exceeding 2 cm in maximum dimension, and its composition depends entirely on what was contained in that particular eruption by that particular volcano. As a volcanic rock, it may well be directly datable (*see* **Chronometric Dating**), and because of the gentle nature of its air-fall descent, it may seal in and protect an archaeological site with little or no disturbance, as well as offering a means of dating it: highly favourable circumstances for an archaeologist. Tuffs are of great importance as datable marker horizons in the Olduvai archaeological sequence, while at **Laetoli** the famous hominid footprint trails were actually left in volcanic ash which hardened to form a tuff, datable to some 3.68 million years ago.

UNCONFORMABLY. If one deposit overlies another unconformably, this implies a clear break between the two in the depositional sequence, often of unknown duration: an 'unconformity' or 'disconformity' is said to exist. Thus, for example, in sediments deposited by a river, a gravel with heavy components might pass upwards conformably into a finer grained sand, the heavier particles having been deposited first and the lighter ones later, in the same cycle of deposition. But if the upper part of a deposited gravel were removed by erosion, and then in a new cycle of river activity a different gravel were deposited directly on the remains of the first one, it would lie on it unconformably. Unconformities can represent either a period of time in which no sedimentation takes place, or a drastic change in the nature of deposition.

UPPER PALAEOLITHIC. The youngest division of the **Palaeolithic** period or Old Stone Age, particularly in the terminology used in Europe, Asia and the northern part of Africa: while it overlaps with the **Later Stone Age** as that term is used in sub-Saharan Africa, it is by no means an exact equivalent. In Eurasia, it is the period which sees a rapid spread by fully modern humans, *Homo sapiens sapiens* (see **Homo sapiens**), replacing all surviving archaic human forms and bringing major advances in many aspects of technology, and in social, economic, artistic and even spiritual life. Settlement is expanded within the **Old World** and extended into the **New World**. While the dating of the Upper Palaeolithic varies from area to area, general dates to encompass the whole period would be from c 45,000 to c 10,000 years ago.

ZINJANTHROPUS, 'ZINJ', see Australopithecus (Zinjanthropus) boisei.